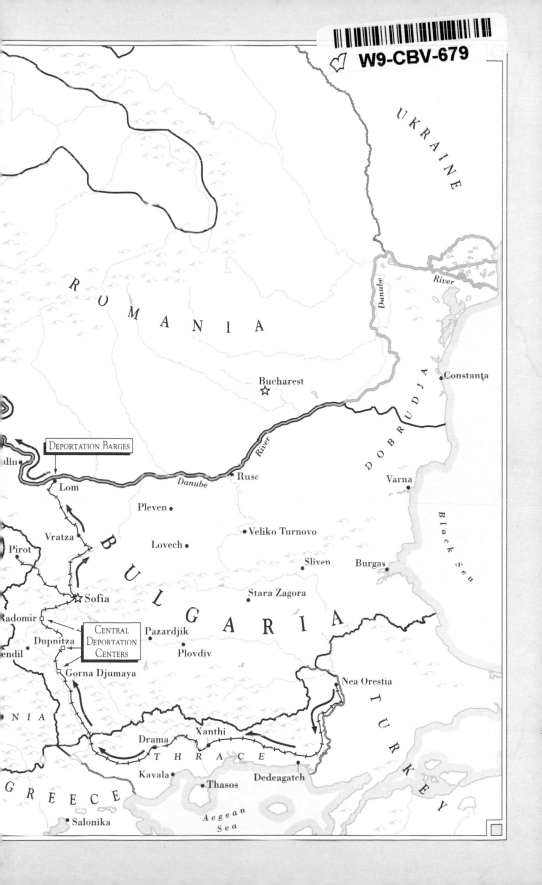

UKRAINE

ROMANIA

Danube River

Bucharest ☆

DOBRUDJA

Constanţa

Deportation Barges

dln

Lom

Danube

Rusc

Varna

Pleven

Veliko Turnovo

Black Sea

Vratza

Lovech

Pirot

Sliven

Burgas

Sofia ☆

Stara Zagora

Radomir

Pazardjik

Central Deportation Centers

Dupnitza

Plovdiv

endil

Gorna Djumaya

BULGARIA

Nea Orestia

TURKEY

NIA

Xanthi

Drama

THRACE

Kavala

Thasos

Dedeagatch

GREECE

Salonika

Aegean Sea

# BEYOND
# HITLER'S
# GRASP

ALSO BY MICHAEL BAR-ZOHAR

Non-fiction Titles
*Suez Top-Secret*
*The Hunt for German Scientists*
*The Avengers*
*Ben-Gurion, the Armed Prophet*
*Embassies in Crisis:*
*Diplomats and Demagogues behind the Six Day War*
*Spies in the Promised Land*
*The Quest for the Red Prince (with Eitan Haber)*
*Ben-Gurion, the Centennial Edition*
*Arrows of the Almighty*
*Facing a Cruel Mirror*
*Bitter Scent*
*Lionhearts*

Fiction Titles
*The Third Truth*
*The Spy Who Died Twice*
*The Secret List of Heinrich Roehm*
*The Enigma*
*The Deadly Document*
*The Phantom Conspiracy*
*Double Cross*
*A Spy in Winter*
*The Unknown Soldier*
*The Devil's Spy*
*Brothers*

# BEYOND HITLER'S GRASP

## The Heroic Rescue of Bulgaria's Jews

MICHAEL BAR-ZOHAR

Adams Media Corporation
HOLBROOK, MASSACHUSETTS

Published by
Adams Media Corporation
260 Center Street, Holbrook, MA 02343

ISBN: 1-58062-060-4

Printed in the United States of America.

FIRST EDITION
J I H G F E D C B A


Library of Congress Cataloging-in-Publication Data
Bar-Zohar, Michael
Beyond Hitler's grasp / Michael Bar-Zohar. — 1st ed.
p.        cm.
Includes bibliographical references and index.
ISBN 1–58062–060–4
1. Jews—Bulgaria—History—20th century. 2. World War, 1939–1945—Jews—
Rescue—Bulgaria. 3. Bulgaria—Ethnic relations. I. Title.
DS135.B8B38        1998
949.9'004924—dc21                98–8407
                                CIP


Endsheet map by Jeffrey L. Ward.

*This book is available at quantity discounts for bulk purchases.*
*For information, call 1-800-872-5627 (in Massachusetts, 781-767-8100).*

Visit our home page at http://www.adamsmedia.com

# CONTENTS

Introduction . . . . . . . . . . . . . . . . . . . . . . . . . . . . . . vii

Acknowledgments . . . . . . . . . . . . . . . . . . . . . . . . . xi

CHAPTER ONE: Alarm . . . . . . . . . . . . . . . . . . . . . . . . . . . 1

CHAPTER TWO: The Fox . . . . . . . . . . . . . . . . . . . . . . . 9

CHAPTER THREE: The Law for the Defense of the Nation . . 27

CHAPTER FOUR: The Commissar . . . . . . . . . . . . . . . 41

CHAPTER FIVE: An Order for Deportation . . . . . . . . . . . . 63

CHAPTER SIX: The Lovers . . . . . . . . . . . . . . . . . . . . . . 77

CHAPTER SEVEN: A Thracian Nightmare . . . . . . . . . . . . 87

CHAPTER EIGHT: Boxcars at the Station . . . . . . . . . . . . . . 101

CHAPTER NINE: An Order from the Highest Place . . . . . . 113

CHAPTER TEN: Trains . . . . . . . . . . . . . . . . . . . . . . . . . . 131

CHAPTER ELEVEN: Forty-Three Signatures . . . . . . . . . . . . 145

CHAPTER TWELVE: The Bluff . . . . . . . . . . . . . . . . . . . . . 157

CHAPTER THIRTEEN: The Metropolitans . . . . . . . . . . . . . 165

CHAPTER FOURTEEN: Belev's Devious Plan . . . . . . . . . . . 179

CHAPTER FIFTEEN: Despair ........................ 185

CHAPTER SIXTEEN: The King Has Vanished .......... 205

CHAPTER SEVENTEEN: Belev's Revenge .............. 215

CHAPTER EIGHTEEN: The Last Effort ............... 219

CHAPTER NINETEEN: The Mysterious Death of Boris III ... 229

CHAPTER TWENTY: A Body in a Ditch .............. 241

CHAPTER TWENTY-ONE: The Hour of Reckoning ....... 249


Epilogue ................................... 259

Notes ..................................... 269

Index ..................................... 289

# INTRODUCTION

On a glorious November day in 1948, a long freight train ground to a halt at the Bulgarian-Yugoslav border. More than a thousand Jewish passengers stepped out of the crowded boxcars, stretching their numb limbs. The night before, at Sofia station, they had set off on their long journey to a secluded harbor in neighboring Yugoslavia, to board a ship sailing for Israel. They were part of a massive wave of immigration that, in a short period of time, would carry to the newborn state of Israel more than 90 percent of Bulgaria's fifty thousand Jews.

I was one of these thousands, a little boy immigrating to Israel with my parents and baby sister. I jumped out of the dark, foul-smelling boxcar and looked around. We were in a lush green valley, breathtakingly beautiful. Alongside the locomotive, Bulgarian and Yugoslav border guards examined stacks of papers. Beyond them lay Yugoslavia.

Almost as one our fellow passengers turned back, casting a long last look at the land of their birth. One began to sing, another joined him, then a third, and a fourth. Soon, hundreds of voices, male and female, young and old, joined together and echoed down the valley. They sang a tuneful Bulgarian anthem, *"Mila Rodino"* ("Dear Homeland").

"Dear homeland," the huge choir sang with deep emotion, "you're paradise on earth. Your beauty, your charm, are endless."

I remember looking up at my parents. Both were crying. Many people, standing beside us, were singing with hoarse, choking voices, tears streaming down their faces.

"Why do you cry?" I asked my parents.

"Because we love this country," my father said softly. "It's been good to us."

I thought of the last days before our departure, in Sofia. Bulgarian friends and patients of my father kept coming to his clinic. "What's the matter, Doctor?" they would ask. "Why are you leaving?"

"We want to have our own country," my father would answer.

With a hurt expression on their faces, they would say, "But this is your country. Bulgaria is your country!"

The memory of Bulgaria clung to many of us when we crossed the stormy Mediterranean and settled in Israel. We carried a deep sense of pride in our Bulgarian origins. When other children would ask whether I too was a refugee, I would respond with an angry outburst and a fist-fight. "I am not a refugee," I would shout. "I am an immigrant!"

Most of us clustered in the abandoned city of Jaffa, Tel-Aviv's twin. We soon transformed the former Arab city into a Bulgarian enclave. In Jaffa everything was Bulgarian—the signs on the stores, the language spoken in the streets, the food and drink sold by street vendors, the daily newspapers, the books in the public libraries, the newly formed Maccabee-Jaffa soccer team, the excellent Tzadikov choir.

While becoming ardent, patriotic Israelis, learning the language, serving in the army, discovering the Ashkenazi Jews—we still remembered Bulgaria. We recalled its rugged landscapes, its vibrant artistic and intellectual life, its picturesque villages, its yoghurt and cheeses, its majestic, snow-topped mountains, its deep blue sky. We remembered the beautiful capital of Sofia, the golden beaches of the Black Sea, the long and narrow Valley of Roses that every spring turned into a fragrant carpet of flowers in many shades of pink and red.

We remembered our Sephardic heritage. We competed at reciting proverbs and verses in Ladino, our ancient Spanish dialect. We longed for the spicy flavors and the tantalizing aroma of our traditional,

Mediterranean food. We hummed the tuneful lullabies our mothers and grandmothers used to sing to us in the soft language of Cervantes.

We remembered the friends we had left behind, our homes, schools, and neighborhoods.

And most of all we remembered our rescue from the Holocaust.

Many recall, to this very day, that dreadful night in March 1943, when we were ordered to pack a few belongings into a bag and get ready to be taken away by the police. We remember the tragedy of the Thracian and Macedonian Jews who were deported, through Bulgarian territory, to the death factories of Treblinka. We can still describe the long trains of boxcars waiting for the Bulgarian Jews at the railway stations. We remember the crying, the despair, the terrible feeling of doom and impending death, and the ominous mention of "camps in Poland," which meant cruel annihilation.

But we were not taken away. The boxcars left the stations, empty. We didn't know exactly what had happened, but the Jews of Bulgaria were saved at the very last minute.

In May 1943 a second deportation attempt was made, and the orders were canceled once again. Not one Bulgarian Jew was deported from the kingdom. The entire Jewish community survived the war, beyond Hitler's grasp. As the years went by, and the true facts about the war years surfaced, we were amazed by the incredible story of our rescue.

In 1993 I came to Emory University in Atlanta, Georgia, as a visiting professor. I met with scholars, historians, and political scientists from throughout the United States. I was amazed to discover that the rescue of the Bulgarian Jews was almost completely unknown. There were publications concerning the Danish rescue, the Italian rescue, about Raoul Wallenberg, Chiune Sugihara, and Oskar Schindler, but nothing about Bulgaria.

I spoke about the Bulgarian rescue at several occasions. People would stand up and say: "This is a wonderful story, but it can't be true. If it were true, we would have known about it."

I thought that the unique story of the Bulgarian rescue, the largest and most dramatic rescue during World War II, deserved to be told.

# ACKNOWLEDGMENTS

For four years I carried out my research in the United States, in Israel, and mostly in Bulgaria. The timing was right. For years Bulgaria's Communist regime had tried to suppress the real story about the rescue for a very simple reason. The Bulgarian rescue had been carried out mostly by Communism's three worst enemies: the Church, the royal court, and pro-Fascist politicians. The Communist regime couldn't admit that fact because it contradicted its basic beliefs. Therefore the Communists attributed the rescue to "the Bulgarian people" and the valiant Communist underground, an unsatisfactory explanation that left most questions unanswered. Only now can the real story be told.

I was fortunate enough to have obtained access to an array of documents and testimonies that had not previously been published. I tracked down former officials of the Commissariat for Jewish Questions and other branches of the king's regime, met close relatives of the main characters in my story, and interviewed a large number of survivors, among them Queen Giovanna and President Todor Jivkov of Bulgaria, who had not previously been interviewed on this subject.

I am deeply indebted to my research assistants, Dr. Sonia Levi and Ms. Albena Taneva, both university professors, who did the impossible to obtain the necessary material and graciously weathered my stormy outbursts.

My project was wholeheartedly supported and encouraged by Emory University. Dean David Bright of Emory College and Mr. John

Ingersoll, director of development at Emory, endorsed my project and contributed to the research.

I am also grateful to several foundations and individuals without whose support this book would not have been completed: the Maurice Amado Foundation, the Free and Democratic Bulgaria Foundation, the Dorot Foundation, the Anti-Defamation League, the Lucius N. Littauer Foundation, Mr. Enrique Moscona, and the Cultural Fund of Kupat Alia in Tel-Aviv.

I am also very grateful to Professors David Blumenthal, Gordon Newby, Kenneth Stein, and Deborah Lipstadt of Emory University, for their support and invaluable advice.

Mr. Avner Shalev, president of Yad Vashem, and Dr. Yaacov Lazovik and his team gave me every possible support, including access to rare documents and unpublished archives. I also thank the Institute for Contemporary Judaism at Hebrew University in Jerusalem, the archive section of the Diaspora House in Tel-Aviv, Ichud Olei Bulgaria in Jaffa, and the staffs of various centers and archives in Germany and the United States that gave me access to their collections of documents and microfilms.

At Yad Vashem, I gained full access to Benjamin Arditi's private archive. My good friend Ms. Ellis Avrahami allowed me to view the private archives of her husband, the late Dr. Moise Avrahami. Mr. Mikhail Kolarov of Sofia graciously allowed me access to his archive and to read some chapters of his forthcoming book. I am grateful to King Simeon of Bulgaria, who became my "research assistant" for one weekend and flew to Lisbon, armed with my questionnaires, to interview his mother, Queen Giovanna. Princess Maria-Louisa supplied me with books and magazines. Stephane Groueff, the author of *Crown of Thorns*, answered my questions and queries. Ms. Ora Alkalay of Jerusalem guided me through the mazes of many Israeli archives. Professor David Cohen, in Sofia, succinctly described to me the results of his lifelong research on the subject and directed me to numerous sources and vital documents, books, and articles that proved to be of great importance. Mr. Eddie Schwartz, then president of the "Shalom" Jewish organization, and Mr. Yaacov Djerassi, the director of the Bulgaria foundation, helped me to establish contact with important witnesses and institutions.

My research assistants and I gained access to the Central National Archives in Bulgaria, to various ministries' archives, the archives of the Saint Synod, the archives of the Bulgarian Academy of Sciences, and the provincial towns' archives. We obtained the complete sets of minutes of the People's Courts, which passed judgment on the main figures of the *ancien regime* in 1945. We also obtained the police files, the interrogation reports, and the full depositions of the main protagonists.

We used the full diary of former Prime Minister Bogdan Filov, the diplomatic and SS archives of Germany, the diplomatic archives of Switzerland, the political department of the Jewish Agency, as well as documents from other countries and institutions. We also used the published diaries of the Reich's Ambassador Beckerle, the prime minister's wife Evdokia Filova, the king's friend and adviser Liubomir Lulchev, and other main characters. I used a large number of history books, memoirs, diaries, and documents that had been published in the United States, Bulgaria, and Israel. The works of Professor Frederic Chary, Benyamin Arditi, and Haim Keshales, although written before all of the source material was available, were very helpful to my research. The history of Bulgaria's Jews was deftly narrated by Gary Haskell in his 1994 book *From Sofia to Jaffa*. The Godishnik, the Yearbook of the Jewish community in Bulgaria, was an important source of material.

I am grateful to the people in charge of the National Archives in Bulgaria and the various archives in Israel and elsewhere, who gave us full support.

Last but not least, I thank the hundreds of Bulgarians I met during my many visits to Sofia, Plovdiv, Kyustendil, and the countryside. These fine people invariably went out of their way to help me, demonstrating that unique mixture of caring, warmth, and goodness that many of their ancestors had displayed toward my people on that fateful March 9, 1943.

CHAPTER ONE

# ALARM

March 4, 1943.

The sky was clear and the air crisp. A soft wind was blowing from the Macedonian mountains in the west. That evening, a group of Bulgarians gathered in the Kyustendil courtyard of Michael Abadjiev.[1] Friends since high school, long before the war, they often spent evenings together—drinking, singing, smoking hand-rolled cigarettes made of coarse dark tobacco, and discussing local politics. That night they met at a cornhusking, a traditional event in this part of the country, at which guests gather together to husk corn—while drinking the host's fiery slivovitz and munching salty snacks.

Later in the evening, Michael Abadjiev approached Buko Lazarov*. In Bulgaria, the name "Buko" was often used as a nickname for the firstborn son of a Jewish family, beside his given name. In Buko Lazarov's case, he was known only by this name. Buko was a slim, balding man with sharp blue eyes, renowned as a tobacco expert. He and his blond wife, Anka, wore small yellow stars made of thick celluloid on their lapels. They were the only Jews in the group.

"We must talk," Michael Abadjiev said, pulling his friend aside. He revealed that he had thrown the party as a pretext for meeting Lazarov, to avoid attracting attention.

What he had to say would make Lazarov's blood run cold.

A few days before, Zakhari Velkov, a friend of Michael Abadjiev, had come to see him in his Kyustendil office. Velkov was

---

* Buko Lazarov was the author's uncle.

(COURTESY OF THE LAZAR FAMILY)

*Buko Lazarov, the Kyustendil Jew who warned the Jewish community of the planned deportation, and his wife, Anka.*

a civil servant in the Commissariat for Jewish Questions in the Bulgarian capital, Sofia. Abadjiev, a lawyer, since the beginning of the war was in charge of the local properties and buildings requisitioned by the government.

Velkov requested that a tobacco warehouse known as Fernandes—which stood close to the railroad station—be put at his disposal.

"Why?" Abadjiev asked.

But Velkov wouldn't give a reason.

Michael Abadjiev told Velkov that he couldn't approve his request unless he was informed of its purpose.

Velkov hesitated but finally agreed, after making Abadjiev swear that what he told him would be kept secret. It was a matter of state and of the utmost importance, he said.

"We signed an agreement with the Germans for the immediate deportation to Poland of all Jews from Kyustendil, Dupnitza, Plovdiv, and other Bulgarian cities," he said.[2] The agreement had been signed by a German envoy, Theodore Dannecker, and by Alexander Belev, the Bulgarian Commissar for Jewish Questions. The warehouse was needed as a concentration locale for the Jews before their departure. Velkov added many details of the agreement, the deportation plans, and the date: March 10, 1943, shortly after midnight. Freight trains were already on their way to the Kyustendil station. The 980 town Jews were going to be taken to a transit camp established at Radomir, where they would be joined by thousands of Jews from the other cities. A few days later they would be sent across the border.

"I tried to keep my promise to Velkov," Abadjiev said, "but as the deportation date approached, I couldn't stay put anymore. That's why I invited you here tonight."

When the party ended, it was past the "Jewish curfew." Jews were not allowed in the streets after 9:00 P.M. Michael Abadjiev escorted Buko Lazarov and his wife to their home. "You must do something," he repeated urgently. "Don't keep quiet. Alert the Jews, make them fight against this!"

Lazarov parted from his friend, feeling "a deadly alarm."[3] He already knew that the police were rounding up Jews from the newly acquired Bulgarian territories in Thrace and Macedonia. Thrace had been detached by the Germans from Greece; Macedonia from Yugoslavia. The rumors were that the Thracian and Macedonian Jews were being sent to Poland. Buko had no doubt that deportation to Poland meant certain death. The first to go, he realized, would be the Jews from "the new territories", then the Bulgarian Jews.

The fateful event was less than six days away.

●  ●  ●

Buko Lazarov was stunned.

Bulgaria's Jews had lived there for many centuries almost unperturbed. Unlike other European Jews they were integrated in the Bulgarian society. They had not been subject to persecutions, expulsions, and pogroms.[4] The anti-Semitism they had encountered had been rare and had almost never turned violent. Although staunchly Zionist, and proud of their Jewish identity, they deeply loved Bulgaria. After all, some of their forefathers had come to Bulgaria even before the Slavs and the Bulgars.

After the destruction of the Second Temple in Jerusalem in A.D. 70—some claim even before that—Jews settled in this stunningly beautiful land, whose present territory is bounded on the north by the Danube River and Romania, on the west by Serbia and Macedonia, on the east by the Black Sea, and on the south by Greece and Turkey. Ancient coins, archeological finds, and fragments of old letters and documents have established the existence of an ancient Jewish community on Bulgarian territory.

Jews, known then as Romaniots, gradually settled in this crossroads of the Balkans, an area regarded as the gateway to the Near East and Arabia. Jewish merchants and craftsmen had been enticed by the trade potential of the country and the tolerance of the local population. These favorable conditions didn't change when the Slavs moved into the Balkans in the sixth century, followed by the Bulgar warrior tribes that emerged from the plains of Central Asia.

The Jews were still thriving when the Bulgarian kingdom was established. When King Boris I embraced Christianity in 863, the Jews were not persecuted. On the contrary, some of their customs and habits had spread among the new Christians, as witnessed by some of the 106 questions submitted to Pope Nicholas I by a delegation of Bulgarian emissaries: Which day is the day of rest, the Bulgarians asked, Saturday or Sunday? What are the proper regulations for the offering of the first fruits? Which animals and poultry may be eaten? Is it wrong to eat the flesh of an animal that has not been slaughtered? Should burial rites be performed for suicides? For how many days after giving birth is a woman forbidden to her husband?[5]

Certainly the Jewish religious rites performed in Bulgarian synagogues had influenced these and other questions. Jewish influence can also be seen in the names of some Bulgarian princes of that time—David, Moses, Aaron, Samuel [6] And when twenty-five years later the monks Kyril and Methodius devised the Cyrillic alphabet, they probably borrowed two characters—that have no equivalent in Western languages—from the Hebrew alphabet: "Sh" (from Shin) and "Ts" (from Tzadei).[7] Kyril and Methodius also were reputed for having translated the Bible from the original Hebrew into Old Church Slavonic.

In the centuries that followed, Bulgaria became a land of refuge for Jews exiled from Hungary, France, Bavaria, and other countries of Central and Western Europe. They survived an occupation of Bulgaria by Byzance that lasted more than a century. In 1185 Byzance was routed and the second Bulgarian kingdom became the mightiest power in the Balkan peninsula.

When King Yoan Assen II captured Theodorus, the king of Salonika, who had attacked Bulgaria in 1230, he conceived a special punishment for him. As the treacherous Greek was notorious for his cruelty toward the Jews, Yoan Assen charged two of his Jewish sub-jects with the honorable task of gouging his eyes. The Jews refused, and the king, in his fury, ordered that they be thrown to their deaths from a mountaintop. Fortunately for the Jewish subjects, two other volunteers were found to fulfill the grisly act, and Yoan Assen was appeased. The Jews regarded that incident as proof of the king's pro-tection of their people. The act was recorded in a letter from Rabbi Jacob Ben-Elijah to the apostate Pablo Christiani in Spain, as a warn-ing about the fate awaiting people who persecute the Jews. This unique document became known as the Coronel Manuscript.[8]

About a hundred years later, in 1346, King Ivan Alexander divorced his wife and married Sarah, a beautiful and intelligent Jewess from Turnovo, then the capital city. Sarah converted and became Queen Theodora. Not forgetting her Jewish origins, she protected her people.[9] While Bulgaria often followed the written politics of her neighbors, including anti-Jewish legislation and the expulsion edicts toward the Jews adopted in 1355, they were never implemented.

In 1396, the Ottoman Empire conquered Bulgaria. After Turnovo fell into the hands of the Turks, the Sultan ordered that all

Jews be expelled from the city, for having devotedly fought for Bulgaria. A single Jew, who tried to welcome the Sultan, was slain on his orders; the place where he died is marked still today by a stone mound called the Jewish tomb.

For the next five centuries, Bulgaria was enslaved by the Turks. Yet the Jews didn't suffer during the first three centuries of Ottoman rule. The sultans gave them autonomy in their internal affairs, encouraged their business ventures, and employed them as doctors and advisers. In 1492, following the expulsion of Jews from Spain, Sultan Bayazid II opened the gates of his empire to them, hoping to benefit from their knowledge and expertise. Thousands of Jews came directly from Spain to the Ottoman provinces known today as Turkey, Greece, Bulgaria, and southern Yugoslavia. They called themselves Spaniols, or Sephardim, from the biblical name for Spain, Sepharad. They brought with them their version of an older Spanish language, customs, and folklore, which remained alive and strong in their community. They claimed to be the only "pure" Sephardic Jews, as they remained the only Jews in the world that continued to speak their unique dialect, Shpaniol. Only a small minority of Yiddish-speaking Ashkenazi Jews—about 5 percent— survived the Sephardic melting pot.

For a while, the Bulgarian Jews knew a golden era. They traded with many European nations, especially Venice. Their religious and cultural life flourished as well. One of the greatest religious leaders of the Jewish people, Rabbi Joseph Caro, author of *Shulhan Arukh—The Set Table*, and *Beit Yosef—House of Joseph*, wrote some of his most important works in Bulgaria. In the sixteenth and seventeenth centuries international trade flourished, and some Jews became very rich. They surrounded themselves with luxury, including the finest silk clothes and expensive gold ornaments. This aroused the ire of Sultan Murad III, who decreed that Jews were forbidden to step out of their homes wearing silk and jewelry; Jewish men were no longer allowed to wear the customary Muslim headdress and instead had to wear a distinctive headpiece of green cloth.

Over time, following wars, persecutions, economic crises, and political changes, the Jews of Bulgaria gradually lost their wealth.

Their culture and status also suffered; they lagged far behind their brothers in Western Europe.[10] When the Russian army finally liberated Bulgaria from Turkish rule in 1878, there were very few rich Bulgarian Jews left. Most were small merchants, craftsmen, and workers. And many were poor.[11] They lived in miserable neighborhoods, side by side with poor Bulgarians, and like them earned their living through hard physical labor. The Bulgarians regarded them as equals, both economically and socially, and didn't feel threatened by them in any way.

After Bulgaria's liberation, the rights of the Jews were guaranteed in the national Constitution. Adopted in 1879 in the ancient Bulgarian capital of Turnovo, it was one of the most progressive and democratic constitutions in nineteenth-century Europe. In fact, the Jews obtained full equality. Still, anti-Semitic incidents continued: In Vratza, Pazardjik, Lom, and Russe, Jews were arrested and accused of murdering Christian children and using their blood for religious rites. These were typical cases of "blood libel," identical to similar eruptions of anti-Semitism throughout Europe. This misinformation had apparently been imported into Bulgaria from abroad, as were quite a few anti-Semitic books and brochures that were published at the end of the nineteenth century. But even these outrageous claims had very limited impact on the Bulgarian people. Jews were allowed in every facet of Bulgarian life, except for politics. There was one shameful incident, when the Bulgarian Parliament, the Sobranie, refused to recognize the election of Peter Gabe, a Jew, as a member of Parliament and hastily replaced him with a Christian.[12] Gabe's daughter Dora eventually became one of Bulgaria's most illustrious poets.

Bulgarian Jews felt so strongly for their homeland that they were willing to die for it. Jewish volunteers fought in Bulgaria's first war against Serbia, in 1885, and distinguished themselves on the battlefield. Bulgaria's first ruler, Prince Alexander Battenberg, decorated David Mizrahi, the commander of one of the Jewish Legions, and saluted his soldiers as "genuine heirs of the Maccabean spirit."[13]

In Bulgaria's subsequent wars, many Jewish men were decorated for acts of heroism. As recently as the Balkan Wars and World

War I, many became officers, some even reaching the rank of colonel. For a short while a Jew served as minister of justice; others became well-known writers, poets, musicians, and artists. They were a strong community, published books, newspapers, and magazines, had their synagogues, sport clubs, schools, libraries, a hospital, welfare associations, and a vibrant Zionist organization. Sofia's synagogue was one of the most beautiful in Europe. By the eve of World War II, Bulgaria's Jews numbered about fifty thousand, less than 1 percent of the Bulgarian population of about six million. About three-quarters of the Bulgarian people lived in the countryside, yet the Jews had no presence in the villages and concentrated in the cities. Half of them lived in the capital, Sofia.

The main enemies of the Jews were the militaristic Legionnaires, led by a group of aging generals, the extreme-right Fascist organization Ratnik ("Fighter"), and the youth Fascist movement Brannik ("Defender"). They mostly copied anti-Semitic practices from abroad, distributed translated books and brochures, and tried, with no success, to rally the Bulgarian people against the Jews. Average citizens treated their initiatives with indifference; the cultural and political elite reacted with anger and disgust. The Bulgarian society was deeply tolerant by nature, proud of its Constitution, and determined to protect its Jewish minority.

The Ratniks even tried to repeat the notorious Kristallnacht ("Night of the Broken Glass"), the violent attack that German Nazis launched in 1938 against Jewish stores and synagogues. On September 20, 1939, the Ratniks organized a march in the streets of Sofia. It degenerated into a stone-throwing assault on Jewish-owned stores.[14] The police didn't intervene. Some shop windows were broken, but the attack soon ended. Nobody was hurt, and eminent Bulgarians publicly condemned the outrageous incident.

Yet, on the eve of World War II, hostility was beginning to brew. A cabinet minister made some offending remarks about the Jews in a radio broadcast, and when the Jewish leaders complained to the justice minister, he fired back at them, "What do you want, that we sacrifice Bulgaria for fifty thousand Jews?"[15]

CHAPTER TWO

# THE FOX

King Boris III of Bulgaria had not a single drop of Bulgarian blood in his veins. But his father, King Ferdinand of Saxe-Coburg Gotha, descended from an illustrious lineage of royalty.

Ferdinand's grandfather was the last king of France, Louis Philippe d'Orleans. His mother was the French princess Clementine, and his father was a German prince. He was a nephew of Queen Victoria and a cousin of the Belgian and Spanish kings. Born and raised in Germany, for many years he had led the easy, hedonistic life of a European prince.

In 1886 Ferdinand was offered the Bulgarian throne by a delegation of endearingly naïve Bulgarians, who were sent by the Bulgarian Parliament that year to roam the European capitals, searching for a king. According to the recently adopted Constitution, Bulgaria had to be ruled by a prince (who would later become a king) of royal blood. The Bulgarians themselves, having spent five hundred years under Turkish rule, had lost all trace of their royal families. They viewed the entire population as commoners and, therefore, unsuitable to rule. Their first ruling prince, Alexander Battenberg, had been forced by the Russians to abdicate. A new blue-blooded ruler was urgently needed.

And so it was that the small delegation, composed of three respectable Sofia citizens, had been sent to the glittering capitals of Europe, to offer their country to some unemployed prince who would be kind enough to accept it. This strange quest had greatly amused most of Europe. After visiting Belgrade, Berlin, and London, the delegation found the twenty-seven-year-old Prince Ferdinand in Vienna. Ferdinand was a tall, narrow-shouldered man with a receding hairline, a mustache and a goatee, and a taste for splendid uniforms and flashy decorations. He welcomed the Bulgarian offer and became the king of a country he had only vaguely heard about. He was a renowned botanist and explorer and a lieutenant in the Austro-Hungarian army. But he was also a vain, pretentious dandy—who would become an autocratic ruler.

Ferdinand was a conceited, flamboyant man with sybaritic tastes and a condescending attitude, which hardly fit the rough, unsophisticated atmosphere of Sofia. He built or acquired palaces around the country, in Vrana, near Sofia, Cham Koriya, at the foot of the Rila Mountains, and Evksinograd, on the Black Sea coast. He married an Italian princess: the sweet, ethereal Maria-Louisa of Bourbon Parma. They had four children, of which Boris was the eldest. The last Tzar of Russia, Nikolai II, was Boris's godfather.

Maria-Louisa died giving birth to her fourth child when Boris was only five. Ferdinand remarried an older German princess, who became Queen Eleonore. The Queen was self-effacing and gentle. She played the role of a governess to her stepchildren, who liked and respected her. Ferdinand was anything but gentle. The despotic, demanding father struck fear in the hearts of his children. "Bo" (Boris), "Kiki" (Kyril), "Koka" (Evdokia), and "Micky" (Nadejda) were raised behind the tall fences of the royal palace by foreign tutors. They learned to speak flawless Bulgarian, French, and German and were light-years away from the harsh, simple life of Bulgaria at the turn of the century. The royal children, raised according to strict Western standards, would have been more at ease in Windsor Palace than in the brutal reality of an emerging Balkan nation.

The children desperately missed the love of their mother, whose presence might have tempered the severity of their demanding father. Throughout most of their lives they would be dominated by

Ferdinand, whom they called *Le Monarque*, "the monarch." They grew up feeling insecure and inadequate, in vain trying to please the overbearing king.

Boris, born in 1894, was a shy and sensitive youngster, good at his studies, excelling in languages. He was a lonely boy. He missed his mother more than his brother and sisters, as he was the only one to really remember her. His closest friend was his brother Kyril, a year younger, but stronger and bigger than the Crown prince. The two brothers often had to endure together the eruptions of their father's ill temper, especially when he scolded them for their scholar achievements, which he deemed unsatisfactory. They regularly went horseback riding together, as this was an essential part of the princes' education. When Boris became fifteen, a tutor for him and Kyril was brought from Switzerland.

The following year, Boris and Kyril went for their first trip abroad alone. They visited Istanbul, met with the Sultan, and went butterfly hunting in the fields outside Smyrna. Boris's first official trip was to England, where he represented his father at George V's coronation.

Boris had to get acquainted with the life of a future Head of State, and that included wearing uniforms, attending official ceremonies, receiving and giving medals and distinctions—duties that he disliked thoroughly. In London George V presented him with the Victoria Cross, and in Paris President Fallieres bestowed upon him the Grand Cross of the Legion D'Honneur. But Boris enjoyed most escaping for a few hours from his hosts and strolling incognito with his tutor on the Grands Boulevards, or traveling with the Parisians on the Metro underground trains.

In January 1912, all Balkan Crown Princes and a host of European Dukes and Archdukes attended the celebration of Boris's coming of age. To the sound of canon salvoes, the eighteen-year-old Boris, dressed in a lieutenant's uniform, swore allegiance to the oldest Bulgarian flag, and reviewed a parade of army units. But his real acquaintance with his soldiers would take place elsewhere—in the muddy ditches and bloody battlefields of the forthcoming Balkan wars.

• • •

Ferdinand wasn't a great admirer of democracy. Yet Bulgaria had already adopted a very progressive and liberal Constitution. It placed a prince or a king at the head of the State, which was held in check by the Sobranie (the Parliament). The prime minister's main task was to curtail and limit royal power. Ferdinand bluntly ignored the constitutional restrictions upon his reign, clashed with his more independent prime ministers, and more often than not chose his ministers from his circle of aides and royal advisers.

Yet, there was another side to Ferdinand. When he came to Bulgaria, the country was backward, underdeveloped, painfully emerging from five centuries of debilitating Turkish rule. Communications were almost nonexistent, transportation was antiquated, and government services hardly functioned. Sofia was a lethargic, Oriental town, lacking elementary services and cultural facilities. Parts of the city still looked like large, sleepy villages.

But after thirty years of Ferdinand's rule, Sofia had become a beautiful European capital, with magnificent public buildings, theaters, an opera, public gardens, museums, and a university. Tramway lines connected the various parts of the capital. The center of the city was paved with beautiful yellow tiles, which became the trademark of the Bulgarian capital. Ferdinand and his ministers organized the country administration, the education and health services, a diplomatic corps, and a modern army. They built roads and railroads and introduced electricity and running water to large parts of the country.

Ferdinand also envisioned himself a conqueror. The swashbuckling king, seized by delusions of grandeur, foolishly followed his dream of a Greater Bulgaria. From 1912 to 1913, he led his country in the Balkan wars, hoping to take from the Turks large territories that the Bulgarians considered theirs. But the Balkan wars ended badly for Bulgaria; she lost all of her early conquests to her former allies.

However, the frustrated Ferdinand did not give up. When World War I broke out, he joined the alliance of the German and the Austrian emperors. With them, he dreamed of conquests and glory; and with them, he lost the war. In 1918, with his army defeated and on the verge of a rebellion, with the Entente armies bracing for the final onslaught on Bulgaria, Ferdinand had no choice but to capitulate. Several units of the Bulgarian army revolted in the city of Radomir, near Sofia, proclaimed a republic, and tried to march on the capital. The rebellious soldiers advanced to positions that were only four miles from Sofia's center. However, the rebels were routed by Sofia's garrison, which was supported by German units. Besides, the night before, Bulgaria had signed the armistice—and the motivation of the rebels was seriously undermined. The revolt misfired, but Ferdinand had to pay the price of Bulgaria's defeat.

He was forced to abdicate and left Bulgaria, never to return. The peace treaty signed at Neuilly, France, on November 27, 1919, ceded large parts of Bulgaria's territory. Bulgaria was forced to abandon Macedonia, which it had occupied during the war, and to cede Southern Dobrudja to Romania, the border town of Tzaribrod to Yugoslavia, and the Aegean coastline to Greece. The victorious allies also imposed heavy reparations payments of 2,250 million gold francs on the impoverished kingdom.

Thus, Ferdinand's twenty-four-year-old firstborn son became Boris III, king of the Bulgarians.

•　•　•

Boris was a shy, hesitant man, lonely and weak of character. Balding and slim, he had gray-blue eyes, an aquiline nose, and a trim mustache. He was gifted with exceptional charm and easily gained the people's admiration; he exuded good breeding and a refined language, but he could also be quite foul-mouthed. Boris, unlike his father, cared little for protocol, splendid uniforms, and shining decorations. He detested the duties of his office. Happiness for him meant hunting or hiking in Bulgaria's picturesque mountains, playing music with a group of friends, or indulging in his favorite hobbies—driving cars and locomotives.

Brooding, superstitious, and suspicious by nature, he lived in constant fear of assassination. The dread of an assassin's bullet had become an obsession with him, since his visit to Russia at the age of eighteen, when Prime Minister Stolypin was shot dead before his eyes. That could happen in Bulgaria, too, which experienced a long period of unrest and violence. Its main protagonists were the army, the Communists, and the wild terrorists of the Macedonian organizations who left a bloody, murderous trail through Bulgaria's history.

In the turbulent twenties, Boris narrowly escaped several assassination attempts. On June 9, 1923, when a coup d'etat overturned the government, Boris fled to the fields outside his country palace. His prime minister, Alexander Stambolisky, was captured by the insurgents. Stambolisky was tortured and maimed before being brutally murdered.

Boris escaped other assassination attempts. In 1925, political dissidents ambushed his car on a mountain road, killing two of his companions. Upon visiting the families of the slain men a few days after the ambush, he was late to another funeral service for a recently assassinated general. The delay probably saved his life. In the middle of the funeral prayers, the roof of the church, Sveta Nedelya in Sofia, exploded and collapsed on the crowd of notables and senior officials. The bombing, allegedly carried out by Communist agents, left 160 people dead and 320 wounded.

Until 1934, Boris III was a puppet in the hands of the politicians and the military who ruled Bulgaria under the appearance of a parliamentary regime. It was an appearance that didn't fool anybody. The leaders of Bulgaria spoke of Boris with disdain. They forced him to sign large numbers of death-sentence decrees. Some openly suggested that they get rid of him and proclaim a republic.

Boris often burst into pathetic diatribes when in the presence of close friends and trusted aides. He would threaten to leave, to abdi-

(COURTESY OF BULGARIAN STATE ARCHIVES)

*After 1934, the Bulgarian Parliament became a rubber stamp for the king's policies. The Members of Parliament were elected according to the degree of their support for the king's government.*

cate, to commit suicide, declare that he was not meant to be a king, that he was not like his father, but a republican and a democrat. He would claim that he was a good negotiator, but not a leader, that he opposed the death penalty, that he wouldn't sign the decrees imposed on him by the ruling junta, and that he would no longer fulfill their whims. But as always, in the end, he would meekly obey and dutifully sign.

During this period, he acquired some useful personal habits that became characteristic of his behavior: a skill for subtle maneuvering between different factions, an ability to postpone and delay an unpleasant decision, a talent for not hearing about things that were not to his liking, and a knack for conveniently disappearing from the palace and hiding in one of his many retreats, whenever he feared pressure to do or to sign something he loathed.

Yet he was well liked abroad. Kings, foreign ministers, and presidents who met him inevitably succumbed to his charm. Hitler liked him and called him "the fox" because of his cunning. But he was not master of his own house.

The situation changed in 1934. Through smart maneuvering between the different political and military factions, Boris III succeeded in establishing a personal rule. That year, a group of left-wing colonels, supported by the Zveno republicans, seized power. The leaders of the coup were Colonels Damian Velchev and Kimon Georgiev. But after a short-lived and inept regime, the army practically retired from power. Velchev attempted another coup. He was arrested and condemned to death. But the justice minister, Dimiter Peshev, refused to sign the death warrant. The minister was dismissed from his position shortly afterward.

When he regained power, the king adopted several of the reforms carried out by the military junta. He was pleased that the military had shattered the power of the IMRO—the Macedonian organization, whose bloody terrorism had reached alarming proportions. The military also had abolished the party system, and that also pleased the king. Beginning in 1938, it appeared that members of Parliament were elected by the various constituencies according to their personal popularity. But in reality, the political parties were not dead at all. The political sympathies and former affiliations of the candidates were well known, and many were elected depending on their support of or opposition to the government appointed by the king. Henceforth, the majority of Parliament members were supporters of the king and his cabinet, and they had to be docile and obedient, if they wanted to be re-elected.

The former political parties were not allowed to campaign for their candidates. And the candidates for the Agrarian, Communist, Democrat, Radical, and other parties could run only as individuals, without party affiliations. That reduced the number of independent members of Parliament and upset the balance of power in the Sobranie.

On the other hand, in spite of the heavy pressure and campaigning by the government in favor of its supporters, no less than 60 politicians identified with the opposition were elected to the 160-strong Sobranie in 1938. For the first time Bulgaria had a quasi-

(COURTESY OF BULGARIAN STATE ARCHIVES)

*The old monarch, King Ferdinand (in forefront) was an honored guest at the wedding of King Boris and Princess Giovanna, in Italy.*

parliamentary regime, in which some of the staunchest opponents of the government were represented and could freely criticize the policy of the majority. At least one government fell in a classic vote of no confidence. Another election was held in 1940, raising the number of the majority to 115.

Boris held on tight to the reigns of power, appointing and dismissing ministers and prime ministers. Now nothing could be done in Bulgaria against his will. No cabinet minister could be appointed without his approval. Many ministers, even some prime ministers, had no political or public record whatsoever and owed their position exclusively to the king.

Still, Boris III was a democrat at heart and an enlightened ruler. He had nothing in common with people like Mussolini and Hitler, who were now rising in Europe. He was a simple and modest man, devoted to his people. Stories about his incognito visits to faraway villages or industrial sites, his spending time with peasants and workers, and his partaking in their poor meals became legendary.

(COURTESY OF BULGARIAN STATE ARCHIVES)

*The Royal family (left to right): King Boris III, Queen Giovanna, Princess Maria-Louisa and Crown Prince Simeon.*

During the bitter Bulgarian wars he too lived the hard life of the soldier on the military front.

He became immensely popular throughout Bulgaria. But he remained disarmingly simple. "I was not born to be a monarch," he once confided to his friend and assistant Parvan Draganov. "When I attend ceremonies I cannot stand looking at myself sporting these dangling rattles. People treat me like a deity. Little do they know that before I show myself in public, I have to go five times to the toilet so I won't do it in front of them!"[1]

His popularity increased in 1930, when the lonely king married an Italian princess, Giovanna, the daughter of King Vittorio Emmanuele. First a daughter was born to the royal couple, Princess Maria-Louisa, and four years later a boy, Prince Simeon, the successor to the throne.

As World War II approached, Boris strove to assure Bulgaria's neutrality. The basic principle of his foreign policy was to support the League of Nations. He sided with the League against the Italian

*(COURTESY OF BULGARIAN STATE ARCHIVES)*

*King Boris walked a fine line between the Soviet Union and Nazi Germany.*
*Both the Soviet (last in the row) and German (facing center) military attachés*
*were among those he greeted at an official function.*

invasion of Abyssinia. He started a rapprochement with Yugoslavia, although the two countries were bitterly opposed on the Macedonian question. Still, he refrained from joining the Balkan Entente, the alliance of Yugoslavia, Greece, Romania, and Turkey. They wanted to maintain the status quo established in the Treaty of Neuilly; he wanted to disrupt it and take back his lost territories.

Still, he wanted to keep out of the war. He feared Bulgaria might be destroyed if it became involved in the conflict of the Great Powers. "When the horses start kicking each other in the stable," he would say, "the donkeys get hurt."[2] Thus, he found himself in a very difficult situation. "If Stalin had his way," he once confided to the queen, "he would turn Bulgaria into a Bolshevik country. If Hitler had his, he would get rid of me and appoint a Gauleiter in Sofia."

He was haunted by his father's fateful mistake in 1914. "As long as I am king," he once declared to his aide and confidant Pavel Grouev, "no Bulgarian soldier will ever fight in a war again, I swear it! I won't allow any Bulgarian to be forced to fight outside our borders!"[3]

Yet, Bulgaria found itself slipping into the German sphere of influence. As far as internal politics were concerned, Boris feared the growing power of Bulgaria's Communist party, coupled with the deep emotional bond between the Bulgarian people and their Russian "brothers." The danger of "Bolshevization" seemed close at hand, and Boris wanted very much to avoid it.

Boris wanted to spare his people the bloodshed and economic destruction that a war would bring. But mostly he feared that the Bulgarian nation would refuse to fight against the Russians. Only sixty-two years before, Bulgaria had been liberated from Turkish rule by the Russian armies, and the Bulgarian people regarded the Russians as brothers and saviors. Sofia's main church, a splendid neo-Byzantine cathedral—white marble, gold-covered cupolas, stained-glass windows, frescoes, and icons—was named after Alexander Nevski and dedicated to the Russian soldiers who died in Bulgaria's Liberation War. The main square in Sofia was the site of a huge statue of "Tzar Osvoboditel"—the "King Liberator" Alexander II of Russia—sitting on his warhorse. A plaque set at the feet of the statue announced: "To the King Liberator, from grateful Bulgaria."

Boris knew well that the Bulgarians might accept an alliance with Hitler if it were beneficial for them, but they would never raise weapons against the Russians.

In the summer of 1940 both the Soviet Union and Germany, who were courting Bulgaria, declared their support for Bulgaria's claim on Dobrudja, which was now a part of Romania. Boris shrewdly navigated between the two powers, playing them against each other, showing himself worthy of the title "the Fox," pinned on him by Hitler.[4]

Economically, Germany had become the main trade partner of Bulgaria. In 1938 Germany accounted for 54.8 percent of Bulgaria's imports and 43.1 percent of her exports. Germany sold Bulgaria weapons, which Bulgaria needed in order to modernize her army.

Also, Germany contested the peace treaties that sealed World War I. And Bulgaria still felt the frustration and bitterness imposed upon her by the humiliating terms of the Treaty of Neuilly. Germany seemed to be the only great power that would listen sympathetically to Bulgaria's territorial claims.

Boris knew exactly what he wanted to achieve and at what price. He wanted territories, the restitution of the fertile northern plain of Dobrudja from Romania, and the annexation of Macedonia, now a part of Yugoslavia, and Thrace, in present Greece, which would give him the coveted access to the Aegean (known as the White Sea in Bulgaria).

King Boris had long ago realized that neither Great Britain nor the Soviet Union could satisfy his territorial claims. Great Britain and France were committed to the status quo in the Balkans. And the Soviet Union would never agree to divide Yugoslavia.

But Nazi Germany would. She had war interests in the Balkans and almost no commitments toward Bulgaria's neighbors. Besides, Yugoslavia still hesitated about which course of action to take in the war, and Greece was definitely a British ally, and therefore in the enemy camp. Adolf Hitler was the key for Boris to achieve his dream of a Greater Bulgaria.

The stage was set. Bulgaria could proclaim her strict neutrality as much as she wanted; King Boris could obsess over his father's experience—the forced abdication for having chosen the wrong partner. Still, by his deeds, as well as by his inaction at decisive moments, Boris allowed his country to move closer to the side of Germany.

Boris had another fear: If he drew too close to Germany and actively assisted her in the war, he might provoke a British offensive. And finally, he feared for his life and for his family. He believed that extremist elements, mainly pro-German generals, might act against him if he remained neutral. Thus, he had to walk a very fine line between a full-fledged alliance with Germany and a minor involvement on her side.

Therefore, Boris had to win German support, but to pay for it other than with soldiers. His conclusion was clear: to declare an unconditional alliance with Germany in every other way. He would try to delay or temper measures that would be unpopular with Bulgarian public opinion; but, when pressed, the alliance with Germany would prevail. If the Germans wanted him to join the

tripartite pact they had signed with Italy and Japan, he would procrastinate and maneuver to gain time, but eventually, if necessary,
do it. If the Germans desired a pro-Nazi government in Sofia, they
would have it. If the Wehrmacht asked to establish bases in
Bulgarian territory, he would allow it.

Boris was haunted by real and imaginary fears. Colonel
William J. Donovan, the chief of US Intelligence, met with Boris in
Sofia in January 1941.[5] He reported to the White House that Boris
was an honest, but easily frightened idealist, who sincerely wanted
to avoid war.[6] The Bulgarian king feared an invasion by the
Russians and a "Bolshevization" of Bulgaria. He was also haunted
by the memory of his father's forced abdication. Ferdinard had chosen the wrong side and had lost his crown as a result. Could this
also be Boris's fate?

When World War II broke out, Bulgaria's prime minister
announced his country's neutrality. But heavy German pressure to
join the tripartite pact between Japan, Italy, and the Reich was
brought to bear over the small kingdom. The Soviet Union tried to
counter that move and dispatched to Sofia a senior diplomat,
Arkadi Sobolev, to offer Bulgaria a pact of nonaggression and
mutual assistance.

Boris still maneuvered incessantly, refusing to commit himself,
hoping to gain time. His foreign minister, Ivan Popov, tried to explain
Bulgaria's foreign policy to Colonel William J. Donovan, President
Roosevelt's personal envoy to the Balkans, in January 1941. "I'll tell
you a Bulgarian anecdote," Popov said. "A criminal, sentenced to
death, begged the Sultan to postpone his execution for a year while
he taught a camel to talk. To his friends, at a loss to understand how
he was going to do this, he explained: 'I have a whole year at my disposal. God knows what may happen in one year—the camel, or the
sultan, or I may die.'"[7] That was Boris's game in this period of crisis—to compromise, to promise, to procrastinate, to balk, in order to
achieve his goal—gaining time.

But when he finally met with King Boris, Donovan analyzed
Bulgaria's situation with surgical precision. "Please correct me if my

(COURTESY OF BULGARIAN STATE ARCHIVES)

*King Boris with his Prime Minister, Bogdan Filov (center) and his Foreign Minister, Ivan Popov (right).*

conclusions are inaccurate," he said to the king and quoted: "Complete economic dependence on Germany; introduction of anti-semitic legislation; presence of German officers in the country; German uneasiness about my visit; officers expecting the arrival of German troops."[8]

The king didn't correct him. He had neither the courage nor the decisiveness to preserve his country's neutrality. On the contrary. He fired his pro-Western prime minister, Georgi Kiosseivanov, and replaced him with the pro-German Bogdan Filov. He appointed a right-wing Fascist leader, Peter Gabrovski, as interior minister. This was a clear indication of the king's strategic decision. Bulgaria was going to become a passive ally of Nazi Germany, but an ally all the same. And the benefits King Boris expected to reap from his alliance with the Germans had a price: anti-Semitic legislation.

King Boris was far from being an anti-Semite. He had a good relationship with his Jewish subjects. He exchanged warm telegrams with the leaders of the Jewish community at every important

(COURTESY OF BULGARIAN STATE ARCHIVES)

*Bodgan Filov's Bulgarian cabinet was the best friend Germany could hope for.*

Bulgarian holiday. His clothiers, dentists, and court suppliers were Jews. He had nicknamed the head of the royal chancery, Pavel Grouev, "the Jewish Consul," because of his many Jewish friends. He would tease him about "the Rosenbaums, Eliases, Goldsteins, Bakishes and Berahas" that Grouev and his wife often saw.[9] After an audience with Nahum Sokolov, the former president of the Zionist movement, Sokolov reported back to Sofia's Jewish leaders: "You can be proud of your king. He is a friend of ours."

The king also had a close personal friend in Germany, Dr. Arthur Meyer. Boris was utterly shocked when he learned of Meyer's sudden death in 1933. Harassed by the Nazis, roughly interrogated and threatened, Dr. Meyer had shot his wife and then killed himself. On the king's orders, the staff of the Bulgarian embassy came to his funeral and placed a wreath on his grave; it carried the inscription: "From your good friend, Boris of Bulgaria."[10] This gesture apparently didn't endear the king to the Nazi regime. Boris's sister, Nadejda, lived in Germany with her husband, Albrecht. Boris was alarmed to learn of the brutal persecution of the Duke of Wurttemberg, Nadejda's brother-in-law, by Nazi S.A. (Sturmabteilung) storm troopers.

King Boris III was considered by the Jews as their friend. But this friend had recently become the ally of the Führer. After the Germans passed the Nuremberg laws against the Jews, Boris did the same, although the Germans did not even ask for it. "I delayed [the Law for the Defense of the Nation] and I didn't want us to do it," the king admitted to Liubomir Lulchev, his occult adviser and confidant. "But now that they have it in Romania, Hungary and even France, I decided it was better that we did it, instead of having it imposed upon us."[11]

A few days after Germany invaded Poland, Prime Minister Georgi Kiosseivanov declared that Bulgaria would follow a policy of peace and neutrality.[12] A month later, the prime minister resigned and new elections were held. Of the 160 elected Members of Parliament, 115 (some say 121) were government supporters.[13]

After the election, the king appointed a new, pro-German prime minister, Professor Bogdan Filov, a renowned archeologist, art historian, and president of the Bulgarian Academy of Sciences. He had served in Kiosseivanov's cabinet as minister of education. A stout, balding man with a fleshy Mongolian face, bushy mustache, and heavy jowls, Filov was vain, pompous, and ambitious. He was a man of extremes, holding in disdain the art of compromise. He had studied in Leipzig, Freiburg, and Bonn, spoke fluent German, and firmly supported a pro-German policy. Totally seduced by the Nazi ideology, Filov was the best Bulgarian prime minister Germany could hope for.

But Filov's appointment created a strange contradiction at the very top of Bulgaria's government. On one hand, by appointing Filov, Boris became his prisoner. Filov was bound to become Germany's watchdog at the royal palace and to carry out the policy dictated by Berlin. On the other hand, Filov depended on king Boris, who could fire him at any moment.

Filov gradually assumed power. Backed by Germany, he had his way in most cases, even when the king initially disagreed with him.

In his personal diary, which he wrote with the clear intention of aggrandizing his role in history, Filov quoted many instances in which he convinced the reluctant king to follow his advice, mostly concerning Germany.

In Filov's newly formed cabinet, the key interior ministry was entrusted to a staunch Fascist, Peter Gabrovski, a Sofia lawyer, who was a founder of the Ratnik Fascist organization. In 1939 a law had been passed, barring Ratnik members from government positions. Now, one of the founders of this extremist organization had become a senior minister in the king's government.

As the war spread throughout Europe, Bulgaria seemed ready to become Hitler's official ally.

# CHAPTER THREE

# THE LAW FOR THE DEFENSE OF THE NATION

Adolf Hitler decisively moved ahead to win Boris's full allegiance. In the summer of 1940, he hosted diplomatic talks between Romania and Bulgaria in Vienna. On September 7, 1940, an agreement was signed, under the auspices of Germany, for the return of Dobrudja to Bulgaria. The entire Bulgarian nation rejoiced. The enthusiastic Bulgarians renamed streets in their cities after Hitler and Mussolini. The first of Boris's three territorial goals had been achieved.

In late September, Interior Minister Peter Gabrovski announced he was going to present a bill to Parliament. *Zakon za Zashtita na Natziata*, "Law for the Defense of the Nation" (ZZN), was modeled after the Nuremberg racial laws. Bulgaria's Jews were going to pay the price for the return of Dobrudja.

Gabrovski had discreetly started preparing the ZZN months before. In the summer of 1940 he had sent a young lawyer, Alexander Belev, to Berlin to study the Nuremberg racial laws passed in Germany in 1935.[1] Belev, another Ratnik leader, was Gabrovski's protégé. Shortly after Belev's return, the ZZN draft was ready. Even before it was received by Parliament, a copy of the bill reached the offices of the Jewish Central Consistory.

The Law for the Defense of the Nation, the Jewish community leaders realized, was an almost exact duplication of the Nuremberg Laws. The Jews were depicted as the vilest enemies of the Bulgarian nation, a danger to its very existence. The only difference from the Nuremberg laws was that in the Bulgarian version Jews were not defined as such by their blood, but by their religion—probably because even Gabrovski and Belev realized that talk of "Aryans" and "the purity of the Aryan race," in Bulgaria, would be considered ludicrous.

"A Jew" was defined as a person with at least one Jewish parent. All Jews had to register one month after the law was adopted, and declare in detail their property; cash had to be deposited in blocked bank accounts and withdrawn only with special permission. Jews had to use their Hebrew names as recorded in their birth certificates; they couldn't use last names ending with "ov," "ev," or "itch," which were typically Bulgarian.

Bulgarians were not allowed to adopt Jewish children; Jews were not eligible for Bulgarian citizenship. They were not allowed to vote or run for office, serve in a public capacity or in the Bulgarian army, or be employed by state or local institutions. They couldn't marry or cohabit with Bulgarians. They were not allowed to employ Bulgarian domestic help. The number of Jews allowed to study in higher schools, practice liberal professions, or work in commerce and industry was restricted to a quota representing their percentage in the population—which was less than 1 percent!

In addition, they were not allowed to change addresses or settle in Sofia. They couldn't invest in or manage cinemas, theaters, newspapers, or publishing houses. They were not allowed to own rural property, manage the firms in which their money was invested, or be members of boards of directors. They could not be customs officers, train employees, accountants, stockbrokers, dealers in precious metals, entrepreneurs, or suppliers. They couldn't even own pharmacies or drugstores.

The Jews exempted from some or all restrictions were those who had converted to Christianity, army volunteers, war invalids, and war heroes.[2]

The text of the bill was published in mid-October 1940. After the initial shock, the Jewish leaders launched a campaign against the ZZN. Joseph Geron, the president of the Jewish community, dispatched a memorandum, prepared by a group of leaders, to the Parliament speaker. It described the patriotism of Bulgaria's Jews and called the depiction of a Jewish "danger" to Bulgaria and its society an absurd and ridiculous allegation.

In his memorandum, Geron pointed out that the last official census in 1934 established the number of Jews in Bulgaria at 45,558, less than 0.7% of the country's inhabitants. Jews had almost no part in the nation's wealth. Only 75 Jews were farmers, and only 24 of them owned their farms. There wasn't one Jew among the owners of mines, forests, and quarries. There were a few scores of Jews who worked for the government as clerks and employees, out of 200,000 Bulgarians. There were only 84 industrialists, not even one banker. The Jewish Bank, Geula, belonged to a cooperative representing the entire Jewish population of Sofia. Out of 25,000 Jews in Sofia, only 1,422 owned shops, and 723 were merchants whose entire capital consisted of a small crate of cheap goods.

In the professions there also were very few Sofia Jews: 58 lawyers, 84 doctors, 25 engineers, 70 dentists. There were no Jews owning or managing newspapers, theaters, or publishing houses. Most of the Jews in Bulgaria, in Sofia in particular, were poor people, living in misery in the poorest neighborhoods—blue collar workers, craftsmen, technicians, workshop employees.

The conclusion was evident: How could these people be a danger to Bulgaria?

Did Bulgaria need a law to protect herself against them?

Geron also mentioned the high percentage of the Jewish soldiers and volunteers in Bulgaria's wars, 952 of whom had fallen on the battlefield. Recently, the Bulgarian minister of defense had written a moving letter of thanks to the Bulgarian Jews who emigrated to

Palestine, who had volunteered to enlist again in the Bulgarian army "and shed their blood for Bulgaria again if necessary."[3]

Geron's memorandum was circulated among more than 120 influential Bulgarians, including the king, all the ministers, members of parliament, former ministers, journalists, and other public figures. Two other detailed letters followed, in the same month.

Another initiative of the Jewish leaders was to meet with all the ministers, most members of Parliament,[4] and other influential members of society. They dispatched a delegation to the cabinet ministers. All the ministers, except for Gabrovski, met with the delegation.

Prime Minister Filov received the Jewish leaders twice. Before the bill's first reading, he coldly exposed the government's position. One of the delegation members, Dr. Buko Levi, noted that Filov gave the bill "a quasi-scientific explanation, based on German Nazism."[5] He said to the Jews: "Liberalism and Democracy have come to an end. . . . A new world is being born, the world of the 'New Order,' led by Germany, that carries new values and ideas . . . the ideas of the purity of the nation. . . . Restrictions will be imposed on anything that is alien to the nation."

One of the Jewish leaders asked why only the Jews were being persecuted, and Filov replied indifferently: "The others' turn will come."[6] Still, he promised to send the Jewish leaders a copy of the bill, so they would be able to present their grievances and reservations. Instead, he submitted the bill to Parliament the same week.[7]

The second meeting, a few weeks later, was much more dramatic. After Filov again proclaimed his Fascist theories, one of the Jews, Mancho Nissimov, began to describe the plight of Bulgaria's Jews, choked, and burst in tears. Filov reacted with anger and cynicism. "Stop these theatrics," he blurted.[8]

Finance Minister Dobri Bojilov ridiculed his visitors and mockingly spoke of their misfortune.[9] Joseph Geron went to the king's palace to request an audience with Boris. The chief of the king's private cabinet, Pavel Grouev, returned with a disappointing answer. "The king is sorry," he said, "but he feels uncomfortable about receiving a Jewish delegation, and you certainly understand why he feels that way."[10]

(FROM THE AUTHOR'S PERSONAL ARCHIVES)

*In no other country in Nazi-occupied Europe could such a photograph be taken.
In spite of the ZZN, these five women in the Bulgarian village of Gorsko Slivovo
became good friends. Second from right, the author's mother, the only Jew in
the group, wearing a Star of David on her jacket.*

Thus far, for Filov and Gabrovski, there were no surprises. The
chain of events could have been expected, even predicted. The bill
was published, the Jews reacted, their demands were rejected, and
the king distanced himself.

But what the government certainly didn't expect was the angry,
unprecedented public outcry.

"This law and others like it are putting an end to our popular and
constitutional freedoms, for which our forefathers shed their blood,"
wrote several hundred non-Jewish citizens from the fourth and fifth
Sofia electoral districts to the house speaker.[11]

"We most vigorously protest against the passing of this bill,
which is anti-national," seventeen citizens from the Sofia Third
Regional City Council wrote to the speaker.[12]

"The Law for the Defense of the Nation . . . is an attempt to deny the daily bread from our Jewish colleagues," cabled a group of Plovdiv tobacco workers to Parliament. "The patriotic Jewish tobacco workers, who work at our side . . . deserve a more humane treatment." A group of shoemakers telegraphed: "The Bulgarian workers have always stood against the maltreatment of the weak and defenseless." Several tailors qualified the approval of the bill as "a stain after the liberation of Dobrudja." Other Plovdiv workers, ped-dlers, pastry bakers, textile workers, technicians, carpenters, food workers, students at the teachers' academy, dispatched furious telegrams to the house speaker and the cabinet ministers.[13]

Fifty young people from the Zaharna Fabrika district in Sofia protested against "the reactionary theory that there are first class and second class nations. . . . the goal of this law is to mislead the public opinion, by designating the Jews as the cause of all the ills in our soci-ety."[14] Sixty-nine residents of the Losenetz district in Sofia pointed out that 8 percent of the soldiers killed in Bulgaria's wars were Jewish.[15]

The Communist party probably inspired some of the popular letters and telegrams, but many others were spontaneous. Still, Communists and non-Communists alike voluntarily signed the peti-tions and sent letters and telegrams with their signatures.

The protest was as furious in the Bulgarian elite as in the pop-ular circles. The Bulgarian Lawyers Union dispatched to Parliament an unequivocal letter demanding:

> . . . the abandon of that bill, which is unnecessary, harm-ful, and opposed to our principles of right and justice. . . .
> The Bulgarian constitution explicitly forbids the separa-tion of the Bulgarian citizens into lower and higher cate-gories. All Bulgarian citizens are equal before the law. All Bulgarian citizens have political rights . . . and all the inhabitants of the Kingdom have citizens' rights. . . . It is clear that the approval of the bill would be an infraction of the Constitution . . . which the Ministers and the Members of Parliament have sworn to observe and defend.[16]

Similar letters arrived from the Doctors Union, the Painters Union, the Administrative Council of the War victims, and other organizations.

"Poor Bulgaria," mockingly wrote the politician and journalist Christo Punev. "If our country of 7 million citizens is so afraid of the treason of 45,000 people, who even don't hold government or responsible jobs, that she must legislate extraordinary laws!"[17] The letter was countersigned by seven notable personalities, three of whom were former cabinet ministers.

One of the most noted documents was a letter to the prime minister and the house speaker, signed by twenty-one Bulgarian writers and poets. "We are very surprised and embarrassed," they wrote, "that [A Law for the Defense of the Nation] is being considered, when there is no feeling that the nation is attacked or harassed by anybody . . . A Law that would enslave a part of the Bulgarian citizens will remain a black page in our new history." The signatures were those of the greatest writers and poets of Bulgaria, including the eminent Ellin Pellin, one of the king's closest personal friends.[18]

Public figures sent personal or group letters to the authorities. One of the most respected figures in Bulgarian political life, former Minister Dimo Kazasov, wrote to Prime Minister Filov, expressing his deep shock at Filov's behavior:

> At this moment, you combine in your person five of the supreme functions of the political and spiritual hierarchy. You are the Prime Minister of the Bulgarian government. You are the supreme guide of the Bulgarian popular enlightenment. [Filov had kept the portfolio of Education Minister]. You are the President of the Bulgarian Academy of Sciences. You are a professor at the unique Bulgarian University. You are President of the Bulgarian Pen Club.
>
> Because of that, everybody is right to expect of you . . . a respect for the accepted ethical norms . . . a fine

sensitivity to any attempt to sentence defenseless citizens
to moral death, to incite the young generation to shameful
violence, to falsify historical facts . . . In spite of all, the
truth will resurrect, and at her light the surprised world will
see that the President of the Bulgarian Academy of
Sciences, instead of holding a torch in his hand, brandishes
a whip.[19]

No intervention apparently carried more weight than the resolution reached by the Saint Synod, the supreme body of the Bulgarian
church. As the official religion of Bulgaria was Christian-Pravoslav,
the positions of the Church had a very important impact on public
opinion. The head of Sofia's church, Metropolitan Stefan, wielded a
lot of political power. The bearded, outspoken cleric was known for
his hostile views toward Germany and his friendship for the Jews. A
meeting of the Saint Synod was called, with the participation of all
the Metropolitans: Stefan of Sofia, Kyril of Plovdiv, Paissi of Vratza,
as well as the Metropolitans of Turnovo, Varna, Lovetch, Sliven, and
their peers. They published the following statement:

This bill and some of its other decisions against the
Jews include some measures, which cannot be considered
as just and useful to the defense of the nation . . . A harmful impression is being created that this bill's goal is the
special treatment of a national minority in Bulgaria. All
men and nations should protect their rights and defend
themselves against dangers, but in this justified effort they
shouldn't admit injustice and violence against others.

The Metropolitans adopted a recommendation in two paragraphs.
They first demanded that all Jews who had been or would be con-
verted to Christianity be treated exactly as the Christian Bulgarians.
The second paragraph was much more significant. "We ask you, Mr.
Prime Minister and the honorable government . . . not to conceive any

measures against the Jews as a national minority, but to prepare satisfactory measures against any real dangers to the spiritual, economical, social and political life of the Bulgarian people, from whatever source these dangers might come." The resolution was unanimously adopted and signed by all the princes of the Bulgarian church.[20]

The ZZN, however, also had its staunch supporters in the extreme right. The Federation of Bulgarian reserve officers, the Federation of Bulgarian reserve noncommissioned officers, the war invalids—all these right-wing bodies printed and published posters and flyers in

(COURTESY OF BULGARIAN STATE ARCHIVES)

*King Boris standing with Metropolitan Stefan (right), the most colorful, versatile, and independent prelate in the kingdom.*

support of the bill. Those who would gain from the law—among them the Pharmacists Union and the Merchants Union—supported the bill as well. The police closely followed the activity against the ZZN and dispatched furious reports to Peter Gabrovski.[21]

The Fascist National Students Union, in a smear offensive, accused the twenty-one writers who had signed the letter against the ZZN of receiving bribes. The "Otez Paissi" Christian-Fascist youth movement went even further and distributed flyers calling the writers "traitors." The flyers concluded: "The progress of the Bulgarian people goes over the corpses of all those avowed and secret enemies, who impede its free and right development."[22] Encouraged by the government, Fascist writers and journalists published anti-Semitic articles and brochures, but they had a minimal impact on the Bulgarian people.

• • •

Agitated and furious debates marked the procedures of Parliament when the Law for the Defense of the Nation was submitted for its approval. Several independent members, led by the intrepid Professor Petko Stainov and former Prime Minister Nikola Mushanov, exposed the absurd and even ridiculous character of the law and its allegations. They were joined by some other speakers, identified with the Social Democrats and the Communists, and even by one member of the government majority.

At the height of the debate, a tragic event occurred that symbolically illustrated the despair of Bulgaria's Jewish community. On December 14, 1940, a small sailing vessel named *Salvador*, carrying 326 immigrants to Palestine, sank in a violent storm in the Sea of Marmara. Of the 335 people on board, 122 people were rescued; 213, including 66 children, died. The ramshackle *Salvador* had sailed from the Bulgarian Black Sea port of Varna, in spite of the warnings of several Jewish leaders that it was not fit for travel. But as the dark clouds of Nazi persecution gathered over Bulgaria, many Jews were ready to ignore the risk and head for Palestine.

Indeed, Bulgaria had become a departure base for thousands of European Jews, from Czechoslovakia, Hungary, and other European nations, who during the years 1939–1941 fled before the Nazi tide. Under the determined leadership of a controversial Zionist, Dr. Baruch Konfino, more than forty-five hundred of them reached Palestine.

Another controversial sea wolf, a colorful adventurer, painter, writer, revolutionary, and spy named Anton Prudkin served as captain on many of the harsh voyages from Bulgaria. Prudkin, who had been the Sofia governor in the Stamboliski administration, was arrested in 1923 for terrorism and sabotage and sentenced to death. King Boris commuted his sentence to fifteen years in jail. Released in 1936, Prudkin got involved with "Aliya Beth," the illegal immigration for Palestine, and for a while was regarded by some as a hero. But this incorrigible revolutionary got in trouble again, was arrested for espionage for Soviet Russia, and hanged on August 2, 1942.

The fatal voyage of the *Salvador* heralded the end of the illegal immigration to Palestine. Only one more ship, the *Dorian II*, succeeded in leaving the port of Varna, on March 2, 1941, with 170 immigrants on board, hours before the German army marched into the Black Sea port. A month later, sixty-five Jewish children left Bulgaria via Turkey, with official visas for Palestine. They were the last Jews to leave for Palestine before Bulgaria's borders were sealed.

•   •   •

When news of the *Salvador* tragedy reached Bulgaria, in December 1940, the Bulgarian Jews were stunned and shocked. Many of their friends tried to plead their cause before the Sobranie. Weren't the deaths of so many innocent people the result of the cruel persecution resulting from the Law for the Defense of the Nation? Shouldn't Bulgaria regain control and stop this inhuman measure that was so alien to her national character?

But the debate was already lost. The government majority, led by Gabrovski and a group of pro-Nazi backbenchers, hastily approved the law in several short sessions during November, December, and January. Quite a few members of the majority, wrote Deputy Speaker Dimiter Peshev, supported the law because they regarded it as lip service to Germany. They believed that:

> . . . the interest of [our] policy with Germany, policy from which we expected the achievement of basic national and political goals, could justify certain temporary restrictive measures against the Jews, if they could help that policy. Nobody, though, agreed or admitted that these measures could be permanent, or that they would take the dimensions and the form applied by the Germans . . . We also assumed, that the restrictions and the sacrifices, imposed upon the Jews, were heavy but temporary, and not of an excessive nature.[23]

Peshev pointed out that the need for alignment with Germany was felt all through the debate, but no one mentioned it, and all the speakers presented the ZZN as a purely internal Bulgarian matter.

No one ever broached the subject that the new Jewish policy of the government was related to the German alliance. The only hint of a foreign influence was a phrase in the Bulgarian writers' letter that vaguely spoke of "imitation."[24] Still, a look at the political timetable would show that the bill was first published a few weeks before King Boris's first visit to Hitler in November of 1940. The debate and the vote were completed in early January 1941 in the very days when Prime Minister Filov arrived in Germany, supposedly "to consult a doctor"—but actually to hold secret talks about joining the tripartite pact.

On January 15, 1941, Gabrovski sent the law to the palace, for the king's ratification.

But what did the king really think of the ZZN?

None of those who wrote and signed the fiery letters, petitions, and telegrams obtained an audience with the reclusive king, except for Colonel Liubomir Lulchev, his occult adviser and close spiritual confidant. Lulchev was one of the main figures in a strange spiritual-religious sect, the Dunovists, who practiced a unique mixture of Christian percepts with Far Eastern beliefs—sun adulation, diet, strict rites, and mores. The members of the cult would meet before dawn each morning at their village at the fringe of "Boris's Park" in Southern Sofia and welcome the rising sun with a ritual of body movements, songs, dances, and exercises. The leader of the cult was "the Teacher," an old man called Peter Dunov, sporting a long beard and dressed in white. Dunov spoke of peace, love, and a legendary "white brotherhood." Dunov's disciples were mostly Christians, but they also included some Jews. According to many sources, some members of the Royal family were deeply impressed by Dunovism and might have been secret Dunovists themselves. (Today there is a rebirth of Dunovism, and large numbers of pilgrims from all over the world come to Bulgaria to learn the teachings of Dunov's disciples.)

There is no doubt that the superstitious King Boris deeply respected Dunov and his teachings. He had many secret talks with

Dunov's emissary, Liubomir Lulchev, in the royal palace. Boris's door was always open to him, and he listened attentively to his advice, although he did not always follow it.

Shortly before Parliament began debate of the ZZN bill, Lulchev wrote a letter to the king.

> Your Majesty . . . In its present form the Law for the Defense of the Nation is a mistake, for the results of which we all shall pay one day, including you personally . . . Who will defend the Nation and from whom? . . . The Law in question will facilitate one-sided decisions that can't be appealed, and widely open the door to excesses. Why should new sufferings be created, we have too many of them anyway; there is a lot of violence all over . . .

The letter ended with a veiled warning: "In no case would we want you to have the same fate like your father."[25]

The same day Lulchev saw Dunov, "the Teacher," who spoke to him against the law. "There cannot be a state without laws," Dunov said, "but Bulgaria should have the mildest laws."

Lulchev then went to see the king and raised the question of the ZZN bill. The king was obviously embarrassed and ill at ease. He said to Lulchev that he hadn't read it yet but expressed willingness to pay attention to Lulchev's remarks. Lulchev then read aloud several paragraphs and pointed out that the Jews were being abused already and that this law would encourage excesses and unscrupulous decisions.

"I understand," Boris said. "That means there should be installed limits and norms, so there would be no excesses . . . "

Lulchev repeated that the law must be just and "close the door to excesses."

"Yes," the king agreed, "[the law] should be polished . . . I am not a lawyer myself, I don't need to, but justice must be introduced [into the law] as much as possible. This is a transit period."[26]

However, the king didn't fulfill his promise to Lulchev, nor did he ask anybody to "polish" the bill or tighten "its norms and limits."

When the bill became law, more than two months later, Boris meekly signed it without a word.

The law was published in the state *Gazette* under this heading:

We Boris III
with God's Mercy and the People's Will
King of the Bulgarians
declare to all our subjects, that the XXVth People's
Sobranie . . . voted and adopted.
We approved and approve the following
Law for the Defense of the Nation.

On January 26, 1941, three days after the official publication of the ZZN, Lulchev met the king in his palace at Vrana, outside Sofia. Boris himself opened for him the gate leading to the garden, and they went for a stroll. Lulchev again raised the subject of the ZZN. As a bill, he told the king, it had been very unjust, but now that it had become law, it had become very cruel.

"Because of that," the king said, "we left it to be applied with a set of regulations."

"I don't know," Lulchev replied, "but this is something horrible and it can bring only trouble."[27]

The set of regulations was published in February. They were harsh and sometimes much crueler than the original law. The king had not interfered with their preparation, the same way he hadn't interfered with the writing of the bill. Once again, his role was to obediently sign the regulations that were brought to him. Once again, he carefully avoided being associated with the law in any way. Hitler had rightly compared him to "a fox, which mostly chooses such paths, where in case of need it can erase its footprints."[28]

CHAPTER FOUR

# THE COMMISSAR

O n March 1, 1941, in the magnificent hall of tapestries at Belvedere Palace in Vienna, in the presence of Joachim von Ribbentrop and Count Galeazzo Ciano, Prime Minister Bogdan Filov signed the Tripartite Pact. And Bulgaria became an official ally of Nazi Germany.

King Boris successfully postponed joining the Nazi coalition, albeit briefly. In October 1940, in a long letter to Hitler, he had explained his reasons for not signing the pact at that moment.[1] His reticence was sharply criticized in several secret reports of the German security services in Sofia to their superiors in Berlin.[2] Consequently, Boris was invited to meet Hitler at Berchtesgaden, but there he once again evaded Hitler's demand to join the Tripartite Pact.[3] Still, he did it with a lot of charm and parted from the Führer in the best of terms. As he bid his goodbye, he said to Hitler: "You have down there a small true friend [Bulgaria] whom you shouldn't reject."[4]

On his return, King Boris declined yet another offer. This one came from Russia. The Soviets offered to guarantee Bulgaria's security if the king would sign a formal pact with their country.[5]

The Germans continued to apply pressure. Finally, in a formidable snow blizzard, Filov secretly traveled to the Führer's mountain retreat, the Eagle's Nest, where he met with Hitler and Ribbentrop on January 4, 1941. On his return, he told the king that there was no other alternative but to sign the Tripartite Pact. Boris reacted with unusual fury. Filov was amazed:

> At first the king said he preferred to abdicate or throw ourselves in Russia's arms, even if we would become 'bolshevized' by that. He was a Republican king; he cared about the people.
>
> Filov further quoted the king as saying that Bulgaria's involvement in the war was an idea of the 'old timers' . . . with his own father at their head, who couldn't cope with the thought that we had achieved everything so far much better than them, without war.[6]

After the outburst, Filov spent half the night with Boris, convincing him that joining Germany was the only way.

Still it took two more months and extreme pressure until Filov flew to Vienna, on March 1, and signed the pact. A radiant Hitler hosted him for lunch and took seconds from the dessert, which the delighted Filov saw as proof of the Führer's great satisfaction.[7]

After the signing, Ribbentrop and Count Ciano, Italy's foreign minister, handed Filov secret letters stating that when the Balkan frontiers were set at the end of the war, Italy and Germany would recognize Bulgaria's access to the Aegean, between the mouths of the rivers Maritza and Struma, in present Greece.[8]

This was an important step, but it satisfied Bulgaria's aspirations only in part. The documents didn't mention Macedonia. They also promised Bulgaria less territory in Greek-controlled Thrace than she asked for. Finally, the German-Italian promise would become effective only at the end of the war, while Bulgaria dreamed of recovering Thrace in the very near future.

A few hours before the formal signing, the German armies had crossed the bridges on the Danube and marched into Bulgaria. An enthusiastic Bulgarian population welcomed them. In the Parliament building in Sofia, on his return from Vienna, Filov was received with deafening cheers. Nikola Mushanov, Petko Stainov, and a few other opposition leaders tried to protest, but their voices were drowned in the fervent cheers of the majority.

Soon after, the Wehrmacht launched two lightning offensives: one against Greece and the other against Yugoslavia. Both countries collapsed under the German assaults. Six weeks later, the Germans asked the Bulgarian army to occupy Macedonia, in defeated Yugoslavia, and Thrace, in fallen Greece.

*(COURTESY OF BULGARIAN STATE ARCHIVES)*

*Strange allies, King Boris (left) and Adolph Hitler (right) met several times over the course of the war.*

For the time being, that was only military occupation, intended to free German troops for other assignments. (Hitler needed them for Operation Barbarossa, the invasion of the Soviet Union, which was launched on June 22, 1941.) But for Bulgaria, this was the realization of her most precious dream. Thrace and Macedonia were returning to Bulgarian rule. They again were part of the Bulgarian kingdom.

Huge demonstrations of popular rejoicing broke out throughout the country. King Boris, yesterday so dejected about the German alliance, was this day at the peak of his glory. First Dobrudja, now Thrace and Macedonia! In a few months Boris had achieved Bulgaria's territorial dreams without firing a single bullet. He was now referred to as Tzar Obedinitel, "King Unifier" of Bulgaria. To a German diplomat he spoke with admiration of the Führer, to whom Bulgaria owed the realization of her national dreams. He would never forget what the Führer had done for Bulgaria.[9]

• • •

> We are the Maccabees' descendants
> with a Bulgarian hero's heart—
> We build the road to the Aegean
> where freely waves our nation's flag.[10]

These verses, published in the Central Consistory Bulletin in the spring of 1941, symbolized the change in the life of thousands of Jewish men in Bulgaria.

Two weeks before the signing of the Tripartite Pact, Gabrovski had published in the state *Gazette* the regulations for applying the ZZN. They included practical instructions for the implementation of the law, ordered the issuing of special (pink) identity cards for Jews, and initiated the immediate discharge of all the Jewish soldiers and officers serving in the Bulgarian army. The only way Jews could serve in the army in the future was in Jewish labor companies. On May 1, 1941, all Jewish men between the ages of twenty and forty were called to the army labor units.

They were sent to build and enlarge roads in the south of the country, close to the Greek border and the newly acquired Thracian territories. They worked with patriotic fervor, as witness the above verses and this telegram, sent by Lieutenant Jacques Levy to the Consistory:

> Called to the lush Rhodope Mountains, to fulfill our duty as work armies to King and Country, we blast rocks, enlarge the road to the azure coast of the White Sea, conscious of our deep historic responsibility to the entire Bulgarian Jewry.
> Long live H.M. the king!
> Long live Bulgaria![11]

*March 1, 1941—the Wehrmacht crosses the Danube into Bulgaria, on it's way to attack Greece and Yugoslavia.*

The Jews tried to overcome the pain of no longer being allowed to fight for their country, and to adjust to the new situation. The official Jewish newspaper declared:

> Those who defend our borders and those who plough the land, build roads or erect bridges—they all serve the motherland . . . True, in the recent past the Jews, together with their Bulgarian colleagues, spilled their blood on the battlefields . . . They now will apply all their physical and spiritual forces in order to fulfill with honor and truthfulness the labor tasks they will be ordered to accomplish.[12]

At first, the Jewish labor units had little to complain about. They were regular units of the Bulgarian army, wore Bulgarian uniforms, and were commanded by Jewish officers. They were treated the same way as similar units of Christian soldiers.[13] In war-torn Europe, where Jews were already subject to inhuman treatment, such "good" treatment was highly unusual. But the situation was about to change.

In July 1941 a new German ambassador arrived in Sofia. Adolf-Heinz Beckerle, an SA. The SA (Sturmabteilung) were the storm troop companies of the Nazi party. Obergruppenfuhrer and a former Frankfurt chief of police, owed his appointment to the Führer himself.[14] Hitler, indeed, unhappy with the "incompetent" diplomats representing the Third Reich in the Balkans, ordered Ribbentrop in January 1941 to appoint efficient people to these countries. Ribbentrop asked the SA headquarters for the names of some gifted commanders. Beckerle, a fanatic Nazi and a staunch anti-Semite, was dispatched to Bulgaria, to replace an old-school diplomat, the Baron von Richthofen. King Boris was outraged. He considered Berkerle's experience as a police chief to be an insult. He told his cousin, Prince Dietrischsein, in Vienna, that he had no use for police chiefs as envoys to Sofia. He felt that the Balkan countries shouldn't be used as guinea pigs, to test decorated SA men as diplomats.[15]

Beckerle promptly discovered an intolerable situation: Jews were serving in the Bulgarian army! Wearing Bulgarian uniforms,

*Jewish workers in a Bulgarian labor gang did not appear to be mistreated. In these two photographs, workers pause for a moment with a camera. The smiling man with the peaked cap in the bottom photo is the officer in charge. The author's father appears in both these photographs.*

led by Jewish officers, these inferior beings were soldiers in the military forces of Germany's ally!

Beckerle urgently requested an audience with the Bulgarian minister of foreign affairs, Ivan Popov, and demanded that he put an end to that "situation."[16] A week later he saw Popov again and demanded not only that he detach the Jewish labor units from the army but also that he charge them with extremely hard work. Ivan Popov hastily agreed.[17]

Popov reported to Filov,[18] who immediately complied. On August 12, the cabinet decided to separate the Jewish labor units from the army and attach them to the Ministry of Public Buildings, Roads, and Public Works. It was also decided to deny them military benefits and salaries, to raise the age of service to forty-six, and to force them to wear a distinctive sign—a yellow armband—in order to be recognized as Jews.[19] The decision was promptly reported in the daily papers.[20]

The living conditions of the Jewish laborers quickly deteriorated. They were placed under the command of Bulgarian officers, many of them known for their cruelty. Their food was bad, and the living conditions degrading. Still, with their unfailing optimism and deep love for their country, the mobilized Jews in the labor units continued to strive to do their best. They worked hard by day, and at night some of them still wrote poems by the light of gas lanterns in their miserable tents. They didn't give up.

> Our toil, even when it's cruel
> and raw and rough, and so-called hard
> is the eternal horn of plenty
> when you are not a slave oppressed,
> but a free man, with real hope blessed—
>
> So blast the rocks and build the roads,
> in rain, and cold, and scorching heat . . .
> you worthy are of brighter days
> for them with courage you will fight.[21]

● ● ●

But courage was not enough. In that summer of 1941 more restrictions were applied against the Jews. Bulgaria agreed, most obediently, to any German demand—expulsion of Jews who were foreign nationals, removing her protection from Bulgarian Jews who were out of the country, closing her gates to immigration to Palestine.

The ZZN financial clauses were doggedly applied. Heavy taxes were imposed on all the Jewish properties; if the owners didn't pay half of the taxes right away and the other half in six months, the properties were confiscated. The Jews had to file tax declarations on all their properties. In the following weeks they filed 29,432 declarations on their properties, whose total value can be estimated at about 6.2 billion leva (roughly equivalent to $75 million, as the rate of exchange was 82 leva to the U.S. dollar). The government assessed the tax on this property at 1.7 billion leva ($21 million), calculated at the rate of 20 to 25 percent of the total value. The Jews paid most of this tax in the following year.[22]

The Jews were confined to certain cities and neighborhoods. Some businesses were expropriated, and in many cases Jews had to give up their apartments. Radio sets and automobiles were confiscated. (When the order to deliver all radio sets to the authorities was published, the author's father refused to comply. He grabbed an ax and smashed the radio set in their home. His sister filled a bag with the radio lamps and other recognizable parts and threw them in the Sofia river.) Jews couldn't use the telephone lest they received a special authorization. Interior Minister Gabrovski issued a strict order forbidding Jews to discuss political and public matters "in order not to upset the Bulgarian nation," and imposing on them a curfew between 9:00 P.M. and 6:00 A.M. Gabrovski warned that Jews who didn't comply would be severely punished by the stripping of their Bulgarian citizenship and even by expulsion from the national territory.[23]

Gabrovski's long-contained hatred of the Jews had finally exploded, and he didn't hesitate to enforce draconian measures that

(COURTESY OF BULGARIAN STATE ARCHIVES)

*Following the publication of the ZZN (The Law for the Defense of the Nation), Jews were ordered to deliver their radio sets to the authorities.*

would please Germany. He felt free to do so: a major restraining factor in Bulgarian internal policy had been removed. Three days earlier, on June 22, Germany had treacherously attacked the Soviet Union. Operation Barbarossa was launched. Bulgaria was locked into her status as a German satellite.

As thousands of German tanks trampled the Russian wheat fields, as Luftwaffe Stuka bombers dived over the fleeing Soviet troops, and as news of astounding victories filled the front pages of the papers, Bulgaria acted swiftly. Its tolerant attitude toward the Communists ended abruptly. The Communist party was declared illegal; Communists and Communist sympathizers were expelled from Parliament. Political concentration camps were established. The Communists, for their part, reacted by forming small partisan units and starting guerrilla warfare against military targets. They were supported by the Soviet Union and later, intermittently, by the Western Allies. Four percent of the freedom fighters—more than four times their proportion in the general population—were Jewish.

The Communist radio station, Christo Botev, named after the nine-teenth-century revolutionary poet Botev—a hero of Bulgaria's strug-gle for freedom—intensified its broadcasts from Russia.

And still, something unique happened, an event that had no equal in Nazi Europe. Bulgaria did not declare war on the Soviet Union and did not cut off diplomatic relations with Moscow. Until the very end of the war and despite heavy and persistent German pressure, Bulgaria stubbornly refused to declare herself the enemy of her Russian brother. She became the only German ally in which a Soviet embassy continued to function, openly and officially. The embassy stayed in its sprawling building, a few yards away from the grounds of the royal palace. The red Communist flag, stamped with the hammer and sickle, continued to fly in Sofia's sky very close to the Nazi swastika until the very end of the war.

●　●　●

On December 29, 1941, a handsome forty-two-year-old Bulgarian lawyer was sent by Interior Minister Gabrovski on a special mission to Berlin.[24] His name was Alexander Belev. A slim, elegant, dark-haired bachelor (some police reports maintained that he was divorced), he had been born in Lom, a small but thriving port on the Danube, and studied law at Sofia University before working as the Saint Synod secretary. According to certain sources, his grand-mother, who had been born in Dalmatia, made her living by dancing in the Lom inns; his father, a schoolmaster in Burgas, on the Black Sea, had been fired from his job and tried for theft.[25] One of his grandfathers was Italian, Melanese, and this fact was later to insti-gate persistent rumors that Belev was of Jewish blood.

Of course it was a ludicrous allegation. Bulgaria probably had not known a more fanatic Nazi. He boasted that he had organized the Bulgarian version of "the night of the broken glass."[26] As a member of the Ratnik organization, Belev had followed his former boss and fellow Ratnik Peter Gabrovski from his private law firm to the Ministry of Interior. For a short while he had worked at the Research and Surveys Department, then had been appointed legal counsel to the ministry and sent to Germany to study the Nuremberg laws.

Back in Sofia, he had been charged with preparing the ZZN; he was not pleased with the final result, judging it "too soft."[27] A witness reported that "he was dedicated to the annihilation of the Jews"; in the ministry he was known as a workaholic and a loner, always bent over his desk, to the point "that nobody even knew the color of his eyes."[28]

On December 29, 1941, he traveled to Berlin, returning on February 14, 1942. He submitted to Gabrovski a detailed report proposing to correct the flaws in the ZZN by promulgating a new anti-Jewish law giving the cabinet full freedom of action.[29] He also suggested other means to assure "the radical solution of the Jewish question . . . by deportation of the Jews and simultaneous confiscation of their property."[30]

When he spoke of the "radical solution," Belev apparently knew what he was talking about. During his stay in Berlin, the most momentous decision about the Jewish question had been reached; and Belev's close friends in the Gestapo and the SS had informed him of the secret, horrendous task the Reich had decided to undertake.[31]

On January 20, 1942, a relaxed meeting took place in Berlin, chaired by Reinhard Heydrich, the head of the RSHA (Reichsicherheitshauptamt), the Reich's main office for security. In this meeting, which was followed by a light meal, a group of Nazi leaders decided to apply "the final solution" to the Jewish problem. The businesslike, almost casual meeting was to be remembered as the Wannsee Conference, so named after the address of the building where the gathering took place—the RSHA offices at 56–58 am Grossen Wannsee in Berlin. The *endlosung*—final solution—of the Jewish problem was going to be carried out in huge death camps, to be built in the East.

Two months later, the annihilation factory at Belzec began functioning; it was followed, a month later, by Sobibor, then Treblinka, Maidanek, Auschwitz. And as the trainloads of Jews from occupied

Europe started moving toward the gas chambers, Germany turned to Bulgaria.

Bulgaria at this time seemed ready to do almost anything to satisfy her German ally. Of all Germany's vassals, she seemed to be the most willing to cooperate with the Reich on Jewish matters.[32] She promptly agreed that Germany would treat Bulgarian Jews living in other countries as these countries' citizens, without any special privileges. By doing this, she removed her protection from these poor people, who became easy prey for the perpetrators of the final solution. Bulgaria's foreign minister even suggested to the Reich that they establish uniform regulations for all the Jews residing in its territories and its allied countries. That would facilitate the confiscation of their property and their deportation to the East. Berlin warmly complimented Foreign minister Ivan Popov for his helpful ideas.

In July, following the detailed report by Belev, Bulgaria took another step. Filov urged the docile Parliament to vote on a new decree-law, giving the cabinet full authority to pass regulations and decrees concerning the Jews, and even modify existing legislation.[33] That meant that the cabinet could do with the Jews whatever it wanted, without even having to bother with a formal parliamentary vote.

On August 26, soon after the law was approved, the cabinet issued a long list of harsh anti-Jewish regulations. Among others, the new decrees reduced the privileged categories of Jews, changed the definition of Jews from one based on religion to one based on ancestry, laid the foundation for the confiscation of all Jewish property, and declared that the Jews of Sofia would be deported "to the provinces or outside the kingdom."

They also established a *Komisarstvo za Evreiskite Vuprosi*, "Commissariat for Jewish Questions," or KEV. The cabinet unanimously approved Gabrovski's proposal to appoint Alexander Belev as the commissar.[34]

With the appointment of Belev, a pro-German and anti-Jewish triumvirate was established in the Bulgarian government. At its head was the eager German vassal Prime Minister Bogdan Filov. Beneath him, contributing the enormous power of the police, the secret services, and the internal infrastructure, was Peter Gabrovski. And

*(FROM THE AUTHOR'S PERSONAL ARCHIVES)*

*Jews from Sofia were relocated to the mountain villages of Bulgaria. Here, the author's family (center) poses with new Bulgarian friends in Gorsko Slivovo.*

fueling the flames, generating new measures, new plans, new fiendish plots against the Jews, a fervent anti-Semite, suddenly invested with enormous powers, Alexander Belev.

Belev acted swiftly and decisively. He moved into a confiscated building on Boulevard Dondukov, one of Sofia's main arteries. He brought with him a group of Ratnik anti-Semitic activists that had clustered around him in the interior ministry. Then he hired clerks, secretaries, and officials, luring them with high pay. He soon had 113 people working in four departments: administration, public and professional activity, economic activity and agents, and treasury. Belev surrounded himself with bodyguards. He was driven around town in two luxury cars and had use of another one for his out-of-town trips.[35] He changed his work style. Before, when he still was an official of the interior ministry, his door was open to visitors, including Jews, whom he treated politely. Now, he entrenched himself in his inner office, rarely receiving visitors, behaving brusquely and rudely.[36] He wouldn't listen to criticism; he became "utterly nervous, dynamic, even demonic."[37]

The KEV managed all aspects of Jewish life. KEV employees registered all Jews throughout the kingdom. The KEV moved Jews out of certain residential sections and concentrated them in others, yet did not establish ghettos. It was in charge of distributing yellow stars to the Jews, and indicting those who didn't wear them. It coordinated the departure of Jews to the provinces and was in charge of all questions concerning the Jewish residences, employment, traveling, and taxation. According to the new regulations, it also confiscated Jewish property. It collected tax declarations from the Jews and issued all the necessary documents.

The KEV's budget was financed by taxes imposed on the Jews, frozen Jewish bank accounts, and confiscated Jewish property.[38] The commissariat collected between 5 and 12 percent of all the frozen Jewish moneys; it also charged fees for all certificates, documents, and affidavits issued to people of Jewish origin. The moneys collected were used to finance the enforcement of more restrictions against the Jews. In a few days after its establishment, the KEV collected from the Jews more than 300 million leva, ($3.7 million), "money which was earmarked for the destruction of its owners."[39]

The KEV controlled the Jewish communities throughout Bulgaria. It governed their activities by appointing special commissars, who participated at the meetings of the local Jewish consistories. In many places, the Jews formed underground committees that met in private apartments, made decisions, and implemented them, bypassing the KEV watchdogs.

Soon after its establishment, the KEV began marking Jewish homes and businesses with special signs and ordering the Jews to wear yellow stars.[40] In carrying out that task, however, Commissar Belev encountered unexpected difficulties. Privileged and christened Jews were exempt from wearing the stars; also, the Jewish stars in Bulgaria were the smallest ever produced in Europe. An angry German report, based on RSHA sources, claimed that by

November 1942 the manufacturing plants had supplied only 20 percent of the yellow stars. Some Jews had devised their own stars, inset with the pictures of the king and queen. The report blamed for these "arrogant" initiatives the indifference of the Bulgarian people, who didn't take part in the segregation of the Jews. It also noted the interventions of the royal palace on behalf of individual Jews; senior palace officials had allegedly asked Belev to soften some anti-Jewish measures.[41]

The RSHA had good reasons to be angry, not only because of the laxity of the anti-Jewish measures but also because of some much more significant developments. On June 16, 1942, while Parliament was busy voting new anti-Jewish measures, the president of the Jewish community sent a telegram of congratulations to the royal palace, on the occasion of the birthday of the king's son, Prince Simeon. The king immediately sent a telegram of thanks: "I am truly grateful to you and the Bulgarian Jewry for the congratulations and the kind wishes you have sent [us] on the occasion of the Crown Prince's birthday. The King."

The exchange of telegrams was printed in the next issue of the Bulletin of the Central Consistory and, when reported to Berlin by Beckerle, caused anger and consternation.[42] After the German protest, the court no longer answered the Jewish community's telegrams.[43] Another event that angered the Germans was the news that King Boris had received Bulgaria's chief rabbi, Dr. Asher Hananel, and explained to him the new anti-Jewish law.[44] Beckerle lodged a protest with the prime minister. The prime minister reported back to Beckerle the king's reaction to his protest. "The king got furious," Beckerle wrote in his diary, "and said [to Filov] that if I wanted something like that [to lodge a protest against his actions], I should turn to him directly. In what I am doing, I am going too far."[45]

Beckerle was not the only one upset about Bulgaria's laxity toward the Jews. Walter Schellenberg, the chief of RSHA espionage, reported to the Reich's foreign ministry that the high political spheres in Bulgaria believe that the August 1942 anti-Jewish law had gone too far. He claimed that many of the law's provisions had not been fulfilled. He then meticulously listed government personalities and dignitaries of the royal court who were implicated in Jewish connections, mixed marriages, or blood relations with Jews—the godfather of Princess Maria Luisa, the king's daughter, had been married to a Jew; the granddaughter of Prince Simeon's godfather was married to a Jew as well!

The report didn't spare anybody. It attacked Sofia's church metropolitan, Stefan, described interventions of top court officials in favor of individual Jews, and even quoted Interior Minister Gabrovski trying to calm down a group of Jews, who came to protest against the new restrictions, by saying that "they should not be disturbed. The government has noticed everything and the worst has already passed."[46]

It is hard to believe that such a meeting ever took place and that Gabrovski had made such a declaration to a Jewish delegation. Shellenberg's report was biased and inaccurate, as it had been inspired by extreme right activists of the Legionnaires and Ratnik organizations, who wanted German support for a possible pro-Nazi coup in Bulgaria. The leaders of the extreme right organizations were critical of the government's policy, which they regarded as too moderate. They would have welcomed Germany's support for a coup, that would enable them to seize power. Therefore they kept feeding the German secret services with provocative reports about the government's policy. King Boris was very worried by the close relations between the right wing and Germany's embassy.

Still, other news pointed out that Gabrovski indeed was backing away, at least verbally, from his extremist positions. At the meeting of the pro-government majority in Parliament, on September 19, 1942, the interior minister declared that "the Jewish question should . . . get off the scene," and the law concerning it should be applied "humanely, sensibly and morally." This declaration calmed many members of Parliament, who were worried about a new wave of anti-Jewish measures.[47]

Still, Berlin should have been much more worried by the early negotiations with Filov, concerning, for the first time, the final solution.

On September 24, 1942, Joachim von Ribbentrop instructed State Undersecretary Martin Luther, director of the Department for Jewish Questions at the Foreign Ministry, to get in touch with the governments of Bulgaria, Hungary, and Denmark, in order to put in motion, right away, the deportation of their Jews to Poland.[48] Luther sent a coded telegram to the German ambassador in Sofia. "Will you please . . . discuss with the Bulgarian government the deportation of Jews to the East . . ." Luther also demanded that the Bulgarian government pay two hundred fifty deutsche mark as travel expenses for every Jew taken in charge by Germany. In order to facilitate the deportation he offered to send to Bulgaria an "adviser for Jewish questions."[49]

Beckerle requested a meeting with Prime Minister Filov, who had assumed the functions of foreign minister as well. Before receiving Beckerle, Filov met with the king and discussed the Jewish question with him.[50] When Filov met with Beckerle, his answer about the deportation was ready.

> He [Filov] pointed out that the Bulgarians are relying on the Jewish work forces that they mobilize and they would use for road construction. Otherwise, he congratulates us for our offer about the rest of the Jews . . . As the shortage of manpower, especially for road construction is great, it seems that so far there has been no decision in the cabinet on that matter.[51]

There is no doubt the king had instructed Filov and Gabrovski to object to the Jews' deportation on the grounds that Bulgaria needed them for road construction. Two weeks later, Filov met with Beckerle again and welcomed the idea of Germany sending an "adviser for Jewish questions" to help with the deportation project.

Yet, he repeated his statement "that [Bulgaria] cannot give up a part of the Jewish men as manpower for construction."

In his report Beckerle hopefully added that "there is a possibility that the deportation would include the majority of the Bulgarian Jews, with the exception of some men who will remain behind for a while, to achieve work goals."[52]

• • •

In every other field, the preliminary negotiations for the deportation of the Jews continued. Filov objected to the price of two hundred fifty deutsche mark per Jew, judging it too high, again congratulated the Germans for helping the Bulgarian government to bring the Jewish question to a final solution, and promised full cooperation with the Reich's deportation adviser.

On December 10, 1942, SS Obersturmfuhrer Adolf Eichmann, the Nazi colonel in charge of the final solution, appointed his envoy to Bulgaria: SS Haupsturmfuhrer Theodore Dannecker, a thirty-year-old specialist on Jewish questions who had been very active in the final solution in France. He had handled the deportation of scores of thousands of Jews to the concentration camps. Dannecker, an aggressive, vain, and irritable officer, was appointed by Eichmann as assistant to Adolf Hoffman, the police (Gestapo) attaché at the German embassy in Sofia.[53] As Eichmann mentioned in his letter that he didn't care about the sum Bulgaria would pay for each Jew, the price fell immediately, and Ambassador Beckerle was instructed to ask for one hundred deutsche mark.[54] Even this payment would be suspended at a later stage.

On January 21, 1943, Theodore Dannecker arrived in Sofia.

The following day Interior Minister Gabrovski had a long and frank discussion with Ambassador Beckerle about the Jewish question. In this most important dialogue, Gabrovski exposed his real views on the Jewish problem in Bulgaria. "I think it will be false [a mistake] to discuss the question in public. I believe in actions. Talking about the Jewish question doesn't matter; what matters is— to act. In the past I acted very strongly and I shall do that in the future as well." Gabrovski pointed out that the economic measures he had taken against the Jews had not provoked strong reactions in the Bulgarian population.

Yet, Gabrovski added, everything must be done quietly.

Beckerle, eager to prepare the public for the deportation, offered to organize an anti-Jewish exhibit in Sofia. Gabrovski rejected the idea and suggested an exhibit showing the social achievements of Germany.

Beckerle didn't like that. Since his arrival in Sofia, he had realized that the Bulgarians, even those in high places, were not anti-Semitic. Beckerle mused, in his later report to Berlin:

> The Bulgarian society doesn't understand the real meaning of the Jewish question. Beside the few rich Jews in Bulgaria there are many poor people, who make their living as workers and artisans. Partly raised together with Greeks, Armenians, Turks and Gypsies, the average Bulgarian doesn't understand the meaning of the struggle against the Jews, the more so as the racial question is totally foreign to him. [This observation in an official diplomatic report, was highly unusual, and shows that Beckerle was shocked by the lack of anti-Semitism in Bulgaria.]

The conversation between Beckerle and Gabrovski went on. In spite of Beckerle's pressure, Gabrovski stood fast and dismissed the idea of an anti-Jewish exhibit. Beckerle came right to the point. He raised the matter of the deportation of the Jews to the East, as he had been instructed.

Gabrovski answered that "all the [Bulgarian] Jews should be deported." Yet, he said, repeating Filov's argument of three months ago, that he would like to delay the date of their deportation because

*In this map, first published in the Berlin magazine* Das Reich, *Thrace and Macedonia are described as "under Bulgarian administration" (unter bulgarischer Verwaltung).*

of the need for their labor in Bulgaria. The country needed the Jewish men to build roads and railroads, he explained. For the time being they could not be sent away. "Right now we can deport the Jews from the newly liberated lands," he stated.[55]

By that Gabrovski meant the Jews from Thrace and Macedonia. The twelve thousand Thracian and Macedonian Jews were not Bulgarian citizens.[56] When the Sobranie passed a law offering Bulgarian citizenship to the population of these lands, it explicitly excluded the Jews. They were a forgotten community: They had no protectors, no friends in the political circles in Bulgaria, and no connections with the Bulgarian elites. They were not regarded as Bulgarians, and even their contacts with the Bulgarian Jews were limited. Gabrovski was very sensitive to the reaction of the public to the anti-Jewish measures. He was worried that the deportation of the Bulgarian Jews might trigger an outcry in the influential circles in Sofia. He could assume, however, that a deportation of the Thracian and Macedonian Jews would pass almost unnoticed and would be viewed with indifference; it would not stir a heated reaction in the Bulgarian public. He therefore agreed to hand them over to the Germans immediately.

Ten days later Gabrovski received Haupsturmfuhrer Dannecker. "The deportation of the Jews from the old boundaries of Bulgaria is out of the question," he said to Dannecker.[57] "We want to use them in the future for public works." On the other hand, he was willing to deport right away, "with German support," the Thracian and Macedonian Jews, whose number he estimated between ten thousand and twelve thousand people. He was ready to act there, because the Jews in Thrace and Macedonia were fomenting "unrest."

"The planning of all the details should be coordinated with the Commissar for Jewish Questions," Gabrovski concluded.[58]

Dannecker didn't waste time. He parted from Gabrovski and without even calling ahead for an appointment, drove straight to Belev's office.[59] There he discovered an enthusiastic ally, a fanatic like himself, who was ready to start working right away.

# CHAPTER FIVE

# AN ORDER FOR DEPORTATION

On February 2, 1943, Belev's private secretary, Liliana (Lily) Panitza, was busy typing letters in her office, when two Germans walked in. The younger man was SS Obersturmfuhrer Dannecker; the older one was Gestapo attaché Adolf Hoffman.[1] They asked to see Belev at once.

Liliana, who didn't speak German and didn't understand who she was dealing with, told them that there were people with him in his office. The confusion continued until, finally, Panitza called one of her colleagues, Christo Bakerdjiev, to interpret. "Tell the Commissar that these gentlemen from the German embassy want to see him right away," Bakerdjiev said. Panitza informed her boss, who immediately cut short his meeting.[2] Dannecker and his companion entered Belev's inner office.

About twenty minutes later, the Germans left. Belev walked into Liliana's office. He was exhilarated. "Panitza" he said, "call all the department heads and the chief inspectors right away." Panitza told him that his deputy, Yaroslav Kalitzin, was home, sick. He ordered her to call him in.[3]

The meeting seemed to last for hours. After everyone had left, Belev called Liliana to his office. "Tonight you'll stay late," he said. "I have to write something that you'll retype later. But I warn

*Liliana Panitza.*

you right now—if any of this gets out, it will cost you more than just your job."[4]

That night Belev called a second, larger meeting of the top KEV officials; he then instructed Liliana to type a report addressed to Interior Minister Gabrovski.[5]

The report was sent to the interior minister on February 4. It was a chilling, detailed plan for the deportation and annihilation of thousands of Jews.

Belev described Dannecker's visit and their conversation about the deportation of the Jews:

The Reich is ready to receive the Jewish population of Thrace and Macedonia as well as the undesired Jews from the old boundaries [of Bulgaria], in a number that will be indicated by the Commissariat . . .

The deportation should start at the beginning of March; 10,000–20,000 people can be deported each month, equivalent to 10–20 special deportation trains . . .

The gathering of the Jews in concentration camps and their transport to the relevant train stations is under the responsibility of the Commissariat . . .

Once the Jews are delivered to the German authorities, they lose their Bulgarian citizenship, if they are Bulgarian citizens . . .

Belev stressed that the Jews would only be allowed to take clothes and food for the journey; they could take no valuables or money; they would be assembled in transit camps close to the departure train stations; the Jews deported from Thrace would not pass through Turkish or Greek territories but would be concentrated inside Bulgaria's old borders, before leaving for German territory; the deportation of the Jews from each town and city would be carried out simultaneously to prevent them from escaping and joining partisan units.

Belev continued:

> If we start the deportation of the Jews it will be good that it includes the Jews from the old boundaries as well. After the deportation of the Jews from Macedonia and Thrace, the Bulgarian Jews will live in constant fear that at any moment they might be deported, and they would react accordingly. In such case they might cause all kinds of troubles.
>
> If the deportation includes only Macedonia and Thrace, preventive measures should be taken against the Jews of the old boundaries. In the first place, all Jewish men between 18 and 48 years of age should be immediately drafted to work units, and put under strict control, to prevent escapes.

(Many of the Jews in the labor units had been discharged temporarily. During 1942, nine thousand Jews were called again to labor units, and assigned to fourteen batallions. They were released on December 5, 1942.)

Belev described in detail how the Jews from Thrace and Macedonia would be arrested and sent to transit camps in old Bulgaria; he precisely enumerated the steps that would be taken. He discussed the location of the camps, the equipment needed, the building material, the financing (from the Jewish communities fund, established with money and property confiscated from the Jews), the cooperation of the army, the police, the railroad authority. He stressed that all Jewish property would be confiscated.

He also thought up a ruse, to avoid trouble: "The deportation must be kept secret. . . . At the roundup of the Jews from the cities, they shouldn't be told that they are deported outside the country, but we should explain to them that they are moved to other parts of the country, and until places for them are found they will be stationed in camps."[6]

But what mattered to him most, apparently, was the deportation of the Bulgarian Jews. "If the deportation of the Jews from the old boundaries is not decided, we should still seize this opportunity, and deport the undesired Jews from the old boundaries. Therefore the number of Jews, whose deportation should be agreed upon, should be raised, for instance to 20,000 people."[7]

This amazing paragraph in Belev's report has been strangely ignored by entire generations of historians. Most modern historians claim that the agreement between Bulgaria and Germany was about deporting 20,000 Jews from Macedonia and Thrace and that when the KEV realized that in Thrace and Macedonia there were less than 12,000 Jews, they then decided to add 8,000 Jews from Old Bulgaria, in order to make up the difference. However, Belev's report proves that the opposite was true. Belev and Gabrovski knew from the beginning that Macedonia's and Thrace's Jews numbered only 12,000. But they agreed to deliver to the Nazis 20,000 people so that they could add another 8,000 "undesired Jews"—active leaders, rich men, opinion makers, left-wing sympathizers. Dannecker was only too willing to comply.

•  •  •

On Saturday, February 13, 1943, assassins shot and killed the Bulgarian right-wing extremist General Christo Lukov. Lukov was the founder of the Legionnaires Fascist movement, and his assassination triggered frustration and fury in right-wing circles. Some Legionnaires even distributed flyers, accusing the government of the murder.

King Boris was very upset by these accusations. A year before, during a visit to Berlin, he had complained to Ribbentrop about Lukov's activities against his government, and his secret connections with Germany.[8] Ribbentrop ordered a thorough investigation, and soon it was established that Lukov indeed was reporting to Reichsmarshall Goering via the air attaché in Sofia, Colonel von Schoenebeck; he also had other connections at the German embassy in Sofia. Ribbentrop ordered these connections to be severed immediately.[9] Boris's complaint was very significant. The fact that the king himself had found it necessary to raise this subject with the Reich's foreign minister (whom he disliked) indicates how disturbed he was by the right-wing activities. Lukov and his followers were a threat to the king's regime, perhaps even to his throne and his life. And now Lukov was dead and Boris's government was accused. The king feared the assassination might provide the opportunity for a right-wing coup, supported by extreme Nazi circles.

Two days after Lukov's funeral Filov came to the king. He, too, was deeply disturbed by the assassination and offered the king a solution. "We shouldn't maintain that Lukov's murder has been perpetrated by "a foreign hand" or by "Bulgaria's enemies . . . We should use this assassination to step up the struggle against Communism and against the Jewry."[10]

At the same meeting, Filov spoke to the king about a British offer, recently relayed by the Swiss embassy, to admit in Palestine four thousand Jewish children and five hundred adults. Ambassador Beckerle had vigorously objected to this plan. (A few weeks later, the obedient Filov would reject the British offer under false pretexts.) Then he added: "The Germans don't want to interfere in our internal affairs and they are ready to support any government which would be able to handle the Communists and the Jews, who have no place in the new Europe." Filov clearly meant that the Bulgarian government should take more decisive measures against the Communists and the Jews. At this meeting, Filov probably obtained the king's approval for the first deportation of Jews out of Bulgaria's boundaries.[11]

Filov noted in his diary: "The king agreed with me, although he didn't seem very convinced by my position."[12] This note probably indicates that although the king didn't approve of the deportation, he bowed to Filov's pressure, as he had always done in the past.

Prime Minister Filov therefore decided to use Lukov's murder as a pretext for launching a propaganda assault against the Jews. He summoned Interior Minister Gabrovski, and they agreed to "start a press campaign against the Communists and the Jews and to recur to harsher measures against them." They also decided to establish a "united front" with the extremist Legionnaires.[13] That meant that the government was about to adopt a more pro-Nazi position.

The Jews were going to serve as scapegoats once again. They "had no place in the new Europe," indeed, and a hostile public opinion could serve Filov and Gabrovski's goals, for good reason: Five days before, in absolute secrecy, Filov's cabinet had approved Belev's plan for the deportation of twenty thousand Jews.[14]

● ● ●

Belev was like a man possessed; he was restless and extremely nervous, yet fanatically dedicated and enthusiastic.[15] He toiled at his task. To Lily Panitza he seemed absolutely euphoric. She had told Belev that what they were doing was wrong. "The Germans would take them anyway, even if we object," Belev answered. "The Thracian and Macedonian Jews are their subjects."[16] His deputy, Kalitzin, asked him: "Why do the Germans want these people? What will they do with them?" Belev answered: "Let them make soap out of them, if they wish."[17]

Belev began work on this operation even before getting Gabrovski's authorization. On February 3 he cabled the KEV representatives throughout the kingdom asking them to send him detailed lists of the Jews in their cities by February 9.[18] A week later, he approved the three main concentration areas—Radomir, Dupnitza, and Gorna-Djumaya, three southern cities built around important railroad junctions[19]—which had been conceived by his deputy, Yaroslav Kalitzin. On February 22, Belev signed the official agreement with Dannecker authorizing the deportation of twenty thousand Jews.

It was a unique document. In the tragic history of the Holocaust, this was the only case in which a contract was signed between Germany and another nation. "Bulgaria," wrote Gideon Hausner, the prosecuting attorney at the 1961 Eichmann trial, "has the distinction of being the only country that signed a written contract to supply Jews to Germany, undertook to pay for their transport, and stipulated that she would never and under no circumstances request their return."[20]

This extraordinary document deserves full reproduction. The agreement was originally written in German and later translated into Bulgarian.

## AGREEMENT

For the deportation at first of 20,000 Jews from the new Bulgarian lands Thrace and Macedonia to the German eastern regions,

concluded between

the Bulgarian Commissar for Jewish questions, Mr. Alexander Belev, on one side, and the German plenipotentiary, Captain of the Defense detachments (SS-Hauptsturmfuhrer) Theodor Dannecker, on the other side.

1. After approval by the Council of Ministers, in the new Bulgarian lands Thrace and Macedonia, 20,000 Jews—regardless of age and sex—will be prepared for deportation. The German Reich is ready to accept these Jews in its Eastern regions.

2. Departure railway stations, figures and number of trains are established as follows:
   a) in Skopje            5,000 with 5 trains
   b) in Bitolya           3,000 with 3 trains
   c) in Pirot             2,000 with 2 trains
   d) in G. Djumaya        3,000 with 3 trains
   e) in Dupnitza          3,000 with 3 trains
   f) in Radomir           4,000 with 4 trains

In view of the fact that complete accommodation of the last 12,000 Jews in camps is possible only until 15 April 1943, the German plenipotentiary will take action so that these 12 trains—as far as this will be possible technically—are ready to depart in the period between the end of March and 15 April 1943. The Jews assembled in Skopje and Bitolya will, consequently, be deported after 15 April 1943.

3. The Bulgarian Commissariat for Jewish Questions, as an organ of the Ministry of Interior and National Health, guarantees the German Reich that the following basic conditions will be fulfilled:
   a) Only Jews will be included in the transports.
   b) Jews in mixed marriages will not be included.
   c) In case the Jews being deported are not yet deprived of their citizenship, that should be done upon their leaving Bulgarian territory.
   d) Jews with contagious diseases will not be included.
   e) The Jews may not carry with them weapons, poisons, foreign currency, precious metals, etc.

4. For every transport a list of the persons included in the transport will be prepared in triplicate. This list must include the name, surname, date and place of birth, last residence, and profession of the Jews. Two copies will be remitted to the German escort of the transport, and one to the German plenipotentiary in Sofia. The Bulgarian government will provide the necessary food supplies for fifteen days, counting from the day of the train's departure as well as the necessary number of water casks.

5. The question of the guard for the transports will be decided later. Possibly a German guard command will take over the transports already at the departure station.

6.  a) The amount of a monetary compensation to be paid by Bulgaria, calculated according to the number of depor-tees, will be decided by a special agreement. This will not affect the timetable of the transports' movements.
    b) The expenses for the transport from the departure railway station to the destination will be covered by Bulgaria.

7.  The Bulgarian State Railways and the German State Railways will agree directly on the trains' schedule as well as on the disposition of the means of transport.

8.  In no case will the Bulgarian government demand the return of the deported Jews.

9.  The present agreement will be prepared in two copies in German and two copies in Bulgarian, with each of these copies being regarded as an original.

Sofia, February 22, 1943

A. Belev
T. Dannecker

•   •   •

Dannecker signed the agreement with green ink, Belev with black. At a certain moment, perhaps during the signing, or later, Belev, with the same black ink, crossed out the words *from the new Bulgarian lands Thrace and Macedonia* in the title and *in the new Bulgarian lands Thrace and Macedonia* in the first paragraph of the text. That change had far-reaching significance. The agreement, as modified by Belev, was for the "deportation of 20,000 Jews to the German Eastern regions." The change meant that the deportation would not be limited to the Jews of the newly annexed territories but would include Jews from the old boundaries of Bulgaria.

The document was signed, almost casually—no ceremonies or festivities, and no protests, soul searching, petitions, or moral dilemmas. Lily Panitza typed it, as she did all the documents that followed. Dannecker and Belev signed it, probably standing alone in Belev's small office. Gabrovski read it, and didn't mention a word to anybody. Filov didn't devote even a single line to it in his diary. Filov or Gabrovski certainly informed the king, as they would never have concluded such an agreement without his approval. And if there were details about which the king didn't know, it was not because he wasn't told, but because he didn't want to know.

Undoubtedly, Boris III was deeply distressed by many of the things he did to prove his loyalty to Germany. But there is no doubt either that, as repulsive for him as these acts were, he did nothing to stop them. The return of Dobrudja, Thrace, and Macedonia to the Bulgarian flag had changed Boris III into a modern Pontius Pilate.

Boris also believed that he had no legal authority to object to the deportation of the Thracian and Macedonian Jews. Officially he was the "King Unifier" who had brought back Thrace and Macedonia into the Bulgarian kingdom. Officially he passed parliamentary laws about Greater Bulgaria. Officially the Macedonians and the Thracians were now Bulgarians. But deep in his heart the king knew the truth. He knew that the annexation of Thrace and Macedonia had not been accepted by anybody, and certainly not by Germany. He knew that Germany accepted Bulgaria's presence in these areas because it freed German troops for other ventures and protected her rear. In a map published in the Nazi magazine *Das Reich* in Berlin, Thrace and Macedonia were separated from Bulgaria's territory and defined as *unter Bulgarischer Verwaltung* ("under Bulgarian administration"). Dobrudja, on the other hand, was shown as an integral part of Bulgaria.[21]

"The Thracian and Macedonian Jews are Germany's subjects," Belev had said.[22] "They belong to us anyway," Dannecker would later point out (see Chapter 10). And Boris himself would write that he couldn't object to their deportation because they were "exiles from Hitler's military command."[23]

●   ●   ●

Belev was extremely happy not only because of his obsession with deporting the Jews, and not only because it was just "a first deportation." He was happy mostly because "he had, in the name of the government, signed an agreement with a great power, Germany."[24]

A delighted Dannecker rushed the photocopy of the agreement to his boss, Adolf Eichmann. "Beside the deportation of Jews from the newly liberated regions," wrote the Haupsturmfuhrer in a report countersigned by Beckerle, "about 6,000 Jews from the old boundaries will be deported as well. At least half of them will be coming from Sofia. The Commissar for Jewish Questions makes a special effort to include [in that number] the influential Jews. Belev means by that affluent Jews, as well as Jews who have good connections with highly placed Bulgarian spheres." Dannecker also reported that after May 1943 Belev would like to deport the rest of the Jews, although it might not be that easy, as Gabrovski wants to use them in labor units.[25]

Ambassador Beckerle was less excited. He knew Bulgaria and was very worried about the plans to deport at least two thousand Jews from Sofia. "I am against the deportation of Jews from Sofia," he noted in his diary,[26] "because it would provoke considerable unrest, and might put in jeopardy the entire project in the future. First the other Jews must be deported, and later the Jews of Sofia, but not all of them together!" Beckerle feared that if only a part of the Sofia Jews were deported in the first stage, those remaining behind might organize protests and various acts of resistance; they also might alert the public. The deportation of all Sofia Jews in one swift operation would prevent such problems.

Beckerle's opinion wasn't heeded. Belev had now an official green light and nothing could stop him. "He exulted . . . He got carried away," remembered Liliana Panitza.[27]

Now that the legal foundation was laid, Belev meticulously prepared and dispatched to Gabrovski several detailed reports and requested that the government pass resolutions giving a foolproof cover to every step and aspect of the planned deportation. Gabrovski, in turn, would rewrite the reports, submit them to the cabinet with a draft resolution, and have the resolution passed as a "warrant," without any problems. And thus, at the cabinet meetings of March 2 and March 5, Belev asked and obtained all the necessary government warrants: a civilian mobilization of all the KEV employees until May 31, 1943, an order to the Bulgarian State Railways for free transport of Jews to the transit camps, a decree to requisition public and private buildings in the various cities as assembly points and temporary camps for the deportees, a resolution to appoint guards to watch over the property of the deportees and pay them with funds collected from the Jews, a decision to confiscate the deportees' property, etc.[28]

The major resolution was Warrant 127 of March 2, by which the cabinet decided that "the Commissar for Jewish Questions is charged to deport from the borders of the country in agreement with the German authorities up to 20,000 Jews, inhabiting the newly liberated lands." The cabinet warrants on the deportation issue were top secret and were not published in the state *Gazette*.

In Warrant 127 the cabinet still stuck to the wording of the original Belev-Dannecker agreement that referred to 20,000 Jews living in the "newly liberated lands."[29] The Jews living inside the old boundaries were not mentioned.

Therefore, the government could pretend, quoting Warrant 127, that it had never authorized the deportation of the Jews from the old boundaries. This excuse was very thin, though. Several reports that were approved by the cabinet, as well as some very significant resolutions, made it clear to all the ministers that they were approving the deportation of Bulgarian Jews as well.

In Gabrovski's report to the cabinet, requesting the approval of one of the proposed warrants, he wrote explicitly: "According to the agreement concluded with the German authorities, 20,000 Jews living in Macedonia and Thrace as well as the undesired Jews from the old borders, will be delivered to the Reich."[30] In another report that Gabrovski submitted to the cabinet, he wrote: "Some members of Jewish families in Macedonia, Thrace or the old borders of the country, who are subject to temporary transfer to camps and deportation outside the country borders, are mobilized in labor units." Gabrovski asked for a warrant ordering the immediate discharge of these men so that they could be deported with their families.[31]

The most substantial proof that the Bulgarian government knew very well that it was ordering the deportation of thousands of Bulgarian Jews was Warrant 116, which stated: "All persons of Jewish origin, who will be deported outside of the state boundaries, are deprived of their Bulgarian citizenship, if until then they had Bulgarian citizenship."[32]

The Jews from Macedonia and Thrace didn't have Bulgarian citizenship. After Bulgaria took over "the newly liberated lands," the government had passed a citizenship law that bestowed Bulgarian citizenship on all the Greek and Yugoslav citizens in these lands (they could, refuse it). The Jews, though, were excluded: "This measure does not include persons of Jewish origin," the law stated.[33] And indeed, all the Jews of Macedonia and Thrace were to be listed in the deportation documents as Greek or Yugoslav citizens.[34] The only Jews who had Bulgarian citizenship were those of Dobrudja, because of its different status. Dobrudja had been officially annexed to Bulgaria by an international agreement with Romania; therefore all its inhabitants, including the Jews, automatically became Bulgarian citizens. This case illustrates the difference in the legal status of the Jews in the newly liberated Thrace and Macedonia and those in the newly liberated Dobrudja.

Therefore, by raising their hands to approve Warrant 116, on March 2, 1943, Filov and his ministers knew well that they were sending eight thousand Bulgarian Jews to their deaths.

Apparently, none of the ministers protested; none raised any objections or voiced any reservations. Everything was accepted, in order to please the German allies who had restored Bulgaria to her ancient greatness. Even the ministers who were not Fascist sympathizers seemed totally indifferent.

However, there was one person who could not remain indifferent to the tragedy that was in the making. It was Liliana Panitza.

# CHAPTER SIX

# THE LOVERS

Blond, blue-eyed, oval faced, and lovely, Liliana (Lily) Panitza was twenty-seven when she became Alexander Belev's private secretary. She had been working as a secretary since the age of eighteen. Despite being highly intelligent, she had gone to school only until sixth grade. Thus, her prospects for promotion or achieving a top position were limited.

Lily came from a family with strong democratic convictions and wasn't at all anti-Semitic. She had moved to Sofia from her native city of Varna and lived in a small room. She didn't have many friends. She worked hard, supporting not only herself but also her brother, who was studying medicine.[1] She had met Alexander Belev at the Interior Ministry when he was a department head, and later the legal counsel. He lured her to the new Commissariat by offering her higher pay and a more senior position.[2]

Lily Panitza was not happy with her new job. She soon learned about many hateful acts being committed in the Commissariat, including the savage beatings of Jews in the guardroom.[3]

She disliked most of the Commissariat senior officials, who were Fascists, and either members or supporters of the extremist Ratnik organization. She also resented the very nature of her work and rejected the racist theories, fervently preached by Belev and his associates. She had been raised to respect the rights of the minorities. She had also been upset by conversations she had had with Belev and his Ratnik friends, who claimed that the Bulgarians were not Slavs at all and therefore had nothing in common with the Russians. "Only the Germans are of a pure race," Belev said to her. "We, the Bulgarians, carry the blood of many tribes—Huns, Tatars, Hungarians, Turks." Lily countered that all the "mixed blood" doesn't change the fact that the Bulgarian people was deeply convinced of its Slavic origins and its strong bonds with other Slavic peoples, mainly the Russians. Belev and his friends dismissed her arguments.[4]

Being secretive by nature, she didn't often discuss her opinions with her colleagues at work. But she did share her frustration with her male friend, Ilya Dobrevski. She dated Dobrevski for about three years, first when they both worked in the Interior Ministry, and later when they were both transferred to the Commissariat.

Ilya, a handsome young man with wavy hair and black-rimmed glasses, confided to her that he too was disgusted with the nature of his work.[5] He told her he couldn't stand "the cruelty of what was being done" and that "they both had to leave that institution."[6] At the end of February 1942, Belev sent Ilya to the Macedonian town of Giumurdjina, as a member of the team charged with the deportation of the local Jews. In spite of what he had said to Lily, Ilya seemed to enjoy his mission. He sent to Belev detailed reports about his activities in Giumurdjina and even stressed that "the deportation of the Jews from Giumurdjina was received by the Bulgarian population with feelings of admiration and relief . . . The black market [for food] went down by 50 percent."[7]

The allusion to the "black market" was part of the KEV propaganda that accused the Jews throughout the kingdom of purchasing food on the black market, thus fueling the steep rise in food prices. The KEV officials didn't miss an opportunity to accuse the Jews of dealing in black market goods, hoping to stir anti-Jewish feelings in the poor population. They also claimed that the deportation of the Jews would bring the food prices back to normal and, thus, food would be accessible to poor Bulgarians again. By mentioning the black market, Ilya Dobrevski could be certain he would please Alexander Belev.

But on his return from Giumurdjina, Ilya told Lily that he was deeply disturbed by what was happening there. He suggested that they both resign their jobs and leave. He said that he could no longer cope with that kind of work, that it was not in his nature or his character. He also urged Lily to leave her job at the KEV, saying that a woman shouldn't work at such an institution. In the end, though, he decided to stay, hoping to be promoted while claiming to work without heart: "You know me, you must understand I cannot work with zeal. I have nothing against the Jews."[8] (Nevertheless, the People's Court, which was established after the war, sentenced Ilya Dobrevski to two years in prison. He had also been accused of grave irregularities in connection with the plunder of the Giumiurdjina Jews. Rabbi Daniel Tzion also testified before the People's Court about the degradation and humiliation of Jewish prisoners in the Somovit camp—May through August 1943—by Dobrevski.)

Panitza didn't leave. She was totally devoted to her boss. Her colleagues complained that she had completely isolated him from others and "kept him like in a cell."[9] Belev's deputy, Kalitzin, said that she was "completely dedicated to her job."[10] After the war, Panitza claimed that she had repeatedly asked Belev to let her resign but was not authorized to do so. This seems improbable. There was nothing to prevent her from leaving her job, if she had really wanted to.

Quite the contrary, it appears that she had fallen madly in love with Alexander Belev and had become his secret mistress.[11] History moves in strange ways; individual lives, emotions, and passions become intertwined with the course of political events and affairs of state. Liliana Panitza's tormented love affair with Alexander Belev was to become an important element in the unraveling of the drama of the Bulgarian Jews.

Except for one fateful moment, the two were never seen together in public. Outwardly, she was the perfect secretary; in reality she was a passionate, emotional, and very lonely young woman. She fiercely protected the secret nature of her relationship with Belev. Yet, persistent rumors began circulating in the Commissariat about their affair. "Her goal was to marry Belev," said her colleague and sworn enemy, Maria Pavlova.[12] Lily vehemently denied the gossip, claiming that Belev was involved with his cousin, Liliana Stoika.

Liliana Stoika was a pretty young woman, approximately Lily Panitza's age. Very often, indeed, she would be seen with Belev. The young woman, a propaganda ministry employee with artistic ambitions, often barged into Belev's office, at all hours, dragging him out with her in the middle of the day. She was even known to call on his junior employees to do chores for her and her mother. She seemed to cast a strange spell over Belev, and that infuriated Panitza. Lily often heard Liliana Stoika raising her voice at the all-powerful Belev, behind the closed doors of his office. Lily hated her fiercely. Several times, she spoke against her to Belev, but he took the side of the other. Once, after she spoke rudely to Liliana, Belev called Lily and said: "I am the boss here. If you don't like the way things are, you can go."[13]

In an effort to conceal her affair with Belev, Panitza continued dating Ilya.[14] Ilya Dobrevski, indeed, saw the young woman quite often, visited her home, and made his serious intentions known to her parents, who were displeased and insisted that he first complete his studies.[15] "From the start our relations became cordial," he said. "Maria Pavlova was always busy gossiping about me and Panitza."[16] However, after a while he disappeared from her life, realizing that she didn't share his feelings and dreams.

Later, Lily Panitza admitted that she had never hidden her "good and beautiful feelings" toward Belev. "I always admired his honesty. I always told him that with his brains he could be very successful if he were more humane. He was cruel, with no sense of proportions . . ."[17] She thought that, the Jewish question excluded, he was respectable and fair. She also admitted that he was more open and sincere when he was with her.[18] "She spoke with rapture of Belev's mind," Maria Pavlova said, "of his beautiful eyes, his goodness, his naiveté and the employees concluded that she was in love with him."[19] Yet, Lily denied any romantic involvement with the commissar.

Still, her behavior, when she worked for Belev and afterward, proved she was not only involved with him but also obsessed with him. At one time, they happened to live across the street from each other, and she would spend hours at night standing on her balcony and watching his windows, waiting for his lights to come on.[20] Even after they stopped working together, she remained his closest confidante and saw him very often, during certain periods several times a day.

At one point, their affair was shaken by a bitter confrontation. Belev stopped seeing Panitza for a while. Her pain was intense, as evidenced by a letter that she apparently wrote to her lover. (She kept a draft of the letter at her home.)

Did I ever love you more than now? Nevertheless . . . I could be so mean toward you . . . I wanted to revenge. I felt my heart was torn. I felt a crazy urge to revenge—on whom? . . . On you, my only love! What happened to my feelings?

No, I didn't hate you that moment but I hurt badly, so much I was driven to madness, and I didn't know what I was doing. I regained control [and] I wanted to fall on my knees before you, to ask your forgiveness. I couldn't . . . Perhaps now for the first time I felt indeed what you have become for me and my life.

I was so confident. Happiness seemed so close. And just then you pulled away from me.

I knew that my love wouldn't meet approval any- where. I knew that it would hardly stir compassion. But do I know how, when and why I fell in love with you? The most irrational, the craziest love.

I love you! And this is so simple. I love you! . . . I felt it coming. For you now my heart exists . . .

I can't give you up. . . . Only in your presence the pain in my heart subsides and some quiet sets in. But when I stop hearing your voice, my heart bleeds again.

This hurts, hurts physically, as strange as it may seem to you.

Something changed in our relationship. But you'll be easily consoled. And you'll leave me with the pain for you

... My life has been broken. My brain is alive, my body is alive, but my soul is dead. I have nothing in this world except my love for you ...

I never wanted to torment you. Perhaps I felt cheated and I tormented myself ... But I know that your soul and your heart never will be mine.

Never. Are you that indifferent?[21]

Lily Panitza loved Belev deeply.[22] And yet, in spite of her total devotion to her lover, she betrayed his confidence by warning the Jews of the impending tragedy.

On February 23, 1943, Belev traveled with the senior employees of the Commissariat to Thrace, to supervise the preparations for the deportation of the Jews. Lily Panitza asked and was allowed to join them, to see the newly acquired "White Sea regions." On her return, Lily became privy to the list of twenty-five hundred "undesired Jews" from Sofia that the Commissariat had started to prepare. All would be deported, as a part of the eight thousand Jews from the old boundaries.

Soon after the deportation of the Thracian and Macedonian Jews started, Panitza raised the subject with Belev. "What is happening to them is very painful," she said.

Belev didn't try to argue with her. "The Germans insist that we send them," he told her. "Even if we refused to cooperate, they would have taken them anyway. Dannecker told me that they are their subjects—Macedonian and Thracian. They would deport them if we want it or not."[23]

At first, Lily Panitza apparently was at a loss as to how to react to the projected deportation. She tried to help some Jews she knew. Some sources claim that at a certain period she had an intimate relationship with a Sofia Jew and tried to help him.[24] She confided in Yaroslav Kalitzin that she wanted to ask Belev to help a Jewish doctor but was afraid the commissar might think she was doing it for money. Panitza wanted to help Dr. Jack Benaroya, a Sofia gynecologist, who had treated her.[25] Kalitzin also noted that the king's junior secretary, Stanislav Balan, began visiting Panitza very often and was several times received by Belev,[26] probably to intervene for some Jewish acquaintances of the king. But such efforts could have only limited results.

Outwardly, Lily remained the same devoted secretary. Some of her colleagues accused her of "nurturing feelings of hatred toward the Jews."[27] They would never have believed that Panitza had made up her mind to warn the people on whose deportation she was so diligently working.

One could imagine the terrible inner struggle of this young woman, torn between her poignant, impossible love and her pangs of conscience; between her loyalty to her employers and her sense of morality; between the trust of her superiors and her anti-racist convictions. Some could assume she was motivated by the ache of a woman scorned, neglected by her lover, and her desire for revenge. Others could claim that her romantic involvement with a Jew, in the past, may have prompted her initiative. Yet, her actions, first in March and then later in May, would prove that her decision to help the Jews stemmed from something much deeper than a rejected love or a past affair.

One night in early March, Lily Panitza rang the bell of a Jewish friend in Sofia who had close ties to the leaders of the Jewish community. She revealed to him the horrible secret.[28]

· · ·

Dr. Nissim (Buko) Levi, a renowned Sofia lawyer, was one of the most active leaders of the Jewish community. Levi was the vice-president of the Jewish Central Consistory. As the winter of 1943 drew to a close, Levi and his colleagues at the Jewish consistory board had begun to suspect that something terrible was in the making. They had noticed several ads in the newspapers, in which the government was soliciting bids for the construction of large numbers of wooden huts.

They assumed the government intended to build concentration camps for the Jews.[29] Their ideas were not far from the truth.

At the end of February 1943, the Jewish leaders in Sofia got wind of rumors that soon the Jews from Thrace and Macedonia would be deported. They tried to verify the rumors, but their contacts at the Commissariat were either silent or hinted that the Jews from the new lands would be deported to camps inside Bulgarian territory. This was, as we now know, a part of the devious plot devised by Belev and Gabrovski, in order to lull the Jews into believing that their transfer was only local, within the boundaries of Greater Bulgaria.

At the beginning of March, a friend of Buko Levi came to see him. The Thracian and Macedonian Jews, he said, were going to be deported to Poland. They would be followed to that destination by transports of Jews from the old boundaries.

"What is your source?" Levi asked.

"Lily Panitza," the man replied.[30]

Lily Panitza was a friend of the Levi family, especially of Levi's wife,[31] and she had previously informed them of new restrictions that were being planned against the Jews.

Levi met with Panitza right away. Their meeting took place in the first days of March 1943. The young woman willingly supplied him with the details of the projected deportation, and even disclosed the dates: March 10 and 11.

Panitza had already warned at least one eminent Jewish figure about the projected deportation. But when she met with Levi, she was well aware that by describing to him the full details of the "monstrous deportation plan," she was warning the entire Jewish community.[32] "She knew I was Vice-President of the Consistory," Buko Levi said later, "and by informing me she would do us a great service."[33]

During the next three months, Levi met with Panitza five or six times.[34] Levi reported the news to the board of the consistory.[35] Lily Panitza also warned Avraham Alfasa, the former president of the Sofia consistory.[36] Panitza's information was detailed, accurate, and credible. She also told Levi that a list of the most notable Jews in

Sofia was being prepared, and he would be among the first to be deported. "You are number two on the list," Lily said.

"Can't you do something and take me off the list?" Levi asked.

"No," she said. "If you were just anyone, a random name on the list, I could have done it. But they know who you are, and they want you to be among the very first to be sent away."

Levi, who had indeed been very active in the struggle against the ZZN, was well known to Belev and Gabrovski. Gabrovski, though, strictly avoided him after his appointment to the ministerial position. When Belev was still a senior official at the Interior Ministry, he often met with Levi, who represented the Jewish community in various conflicts linked to the ZZN. They debated, clashed, and once even had a fiery confrontation. But later, when Belev became the Jewish commissar, he adopted the same attitude as Gabrovski: He didn't want to meet with Levi anymore and was infuriated by his intensive public activity. He wanted to get rid of the "troublemaker" as soon as possible, and the forthcoming deportation was the ideal solution. Lily Panitza told Levi what Belev had said to her: "If I am allowed to deport only one Jew to Poland—I'd choose Dr. Levi!"[37]

In their following meetings, which took place before and after March 10, Lily Panitza warned Dr. Levi that Alexander Belev was determined to deport the Jews from the old boundaries of Bulgaria, "in order to radically solve the Jewish question."[38] She also informed him that Belev was working hand in hand with the German police and that he had signed a secret agreement with Dannecker for the deportation of twenty thousand Jews.

"We were very surprised by this information," Levi testified later. "We started deploying efforts to attract to our defense some of the representatives of the Bulgarian progressive circles, in order to launch a powerful struggle against these measures."[39]

But no struggle could save the Jews from Thrace and Macedonia, whose fate had already been sealed.

CHAPTER SEVEN

# A THRACIAN
# NIGHTMARE

I n the predawn hours of March 4, 1943, fists and rifle butts
pounded on hundreds of doors in the Thracian town of
Giumurdjina. During a fierce, driving rain, heavily armed units of
the Bulgarian army and police had sealed the Jewish quarter. At
4:00 A.M. the raid on the Jewish homes began. Shouting and banging on the doors, the police officers and the special envoys of the
KEV roused the Jewish people from their sleep.[1] "You have a half
hour to pack," they ordered the stunned, scared Jews. "Forty kilos
per adult, twenty kilos per child. Take food, clothes, money and
valuables."

The Jews, bewildered and frightened, grabbed bags and suitcases, stuffing inside every object within reach. Those that dared to
ask where they were being taken were all given the same answer:
"To villages in the interior of the country."

Half an hour later, in the icy March rain, escorted by police officers and soldiers, a sad, desperate procession made its way to the
Chalburov tobacco warehouse. Behind them, police and KEV agents
sealed their homes; this didn't prevent the same police and agents
from looting the meager property left behind.

Inside the Chalburov compound, civilians and police, assisted
by representatives of the local authorities, ordered the Jews to hand

over all their money and valuables. The policemen ripped with knives and bayonets bedspreads, pillows, mattresses, and blankets to look for hidden jewelry and paper money. Clouds of white feathers from torn pillows floated in the air. Men and women were separated, undressed—their clothes searched, the lining of coats and sleeves torn to pieces. Their anuses and vaginas were brutally probed for hidden valuables. Some were savagely beaten and whipped.

Nice clothes, new shoes, and good quality luggage were removed and confiscated by police officers and civilian agents. The policemen squeezed and smashed with their fingers foodstuffs, like marmelade or cheese, lest hidden treasures were concealed within.

The desperate prisoners were herded to the cold, stinking storage rooms and left there, shivering in their wet clothes, with no covers, blankets, medical attention, or food. The latrines were insufficient, water faucets almost nonexistent. The prisoners were not allowed to walk in the yard or to establish contact with people outside the heavily guarded compound.

The following night, at 2:30 A.M., the police returned. The Jews were marched in long files to the small train station. Some of them were half-naked, others barefoot, hungry and thirsty, wailing and moaning, pushed and kicked and slapped by the police officers. In the station, they were packed into open freight cars. The trainload of hopeless men and women, children, old people and babies in arms, shouting and crying, whipped by the rain and the wind, seared by burning sparks carried by the smoke of the locomotive, looked like a convoy of damned souls on their journey to Hades.

That was how the raiders of the KEV and their assistants from the Bulgarian police, army, and local administration, rounded up the 863 Jews of Giumurdjina. They called it Aktzia, similar to the German *Aktionen*—their Teutonic allies' roundup of Jews in Poland and Russia, to drag them to the concentration camps. And in similar Aktzias, the KEV raiders snatched 42 Jews of Dede Agach, 538 Jews of Ksanti, 589 Jews of Drama, 1,471 Jews of Kavala, 499 Jews of Seres; and, with a special squad, 11 Jews of Sara-Shaban.

Everything had been prepared, right down to the last grisly detail. On February 23, Belev had launched his operation.

Accompanied by Kalitzin, Dobrevski, and Liliana Panitza, Belev toured Thrace. He left his deputy, Kalitzin, in the ancient Greek town of Ksanti, from where he would coordinate the deportation in Thrace. Dobrevski was in charge of Giumurdjina. In the following days, Belev and his troop of fanatics toured the rest of Thrace, Macedonia, and several old Bulgarian cities, established contact with the local mayors and police, and checked tobacco warehouses, schools, and camps. They secured the cooperation of the army, police, train authorities, municipalities, health services, finance ministry, and banks. Officials, officers, clerks, and KEV personnel, were mobilized for the operation. (KEV officials got extra pay for their effort.) Hundreds of documents went to town halls, police headquarters, and army camps.[2] Medical teams were formed and supplied with disinfecting and delousing equipment—needed to protect those who would come in contact with the deportees during their trip. Drugs and medicines were not necessary. The Jews were not going to need them where they were going.

Detailed orders specified the exact time of each Aktzia, the forces that would participate in it, the procedure of the search, the sealing of the homes of the deportees, and the collection of their money and valuables. The entire deportation process in the king dom, both in the old and new territories, would be carried out by Bulgarians. No Germans were actively involved.

The KEV officials had calculated the exact number of days the deportees would spend in each camp, the exact number of hours they would spend at the train stations, and the coordinated arrivals of various groups from different cities and villages, in order to board the same trains. They had Jews from remote villages brought to the train stations by trucks. The KEV officials had scheduled several consecutive searches, at different stages of the deportation, so that not a single wedding ring or leva note would escape their attention.

They had prepared several transit camps in Thrace, Macedonia, and old Bulgaria, mostly in tobacco warehouses and schools; three major concentration and departure camps in old Bulgaria—Dupnitza, Gorna Djumaya, and Radomir; and two others in Macedonia—Skopje and Pirot. Train schedules had been drafted,

*Macedonian Jews in a tobacco warehouse in Skopje, before their deportation to the death camp, Treblinka.*

half-price railroad fares (workers group fares) negotiated, and numbers of transported people and families verified.

A detailed timetable had been established. First, from March 4 to March 8, the Jews from Thrace would be rounded up and transferred to the main deportation centers in Bulgaria. On March 10, at 12:00 A.M., eight thousand Jews of old Bulgaria would be arrested (except for twenty-five hundred Sofia Jews who would be seized on March 13). The Bulgarian Jews would join the Thracian deportees in the three major transition camps. All of them would be transported by train to Lom on the Danube and by riverboats to Vienna, where they would be handed over to the German authorities. The Macedonian Jews would be rounded up on March 11 and ten days later would be sent directly to Poland, via Katowicz, their trains traveling through Macedonia, Albania, Serbia, Croatia, Hungary, and finally German-administered territory. Therefore, the handing over to the Germans would be executed earlier, at German-occupied Lapovo.

Between February 22 and March 4, in absolute secrecy, the deportation net was spread over old and new Bulgaria. And on March 4, with stunning cruelty, the Bulgarian raiders, armed to the teeth, started the Aktzia.

The cruel treatment of the Jews shocked even some of the participants in the raids. "The very taking of the Jews from their homes, in the middle of the night, was an appalling picture," wrote later Boris Gheorghiev Bozukov, a police detective stationed in Kavalla:[3]

> Old men, children, women, half-asleep, frightened, laden with suitcases and bundles, incessantly prodded by the police officers to go faster, marched toward the tobacco warehouses. Some of them fell on the ground, collapsing of sickness or fatigue.
>
> In the warehouses where they were jailed, all of them were subjected to the most detailed search. Women were searched by women who probed their bodies for hidden money or jewelry. A very rich Jew, Ashkenazi, was supposed to own three tin cans full of gold. At the search in the warehouse nothing was found, and he was beaten hard to say where the gold was.

Nobody was killed by the raiders. But during the operation several old and sick people died—in the transit camps and aboard the trains.

The trains coming from Ksanti, Kavala, Giumurdjina, Dede Agach, and Drama stopped at the railroad hubs at Demir Hissar and Simitli, where the track changed, and the Jews were transferred to other trains heading to the transit camps in Dupnitza and Gorna Djumaya in the interior of Bulgaria.

At Demir Hissar a medical team was waiting for them, composed of three Jewish nurses and a Jewish physician, Dr. Joseph Konfino. They were part of a special unit of thirty Jewish nurses assigned by the Bulgarian Red Cross to take care of the deportees. Upon the arrival of the Jewish nurses to Demir Hissar, police officers searched them for letters and parcels they might be carrying for the deportees; they also took their personal money. On the following night, one of the trains from Thrace arrived in the station. One of the nurses, Rosa Yakova, wrote:

> We saw children, old people, mothers, all of them helpless, naked, and barefoot. It was dark. A strong wind was blowing. Mr. Ovcharov [the KEV delegate], started yelling: "Get off right away and get into the small open cars!" He ordered the police officers and the soldiers: "Beat them with your rifles, make them hurry. We are not going to waste all night . . ."[4]

The children cried and shrieked, they were hungry, but there was no food.

> We gave them only hot water and some medication. Some sick deportees asked for aspirin, but Mr. Ovcharov forbade it, so that we wouldn't establish contact with them and learn something from them.
>
> During the day we wore our Jewish stars, but in the evenings, when the trains arrived, Mr. Ovcharov forbade us to wear them, so that the deportees wouldn't realize we were Jewish.

And so, night after night, the trains arrived. One night a woman gave birth, and the nurses wrapped the baby with rags. Then the mother was carried back to the open freight car with all the others. Among the deportees were very sick people, some of them crippled or half-paralyzed, who needed help, but didn't get any. "Soldiers and police officers molested the women, touched them, threw their luggage, kicked them, grabbed their breasts, pushed them into the small cars. Ovcharov was watching with pleasure."

The brutality of the officials was revolting. Dr. Konfino wrote:

> The transfer of people from the trains to the open cars on the narrow-gauge railway was done in minutes. Under the blows of the rifle butts, the lashings of the whips, the curses of the commissar, people were transferred from the tall broad-gauged cars to the low, open narrow-gauge cars; people were thrown on baggage, baggage on people, to the sound of the heartbreaking cries of the deportees.

After the transfer, the Jews waited in the cars for four to five hours in the bitter cold before resuming their tragic journey. Then the trains traveled for twelve hours in the freezing night through the Kresnen Pass, exposed to shrieking winds.

> Every morning one or two trains arrived at Simitli.... The sight of these wretches was indescribable. Smeared by soot, covered by rags, with holes burnt in them by the sparks of the engines, with frightened faces, with unfocused looks, having had no food and no sleep for several days, some of them were chewing yellow, stale cornbread, or eating from their palms corn flour, raw rice or raw beans ... The weeping of many of them was accompanied by the despair and the weeping of the doctor who escorted them or the doctor who met them.[5]

At the Simitli train station, another Jewish nurse, Nora Levi, waited for the deportees. She was joined by the devoted Dr. Konfino, who seemed to be everywhere. The KEV official, Ivan Popov, scolded her for not wearing her Jewish star. (She had removed it on Ovharov's order).[6]

Late at night, the first trainload arrived. "Their eyes were swollen, they were dirty, freezing, tormented, and so frightened, that I had trouble communicating with them." Popov refused Dr. Konfino's request to give them some hot water and reluctantly agreed to allow some of them to relieve themselves out of the train. "They still risked to be whipped if they were too long. They were beaten without reason, just for the fun. All the Thracian Jews were hungry." They said they hadn't eaten for thirty-six hours. They told how they were whipped and beaten during their arrest. "Some of the women," Nora Levi wrote, "were dressed in robes and slippers, and some were holding brooms. When I asked them what they needed those for, they answered, 'We don't know what we are doing.'" They spoke of cruelty, beatings, degrading searches. A six months pregnant woman had been beaten so hard that at Simitli she was seized by labor pains. Nora Levi tried to help her but was reprimanded again by Popov. A few days later the woman miscarried and died at the Dupnitza camp.[7]

As the wind blew and the torrential rains beat down on them, the deportees sat unprotected in the open freight cars, huddled against each other in a futile effort to keep warm. But an even worse experience was in store for them. Several Jewish labor gangs were working along the railroad. Some of the men were from old Bulgaria, many others from Thrace. Most of the men from Thrace were later discharged from the labor companies and sent to Poland as well.

At the Kresnen gorge, Jewish workers were awakened by cries that sounded like the "wailing of caged birds." One of them, Dr. Sammy Shakov, was stunned by the "scene of naked horror" that he witnessed.[8] "For one instant we saw the entire tragedy of the Jews of the Belomorie—raw material for the factories of death—unfold before us." He was struck by the image of a white-bearded patriarch, who looked and shouted like an ancient prophet: *No vos spantes, ermanos, la salvacion viene!* (in Ladino: "Don't fear, brothers, salvation is coming!").

Marko Aaron Peretz, a Bulgarian Jew arrested in Thrace with the other Jewish families, and later released, described the heartbreaking scenes he witnessed. He wrote:

*Belev personally supervised all deportations, including this one where he is shown with Jewish women in Macedonia.*

The [Jewish] workers . . . ran toward the railway, to see their relatives. Tears ran on both sides, when [both the deportees and the workers] were shouting: shall we ever see each other again? Even those who had nobody in the trains were crying, and what can be said of those who were parting?[9]

Bulgarian Jews also ran toward the train. Some of the workers were stopped and beaten for approaching the slowly moving train and throwing in bread, money, and canned foods.

One of the Jewish workers along the railway was Harry Nissimov, a twenty-five-year-old Sofia Jew. For the past ten days he and his friends had been discussing rumors that the Jews would be taken to concentration camps. They then heard harrowing descriptions of the roundup of the Greek Jews, the deaths on the road, and newborn babies carried by their young mothers in the freezing cold. Fear and pain spread throughout the camp.

As Harry and his friends were digging a ditch 400 yards from the narrow railway, a train suddenly appeared in front of them, then a second and a third. The open cars were full of people.

> They were Jews.
> Immediately two men, Moni and Gero, grabbed two loaves of bread and ran toward the trains. The first had already passed. They succeeded in climbing on the cars of the next one. A thundering shout erupted. Then another pair of workers took off their shoes, so they could run more easily. In an instant we collected some bread and money, and we sent it to the third train. . . . The sight in the cars was heart-rending. Families, huddled together, hugging each other in despair.[10]

Expecting the arrival of more trains, the Jewish workers began to collect money, contributed half of their bread rations, all of their sausage rations, and bought from the local grocer a hundred packages of cigarettes and all the marmelade he had available. The following night, after a junior officer had forbidden them to approach the railway, they sent a delegation to the camp commander, an officer named Karadjov. "This anti-Semite, who nurtured such hatred toward the Jews, showed that he had a heart." Unofficially, he allowed five of them to go and wait for the trains.

Nissimov had a special reason to be concerned about the plight of the trainloads of people. In one of them, his friends had seen his own brother, who had been evacuated from old Bulgaria to Ksanti not long before. Harry Nissimov became almost crazy with fear, but finally his brother was released as a Bulgarian citizen. "How selfish can a man become?" he wrote in his diary when his brother was sighted in the convoy of the damned. "I am worried about my brother. And what awaits all the other poor devils?"[11]

•  •  •

A never-ending string of telegrams, expressing thanks and congratulations, poured into the offices of the prime minister and the minister of interior in Sofia. The Drama merchants cabled Gabrovski that they welcomed "with relief and enthusiasm, the government's decision to liquidate forever the eternal profiteers and traitors of our people—the Jews."[12] "Long live Bulgaria and the Bulgarian government," stated the artisans of Drama, "for liberating the Bulgarian people from a minority of Jewish predators, who without working but by profiteering and fraud amassed wealth like ticks on the back of the artisans of Drama."[13] The Bulgarian workers of Drama "admire the action taken by the government to remove the Jews and the Jewry from the Bulgarian land—those who for centuries sucked the vital juices of the workers."[14] "The blow on the Jews of Ser and the White Sea region," cabled the veterans of the area, "is a blow on the communist spies and profiteers' nests."[15] The fighters on the fronts from Giumurdjina congratulated the government "on the occasion of the cleansing of Giumurdjina from the Jewry."[16] Mayor Petev of Ksanti expressed the delight of his citizens for "your radical solution of the Jewish question."[17] His colleague from Kavala, Mayor Shipliev, was even more eloquent: "Kavala, the Queen of the White Sea, was liberated from two thousand supporters of the black market, of the eternal robbers of Bulgarian labor and goods, of the Judeo-masons, the most devoted allies to the Anglo-Saxons and Bolsheviks and our vilest enemies."[18]

This outburst of racist fervor would be better understood in the light of a confidential telegram by Dr. Popov, one of the KEV senior officials, to several regional governors: "After the deportation . . . do arrange for telegrams of thanks to the Ministry, copy to the KEV, from the citizens, the mayor, the patriotic organizations, etc."[19] Ilya Dobrevski, the KEV official in charge of the deportation from Giumurdjina, testified later that "first Kalitzin . . . and after him Belev . . . instructed me to take the necessary steps so that telegrams of thanks be sent to the Prime Minister, the Minister of Interior, and to him."[20]

•  •  •

Who were these "profiteers and traitors," these "robbers," these "ticks on the back of the artisans of Drama"? For the most they were poor country Jews, who had lived for centuries in the ruggedly beautiful mountains and villages of Thrace and Macedonia. Many wore the local peasants clothes, sporting bushy mustaches, their faces burnt in the sun, their hands strong, callused, the powerful hands of workers. For centuries they had lived peacefully among Greeks and Macedonians, speaking the same language, eating the same food, suffering the same hunger. In Ksanti and Kavala, in Giumurdjina and Dede Agach, there was no rejoicing at their tragic fate. Only pain and anger and deep empathy on the side of their Christian friends and neighbors, who at night haunted their transit camps hoping to smuggle in a loaf of bread or a jar of water.

Yet, even the modest property the Jews left behind was shamelessly looted by the administration. Officially, the homes of the Jews had to be sealed and guarded. In reality, police officers, local officials, and KEV representatives, walked into the houses and took what they wanted. Some of the property had to be auctioned and the proceeds deposited in the "Jewish communities fund." Most of the auctions were fraudulent; in many cases the proceeds were minimal and often didn't reach the bank accounts of the Jewish communities fund. The personal property, money, and valuables, seized during the searches, was supposed to be deposited under the names of the families from whom it was taken. In most cases nobody registered the names of the owners, and the seized valuables and money were just mixed together by the clerks who found them in the Jews' clothing. This property was later deposited in the very funds used to deport and persecute its owners, or support the ultra-Fascist organizations.

In the rare instances when property— or the proceeds from its sale—was registered under the names of its lawful owners, a bizarre correspondence ensued. For years after the deported Jews had been murdered by the Nazis, formal letters continued to arrive at their homes from the Bulgarian National Bank, informing them of the balances in their frozen accounts.

•   •   •

On February 25, the Jews of Dupnitza, a town in old Bulgaria, were placed under house arrest. Only children were allowed to buy bread and groceries. Members of the Brannik youth Fascist organization were posted in the Jewish quarter, to enforce the curfew, often beating up the children or barging into the homes and harrassing the confined Jews. The local Jews realized something was happening and feared that their fate had been sealed.

On March 7, several trains from Thrace unloaded Jewish passengers at the train station, and from there the deportees walked to the tobacco warehouse, in the outskirts of the town. They would spend about two weeks in that prison, sleeping on the concrete floors or the wooden platforms used for drying tobacco. They were given tiny rations of food and inadequate covers during the cold nights. The latrines overflowed; some of the warehouse rooms became inundated with urine. The Jews of Dupnitza collected money, clothing, and provisions and sent ten carloads of supplies to the camp. But the KEV delegate, Paytashev, would not allow the leaders of the community to distribute the supplies to the deportees. Instead he had them delivered to the police and the local officials; thus, most of the food and clothing disappeared. At least five Jews died in the camp and were buried at the local Jewish cemetery. The KEV officials continued to lie to the Jews about their fate. They told them that they were to be sent to Black Sea ports, where they would board ships for Palestine. Nobody believed them.

About three thousand deportees were sent to another Bulgarian town, Gorna Djumaya, and imprisoned in the junior high school, the economics school, and the tobacco warehouse. They also suffered terribly from the incarceration. In the schools there was one water faucet for every 1,500 people; one latrine for every 300 to 500 people. Many suffered from malaria, pneumonia, influenza, and gastric illness. The six Jewish doctors assigned to the camp were unable to help, for the lack of drugs and medical facilities. "They all were sick after the freezing trip [was] over," wrote Dr. Konfino, who did his best to help. "We were not able to give them any help, except for consolation."[21]

In the dirty-gray headquarters of the KEV on Boulevard Dondukov, the deportation process was followed with utmost satisfaction. Yaroslav Kalitzin, Ivan Popov, Ilya Dobrevski, Atanas Ovcharov, and other KEV raiders, sent to Belev reports of the tremendous success of their operations. The first stage in the Belev-Dannecker agreement was completed. The second stage was about to begin.

In utmost secrecy, Boris Tasev and other KEV envoys completed the preparation of the transit camp at Radomir; they also prepared additional structures in Dupnitza and Gorna Djumaya.

Time had come to hit the Jews of old Bulgaria.

# CHAPTER EIGHT

# BOXCARS AT
# THE STATION

N estled in the slopes of the Hisarluka Hill, overlooking the fertile Struma valley—known as Bulgaria's fruit orchard—Kyustendil was a mellow province town in the southeast, basking in the glory of past centuries. It had flourished under Roman rule. Archeologists have uncovered a multitude of artifacts and more than nine hundred kinds of ancient coins, buried in Kyustendil's millenary ruins. A coin of the third century depicts the magnificent temple of the town patron, Aesculapius, the God of medicine. Neglected by the Slavs, Kyustendil acquired new glory under Turkish rule, when the Ottoman sultans would send their harems to spend the summer in its pleasant climate and lush scenery.

Kyustendil's green fields and orchards—apples, plums, vines, and tobacco—were irrigated by the pure waters of the Struma tributaries. Around the town, the snow-topped Osogovo and Lisetz Mountains etched their jagged contours on the luminous skies. A few miles to the west, across the pre-war border, unfolded the breathtakingly beautiful mountains and valleys of Macedonia.

Kyustendil was a crossroads between the ancient and the modern, between the picturesque Bulgarian village and the bustling European city. Beside the sleek clock tower of the Court of Justice building and the sturdy Bulgarian banks, stood four ancient churches and a sixteenth-century synagogue. From needle-shaped mosques, Muslim priests called the local Turks to the five daily prayers. In the fields, black-robed Greek-Orthodox priests led the seasonal prayers for a good harvest. Many of the town streets were still unpaved, dusty in summer and muddy in winter. Shepherds often crossed the outskirts, leading their herds to pasture.

Horsecarts and phaetons were the main means of transport, and most of the houses were the typical red-roofed, whitewashed low structures, sprawling toward the backyard vegetable patches. Everybody had a cousin in the nearby village, spoke the peasant dialect, and seemed to know how to milk a cow, or at least a sheep. Every Saturday a farmers market was held in Kyustendil. The neat suits and ties and the Paris-inspired dresses mixed with the tall fur caps, the embroidered blouses, multicolored aprons, and leather sandals of the village people. The town also had electricity and running water, a modern center, an active cultural life, libraries, public gardens, schools, a museum, theaters, and fashionable stores.

Proud of its magnificent linden-lined avenue, of its main square surrounded by public buildings, hotels, and restaurants, and of its newly acquired status as the seat of the regional administration, Kyustendil was the home of a diverse population—twenty thousand Bulgarians, Macedonians, Gypsies, Turks, and Jews. The Jews, numbering about a thousand, had roots dating back to the Middle Ages. Mostly artisans, workers, and merchants, many of the Kyustendil Jews lived near their downtown synagogue; many others, however, lived in other parts of the town and grew up among Bulgarian families. It was not rare for Bulgarians to speak some rudimentary Ladino-Spanish, which they had learned from their Jewish neighbors. Under the influence of the town Jews, the representatives of Bulgaria's Jewish community, Colonel Avraham Tadjer and Dr. Buko Levi, had supported the Macedonians' civil rights petitions at the League of Nations Commission of Minorities. The relationship between Jews and Macedonians was close and warm.

Yet, Kyustendil was not a paradise. The Brannik and Ratnik Fascist organizations had quite a following in the small town, although their activity had rarely ventured beyond yelling offensive slogans at their Jewish neighbors. The tension grew when two hundred Sofia Jews moved into the town after the passing of the Law for the Defense of the Nation.

Alexander Belev chose Kyustendil as one of the Bulgarian cities whose entire Jewish population would be deported, in March 1943.

•  •  •

On February 26, the KEV general inspector, Dr. Ivan Popov, traveled to Kyustendil with Borislav Tasev, who headed the police agents group at the Commissariat. Belev himself visited Kyustendil a few days later. Tasev was left in Kyustendil and was instructed to carry out the deportation of the local Jews.

He began his preparations. First he established the transit camp at the tobacco warehouse, which had once belonged to a Jewish family, the Fernandes.[1] Zakhari Velkov, another KEV employee, helped him to obtain the use of the warehouse from the local authorities.[2] The following day Tasev instructed Mayor Efremov and the district governor, Liuben Miltenov, not to deliver any more travel permits to Jews, but refused to disclose the reason why. He didn't know that Miltenov and Tasev's boss, Popov, had spent the previous night drinking together and that Popov had revealed to the governor the deportation plans.[3]

On March 5, Tasev sent an official letter to the mayor, instructing him to collect large quantities of equipment from the town Jews. His list included 300 pails, 300 ladles, 30 coal shovels, 10 kitchen knives, 5 pans, 5 axes, 6 beds, rubber pipes, 20 tables, 20 basins, and 30 coat racks.[4]

That evening the list was sent, for immediate execution, to Pinhas Comforty, the secretary of the Jewish community. On March 6, a large part of the listed items was delivered by the Kyustendil Jews.[5]

Tasev intended to send the equipment to Radomir, where the main transit camp for the old Bulgaria Jews was being established. He thought that he could equip the Radomir camp at the expense of the Jews. However, Tasev didn't realize that as soon as Comforty saw the list, the deportation was no longer secret. Anyone would understand that the equipment was needed for a camp—a deportation camp for the Jews.

Tasev's foolish initiative triggered a wave of rumors among Kyustendil's Jews. They had already heard about the raids on the Jews in the new territories; they knew that temporary camps were being established throughout the country and that the Dupnitza Jews had been kept under house arrest for more than a week. It was not difficult to guess that the KEV was preparing their deportation to Poland.

Confirmations to the rumors came from many sources.

Haim Rahamim (he is also referred to as Rahamimov, and Haim Rahamim Behar), a Kyustendil Jew, heard about the deportation plan as early as February 25.[6] By a strange coincidence, within forty-eight hours, three sources—independent of each other—informed Haim Rahamim of the deportation. On February 25, Rahamim was in Sofia. While walking with his cousin on Dondukov Boulevard, he met Dr. Iosif Vatev, a corrupt optician who was a medical consultant for the KEV. Vatev issued false medical certificates for the Sofia Jews, in exchange for fat bribes. Although some KEV agents knew about his activity, Vatev performed with absolute impunity, as he was a brother-in-law of Interior Minister Gabrovski, and nobody dared to accuse him.[7]

Dr. Vatev greeted Rahamim and said to him: "I shall reveal to you a big secret, for a payment, of course."

Rahamim readily reached for his wallet, and Vatev told him that the Jews of Bulgaria were going to be deported out of the country in the near future. The following day Rahamim met one of his close friends, the Macedonian leader Vladimir Kurtev, who also happened to be in Sofia. Kurtev told Rahamim that he had learned from a senior official at the KEV, Gioshev, about the Belev-Dannecker agreement and the projected deportation of the Kyustendil Jews to Poland.[8] The same day, the Kyustendil district governor, Miltenov, telephoned Rahamim in Sofia, and asked him to be back in Kyustendil by Sunday, February 27, "for he had something very important to tell him."

Miltenov, Buko Lazarov recalled, "was a good man, but he was corrupt and an alcoholic. Haim Rahamim knew his weaknesses. Whenever somebody got in trouble, or was arrested—people gave money to Miltenov, and he helped."[9] Rahamim returned, and Miltenov told him that "there was an oral order by Alexander Belev to prepare the Jews for deportation on March 10 to the city of Radomir. There they would be joined by Jews from Sofia, Samokov and Dupnitza, and sent to their destination." The governor threatened Rahamim with death if he revealed the secret to anyone else. He had intended that Rahamim save his family only.

"How do you want me to keep the matter secret?" Rahamim asked. "I learned it from Kurtev as well!"

Miltenov asked Rahamim to raise 300,000 leva ($3,700). With this money, he, Miltenov, would try to help the Jewish community "as much as he could."[10]

In spite of the governor's warning, Rahamim disclosed the news to his wife, a few friends, and a group of people whom he met in the house of Pressiado Anavi, a Sofia pharmacist who had been exiled to Kyustendil.[11] (Pressiado Anavi was also the author's grandfather.) The group of people were actually members of his family. But Rahamim also informed Pinhas Comforty, the president of the Jewish community, of the forthcoming deportation. Yet, between that day and March 6, apparently nothing was done with this information. (Buko Lazarov claims that Haim Rahamim revealed the secret only to the members of his family—when the other Jews asked about the deportation, Rahamim claimed that it was not serious and that perhaps there might be a deportation inside Bulgaria's borders.)

Rahamim was not the only one who heard the news from Miltenov. The regional governor also disclosed the deportation secret to Samuel Baruch, a pharmacist. Baruch, a citizen of Sofia, was forced to work in Kyustendil, by the Law for Civilian Mobilization. He wrote a short letter that he immediately dispatched with a friend to his brother, Jacob (Yako) Baruch, in Sofia.[12] "Intensive preparations are being made here to round up the Jews on March 9 in the evening. I know that from the regional governor, who told me confidentially that on March 9 the Jews would be taken from their homes and then sent to Poland. See what you can do in Sofia."[13]

Yako Baruch, the leader of the Zionist organization in Bulgaria, was a well-known lawyer, with excellent connections in the capital. But his efforts to thwart the deportation plan failed.

Another Kyustendil Jew, Buko Beracha, received a note from a Bulgarian friend saying that at Radomir railway station a train of twenty-nine boxcars had been prepared to take the Jews "somewhere." That same evening a second message came to Beracha's home: In the Radomir schools, classrooms are being prepared to temporarily house the Jews from Kyustendil, Dupnitza, and Gorna Djumaya.[14]

Panic spread throughout the Jewish community. Beracha and a friend visited the town mayor, Dr. Efremov, at his home. The mayor said to Beracha, "Bad things are in store for you." His eyes filled with tears.[15]

The Kyustendil Jewish leaders were at a loss. What could they do? One of the men, Buko Lazarov, decided to act. Warned by Michael Abadjiev at the cornhusking at his home (see Chapter One), Lazarov knew about the planned concentration of the Jews in the Fernandes warehouse. He alerted the president of the Jewish community and suggested a course of action.

In the meantime, Tasev had collected his pails and pans, confirming the rumors about the impending raids. Following the advice of his friend Abadjiev, Lazarov went to the Midrash synagogue and gathered a group of Kyustendil Jews as well as exiles from Sofia. "We must make some noise," he told them. And noise they made, sending a young man with a tin drum to the streets of the Jewish neighborhoods, to beat the drum and announce that there was an urgent meeting at the Midrash.

The meeting took place on March 7. More than a hundred Jews came. Lazarov, Comforty, Rahamim, and their friends revealed to their audience details of the forthcoming deportation.[16]

The news spread throughout the town, and soon the Bulgarians were offering to help their Jewish friends. Some brought presents, clothes, and food; one woman brought Anka Lazarov good walking shoes. Others told their Jewish friends "to leave with them the houseware they wouldn't need."[17]

In a few hours Haim Rahamim succeeded in raising 900,000 Leva. The Jews gave Miltenov the 300,000 leva he had asked for. They also gave the Macedonian leader and their good friend, Vladimir Kurtev, 320,000 leva to bribe people at the KEV. They gave 80,000 leva for urgent expenses to another friend, the attorney Ivan Momchilov. And Pinhas Comforty himself took 180,000 to attempt to bribe Tasev, who had been charged by the KEV to deport Kyustendil's Jews.[18]

But the money alone would not solve their problem. In the Midrash meeting, the Jews discussed the idea of a delegation that would travel to Sofia and try to influence senior leaders to cancel the deportation. The delegation had to be composed of Bulgarians. Haim Rahamim spoke to Vladimir Kurtev, who immediately agreed. Beracha approached Ivan Momchilov, a local lawyer. Others spoke with Assen Suitchmezov, a wealthy businessman who had grown up in a Jewish neighborhood. A tailor, Georgi Yeremiev, the president of the reserve sergeants union, and Ivan Levkov, a representative at the Sofia chamber of commerce also promised to join the delegation, as well as scores of other businessmen, merchants, and prominent local citizens.

But such a delegation needed a leader. Lazarov went searching for his childhood friend, Peter Mikhalev. Mikhalev was an attorney. A tall, distinguished-looking man, Mikhalev had served in the past as a judge and as district governor of Kyustendil. Now he was a member of the Sobranie, the Bulgarian Parliament, representing Kyustendil. He divided his time between Kyustendil and Sofia. In Sofia Peter and Parka Mikhalev had an apartment in the same building on Exarch Yossif Street, where Buko Lazarov once lived. Mikhalev was a good friend of the Jewish community, had refused to vote for the Law for the Defense of the Nation,[19] and even spoke some Ladino.[20]

(COURTESY OF PARKA MIKHALEVA)

*Peter Mikhalev, a Member of Parliament and a participant in the Kyustendil delegation.*

Buko didn't find Mikhalev at his Kyustendil home. The member of Parliament was touring the neighboring villages, he was told, to meet with his constituents. He was supposed to return later in the day. Buko wandered through the city, looking for his friend. Finally he caught up with Mikhalev at the market, as he was coming back from his tour.

Mikhalev was walking up the street, aware of the strange quiet that had settled on the market. Only a few people were moving around; life seemed to have stopped.[21] He suddenly saw Buko Lazarov, hurrying toward him. Buko looked extremely agitated. "Peter, we are finished!" he cried out.[22]

He then described to Mikhalev the dramatic events of the last few days: the arrival of KEV agents from Sofia, the interdiction to the Jews to leave town, the planned raid on the Jewish homes, then the concentration in the Fernandes warehouse and a departure "to a place of no return."

"Buko," Mikhalev said, "this can't be true. Neither I nor Peshev know anything about this." Peshev was the other Kyustendil member of Parliament and the deputy speaker of the Sobranie.[23]

Everything is being prepared in the utmost secrecy, Buko explained, without any public statements or publication of the decrees in the state *Gazette*.

Mikhalev felt a deep anxiety. The lives of more than a thousand Jews were at stake! "For a moment I imagined all those children, men, women and helpless old people, packed like animals in the freight cars, taken . . . to mass massacre. I felt a strong indignation, but also a determination to do all that was in my power to thwart that infernal project."[24]

He didn't hesitate for a single moment. He told Lazarov that he would go to the governor's office right away, to find out the truth about the situation, "and then we would decide what to do."

In Governor Miltenov's office, Peter Mikhalev met Borislav Tasev, the KEV representative. Tasev confirmed that the deportation of the Jews had been decided and that it was to begin in a matter of hours. The police cooperation had been assured.

Mikhalev waited for Tasev to leave, then assailed the governor with questions. Miltenov confirmed Lazarov's information. A special train had arrived at the station, he said, to take the Jews away, after their concentration at the Fernandes warehouse.

Mikhalev felt that immediate action was necessary, "to prevent the tragic fate of a thousand of our co-citizens." He said to Miltenov: "The deportation means their death. In no case should we allow their departure from the town. Our duty is to do all we can in order to prevent a criminal action and defend their lives." He would depart to Sofia right away, Mikhalev said. "Until you hear from me, you will not allow the police to cooperate [with the KEV], and without the police the deportation of the Jews will not be possible."[25]

Buko Lazarov was waiting for Mikhalev in his brother's home. When Mikhalev walked in, Buko noticed that his friend's face was chalk-white. "Now he knew that we had told him the truth."[26] Mikhalev said he was leaving for Sofia, right away. There are forty others, Buko said, who would like to join the delegation.[27] They decided that the delegation would leave by taxis or by the 5:00 P.M. train.

•　•　•

A few blocks away, Assen Suichmezov also was preparing to leave for Sofia. Suichmezov had grown up among Jews, spoke their language, and regarded some of them as his closest friends. To his son, Gregor, they were "Uncle Oliver, Uncle Haim, and Uncle Sabo."[28] Suichmezov was an affluent businessman, a director at the local bank, and an owner, among others, of a large leather workshop and a coat store. His pro-Jewish views were well known in town, and the Kyustendil Fascists had often threatened to harm him or his business. One evening, at the local inn, he barely escaped a beating. A furious anti-Semite was about to smash a chair on his head, when Suichmezov's friends intervened and whisked him away. "Run," a Bulgarian friend shouted at him. "They'll beat you up because of the Jews."[29]

When Suichmezov heard the news about the forthcoming deportation, he immediately decided to join the delegation that was forming. He recalled that forty-four people had signed up to go to Sofia. The delegation was to travel in a convoy of taxicabs, but the governor (probably acting on orders from Sofia) had refused to release the necessary gasoline.[30] They decided therefore to take the train, but a family friend, a former policeman who worked now for Suichmezov, told him that the railroad station was surrounded by police, to stop the delegation. Suichmezov had a backup plan; he secretly hired the town's phaetons to take him and the members of the delegation to the next train station. That way, they would be able to board the train, if access to the Kyustendil railroad station was denied to them. If they couldn't leave on the evening of March 8, they would depart at 5:00 A.M. the following morning.

Suichmezov also sent his son, Gregor, to the railway station on bicycle, to check if a train of boxcars had arrived. Twice the boy went to the station, but didn't see anything. The third time he saw a long train that almost blocked the railway.[31]

The news of the arrival of the deportation train spread like brush fire. A Bulgarian was sent to speak to the railroad employees. "What are these trains?" he asked.

"They are for the Jews," came the answer.[32]

While many of the town Jews were desperately packing, selling their belongings, and buying suitcases and bags, others came to

Suichmezov's workshop. "Good-bye, Mr. Assen," many said, weeping openly, "we'll never see you again!"[33]

Suichmezov also had other visitors, Bulgarian friends who begged him to go to Sofia with the delegation. The attorney Ivan Momchilov, himself a member of the delegation, burst in tears in Suichmezov's workshop, while pleading with him to go to Sofia, in spite of the Fascist and the official pressure against it. But Suichmezov had no intention to withdraw from his commitment anyway.

(COURTESY OF THE KURTEV FAMILY)

*Vladimir Kurtev, a Macedonian leader and a member of the Kyustendil delegation.*

Ivan Momchilov, a tall, thin man with an oblong face and deep dark eyes, was a Macedonian; he had spent a few years in prison with Vladimir Kurtev. He also had been a member of Parliament in the twenty-fourth Sobranie, together with Mikhalev and Peshev. However, because of his independent views, he had not been re-elected.[34] His family had many Jewish friends. When the rumors about the deportation spread through Kyustendil, his son's Jewish friend came to their home and, bitterly crying, entrusted Momchilov with his violin. Momchilov didn't hesitate for a moment when his Jewish friends asked him to join the group leaving for Sofia.

On March 8, at 5:00 P.M., the delegation met at Kyustendil railway station. Apparently, a high official had done a very effective job of applying pressure on the delegation members. Only four people found the courage to come to the station: Parliament member Peter Mikhalev, Attorney Momchilov, Macedonian leader Vladimir Kurtev, and Assen Suichmezov.

At that moment, as darkness descended upon the empty railway station, the most natural thing for the four delegates to do was admit defeat, shake hands, and go home. What could a delegation of four people do? And why should they take such unnecessary risks? They were about to initiate an action against a government resolution. By doing so they would attract the attention of angry officials, of fanatic Fascists, of a pro-German establishment in the administration, the police, and the army. They would be accused of treason. The action they were about to take might put their very lives in jeopardy. And if they had decided to go home at that moment, who could blame them? The battle seemed to be already lost.

But these four determined people didn't hesitate for a single moment. The thought of giving up never crossed their minds. Without any discussion, they boarded the train. They didn't notice Tasev's agent, who had followed them to the station and was watching them closely. The train began to move, and the four self-appointed delegates were on their way to Sofia—a naïve endeavor to prevent this deportation of Jews, to stop the huge wheels that were already turning.

As the train moved out into the cold winter night, they passed the long succession of boxcars waiting at Kyustendil station.

# CHAPTER NINE

# AN ORDER FROM THE HIGHEST PLACE

The delegation arrived in Sofia in the late evening.*

They put all their faith in one man, a man they all knew and held in profound respect—Dimiter Peshev, deputy speaker of the National Assembly and a former justice minister. He was the only one they knew who possessed both the integrity and the power to effectively intervene and make the government listen.

Peshev was a forty-nine-year-old bachelor; he was an elegant, balding man of average height, his grave, oval face adorned with a square mustache. Born to an affluent family in Kyustendil, he had studied languages in Saloniki and law in Sofia. The outbreak of World War I interrupted his studies. He applied to the Officers Academy and, after being commissioned, bravely fought on the southern front. A year after the war ended he completed his law studies and became a judge, first in Plovdiv and later in Sofia. In 1935 he was appointed

---

* The following description is based on a comparative analysis of the various testimonies concerning that fateful day, March 9, 1943. Unfortunately, many of the testimonies, depositions, and memoirs are inexact, and some very highly praised scientific works based on those inaccurate accounts are distorted and erroneous as well. Only by comparing the various accounts on an hour-by-hour basis and testing them against other facts and evidence were we able to reconstruct the events of that day.

(COURTESY OF KITZA AND KALUDKA KIRADJIEV)

*Dimiter Peshev.*

minister of justice in the Kiosseivanov cabinet, resigning the following year. He was credited with the introduction of civil marriage in Bulgaria. Peshev was strongly disliked by Prime Minister Filov. Right-wing circles couldn't forgive him for refusing to sign the 1936 death sentence against Colonel Damian Velchev, after his failed coup (see Chapter Two).

Since 1938 he had been a member of Parliament, on the majority side. He had challenged the official candidate of his own parliamentary group for the position of deputy speaker of the Sobranie. On the eve of the election, the members of his group were split almost equally between the two candidates. Two of Peshev's friends visited Dr. Liuben Dukmedjiev, a Communist Parliament member, who headed a loose coalition of eighteen opposition members. "You know Peshev," they said to the Communist, "he is an honest and honorable man. You should vote for him." Dukmedjiev convened the group and told them they had interest in electing an objective and impartial deputy speaker. Peshev, he told them, was running against the official government candidate, and anytime the opposition could derail a government initiative, they should do so. Dukmedjiev then spoke to the timid Peshev, who became as "red as a lobster and shy as a maiden," saying, "We shall vote for you."[1]

Peshev won, with the support of the opposition, further poisoning his relationship with Filov.

Peshev was as obsessed with order in his affairs, papers, and books as he was with doing the right thing.[2] He was not talkative.

He would spend long hours with his brother, in their Kyustendil family home, sitting in the living room in absolute silence.[3] He expressed most of his thoughts in writing, spending hours every day scribbling in his diary in his large handwriting. The Constitution and especially the safeguarding of human rights were his top priorities.

Peshev was a good friend of the Jewish community in Bulgaria. Still, he had not objected to the ZZN during the legislative process. He claimed to be against the Law for the Defense of the Nation and that he had helped his colleagues to soften the language of the bill during its preparation.[4] However, there is no evidence to confirm that claim. He told his Jewish friend Jacob ("Yako") Baruch, with whom he had studied law in Sofia: "I don't believe there would be one Member of Parliament who would vote for such a law, because we are a small nation, we have proved that we tolerate the minorities. There is a very slight chance that Gabrovski would pass that law." He also advised his friend to lobby the main "social powers" and make known his opposition to that law.[5]

Still, in the end, Peshev did not vote against the law. In his memoirs of that period, he stressed that those who opposed the bill didn't voice their objections "publicly and sharply," because "they had to consider the political needs of the times and the interests of the grand national policy."[6] Peshev and some of his friends had hoped, afterward, that the question would be "liquidated" without the introduction of new, harsher measures. He had been reassured by Gabrovski's speech at the majority meeting, on September 19, 1942, when the interior minister declared that "the Jewish question must be ended, it must be taken off the stage, and the decrees concerning it applied sensibly, humanely and morally."[7]

"Those [of us] who feared new, harsher measures against the Jews—and the rumors and fears about this abounded—could calm down and recover their breath." So thought Peshev only a few months earlier. And now he was about to discover that he had been cheated, together with the other majority members of Parliament.

•  •  •

Upon their arrival, the Kyustendil emissaries immediately phoned Peshev.[8] They informed him of the latest events in their town and of the goal of their mission: to seek his support in preventing the deportation of the Jewish community.

It was late—about 10.00 P.M.—so they decided to meet the following morning.[9]

For many desperate Jews, March 9 was their last day of freedom. In Kyustendil, a twelve-hour curfew was decreed at 9.00 A.M., and the entire population—Jews and Bulgarians alike—were confined to their homes for the day.[10] The goal was to prevent the Jews from leaving the city. In spite of the curfew, word had spread that by evening the Jews would be taken to the Fernandes warehouse and the authorities would seal their homes. The day passed with nerve-racking tension.[11] Similar despair spread throughout the towns of Plovdiv, Dupnitza, Sliven, Pazardjik, and others, when word spread that the Jews would soon be taken away.

Mikhalev spent the night at his home on Exarch Yossif Street; the others found a nearby hotel. On the morning of March 9, they met at Popov's millinery shop, at the corner of Boulevard Dondukov and Turgovska Street.[12]

However, they had underestimated the speed by which the news would travel throughout the Jewish community. A few hours after their arrival (some say even before they boarded the train in Kyustendil station), the Jews of Sofia knew about the delegation. Early in the morning, two men approached Assen Suichmezov in the hotel lobby. The two men, renowned leaders of the Sofia Jewish community, asked the Kyustendil businessman to escort them to the meeting of the "Jewish committee" that was trying to save a number of Jews by sending them to Palestine. Suichmezov accompanied them to the Jewish community center, where a large crowd of distressed Jews had gathered. They had heard that something terrible was happening but didn't know exactly what.

The lawyer Jacob ("Yako") Baruch, one of the community's most active leaders and the director of the Jewish Agency in Bulgaria, succeeded to clear the way for Suichmezov. Baruch had been among the first to learn about the forthcoming disaster. A couple of days before, a friend had brought him a confidential letter from his brother Samuel in Kyustendil (see Chapter Eight). After receiving the letter, Jacob Baruch plunged into hectic activity. He turned into a one-man task force, launching a personal effort to thwart the deportation. He dragged his feet in the waiting rooms of ministers, Parliament members, royal advisers, and influential public leaders, in a pathetic attempt to obtain the cancellation of the deportation plans.[13] Baruch also met with his friend Dimiter Peshev, on Sunday, March 7, and told him about the news from Kyustendil.

At first, Peshev didn't believe him. "This can't be true," he said. "This is an absolute lie."

"No," said Baruch. "You are not well informed. Here is the letter. The man who brought it came from there."

"As a Deputy Speaker, I should know such a fact," Peshev objected.[14]

According to Baruch, Peshev tried to phone Kyustendil's governor but was not able to find him.[15] Baruch's last hope was the Kyustendil delegation.

He then introduced Suichmezov to the Jewish committee as a member of the Kyustendil group that was about to meet with Dimiter Peshev.* Suichmezov made a short speech, describing the alarming situation, and said that if the deportation couldn't be called off, the delegation would propose to the government that all the country Jews be moved to one of Bulgaria's regions until the end of the war.[16]

---

\* In his memoirs, Peshev claimed that after hearing about the deportation he went to Kyustendil and was told by the regional governor about the preparations to assemble and deport the Jews. This is a mistake. Peshev didn't visit Kyustendil in the days before the deportation; he got his information from Yako Baruch, the Kyustendil delegation, and telephone conversations with Kyustendil senior officials.

Suichmezov then hurried to Popov's store, where, beside the racks of elegant hats, his friends impatiently waited. He telephoned Peshev, whom he knew well, and the deputy speaker invited the delegation to his home. They hailed a taxi, and at ten o'clock walked into Peshev's apartment on Neofit Rilski Street.

In an atmosphere of extreme tension, the delegates from Kyustendil described to Peshev the events in their city. They told Peshev it was a matter of hours before the police started rounding up the town Jews. Suichmezov had tears in his eyes when he spoke of the boxcars waiting at the railway station and of his Jewish friends who begged him to join the delegation. "They told me: 'Mr. Assen,[17] if you don't go, we are lost!' " The delegation told Peshev that the deportation was going to end in a terrible tragedy, that it would be a permanent stain on the Bulgarian nation.[18]

"What does the public opinion think about this in Kyustendil?" Peshev asked.

"There is a widespread feeling of indignation," Momchilov said, "but they don't dare to voice their opinion."

"For me that's enough," Peshev replied.[19]

Peshev didn't tell the delegation that he had already heard from Yako Baruch about the projected deportation. He listened quietly, but his calm exterior concealed a deep inner turmoil. He was haunted by what had taken place in his office only the day before.

The previous night he had been quite surprised when Dimiter Ikonomov, a member of Parliament from the small town of Dupnitza, entered his office without an appointment. Peshev and Ikonomov were not friends. In spite of the respect and the esteem they held for each other, Peshev and Ikonomov were not on speaking terms because of their bitter disagreements on many basic issues.[20] Peshev knew that only a matter of grave importance could compel Ikonomov to overcome his animosity and enter his office in this manner.

"I have just come back from Dupnitza," Ikonomov said.[21] He went on to describe to Peshev what he had witnessed in his hometown.

Many freight trains had come from "the Belomorie."* They unloaded a large crowd of Jews, who were then herded to a transit camp outside Dupnitza. Ikonomov described "the poignant picture of Jews from the Aegean territories passing through the town on foot. All of them—old people, women, children, men, laden with baggage, dejected, desperate, crying for help—painfully dragged themselves in an unknown direction." Ikonomov was deeply disturbed by "the sight of these helpless people, being taken to a place one could only guess, and to a fate about which everybody had dark forebodings."[22]

Ikonomov described to Peshev the effect of that heart-breaking scene of the inhabitants of Dupnitza. They were shocked and revolted and could not sit by and watch the tragic fate of so many people. The scene struck an emotional chord among the people of Dupnitza, and many of them burst into tears as they watched the procession.[23]

Since that meeting, Ikonomov's words haunted Peshev.[24] The report on the projected deportation of the Thracian Jews added credibility to the report by Baruch and the Kyustendil delegation. On the morning of March 9, Peshev's mind was made up. He didn't need to be persuaded to help the Kyustendil delegation.

There was no doubt in my mind about what was going to happen (in Kyustendil and elsewhere). The tragic scene described by Dimiter Ikonomov emerged before my eyes. My human conscience and my understanding of the fateful consequences both for the people involved and for the policy of our country now and in the future did not allow me to remain idle. And I decided to do all in my power to prevent what was being planned from happening; [I knew that this action] was going to shame Bulgaria in the eyes of the world and brand her with a stain she didn't deserve. I couldn't assume any responsibility—moral, political, or

---

* In Bulgarian *Belo Moro* means "White Sea," the name the Bulgarians use for the Aegean Sea. *Belomorie* refers to the White Sea coast areas.

other—for such actions by the government, taken without even consulting the Parliament and securing its support.[25]

At the end of the meeting, it was agreed that Peshev would go to his office in the Parliament and seek an urgent audience with Prime Minister Bogdan Filov. The delegation was invited to come to Peshev's office at 3:00 P.M.[26]

Peshev left his friends and soon afterward reached Parliament, where the rumor of the forthcoming deportation of many Bulgarian Jews had already spread. Parliament was reconvening, after a recess of several days, and many members were arriving from their cities and towns in the provinces, bearing the disturbing news. Ikonomov had told his friends of the events in Dupnitza; Georgi Petrov Kenderov, who still was in his town, Pazardjik, had been informed that the Jews would be rounded up;[27] grim news had arrived from Plovdiv and Lovech; Jewish leaders from Sofia had approached some parliamentarians as well. Several members of Parliament came to see Peshev to ask him what to do.[28]

Peshev decided to speak with Peter Gabrovski, the minister of the interior.

If we were to succumb to temptation and try to pinpoint the exact moment when Peshev entered history, it would be that late morning of March 9, when he walked out of his spacious office and down the arched hallway toward the office of Interior Minister Gabrovski.

Gabrovski was in his office and agreed to see him right away. Peshev told Gabrovski the news from Kyustendil,* but the Interior minister vehemently denied that any deportation of the Kyustendil Jews was planned. "There is no such a thing," he said firmly.[29]

---

* In his testimony before the People's Court, Peshev claims that when he met Gabrovski he was accompanied by several members of Parliament. (Peshev, statement, vol. 69, 10a, handwritten, n.d.). We know that these MPs—Dimiter Ikonomov, Ivan Petrov, B. Kovatchevski, and others—participated at the second meeting of Peshev with Gabrovski, in the afternoon. Peshev might be mixing up these two meetings.

Peshev returned to his office and telephoned the Kyustendil regional governor, who confirmed to him his secret orders to round up the Jewish inhabitants the same night and incarcerate them in the tobacco warehouses. He also confirmed that an envoy of the Commissariat for Jewish Questions had arrived to supervise the operations; special trains were waiting at the station to take the Jews away.[30]

Shortly before noon, Peshev telephoned Mikhalev. He told his Kyustendil colleague about his meeting with Gabrovski and about Gabrovski's denial that a deportation was planned. Mikhalev was surprised. He couldn't believe that the minister didn't know what was happening in Kyustendil.[31]

Mikhalev was not at the Parliament building at that time. He had agreed to participate at an urgent meeting of Sofia's Jewish leaders,[32] who had gathered at the Ohrid café. The participants included Colonel (retired) Avraham Tadjer, the highest ranking and most decorated Jew in the Bulgarian army, the lawyer Jacob Baruch, Benyamin Arditi, and others. Several Bulgarian members of Parliament, and the Macedonian leader Vladimir Kurtev, a member of the Kyustendil delegation, also participated in the meeting.[33]

They discussed at length various courses of action they might take. Kurtev announced that, in the name of the Macedonian organization, he planned to threaten Interior Minister Gabrovski with retaliation, if the Jews were deported outside the boundaries of Bulgaria.[34] Coming from a leader of the Macedonian organization, such a threat had quite an impact; one that could result in bloodshed. As the meeting ended, Mikhalev promised Jacob Baruch that he would let him know the result of the delegation's meeting with Prime Minister Filov.[35]

At 3:00 P.M. the delegation met outside the Parliament building. As they were about to enter, Vladimir Kurtev informed his friends they would have to do without him. He had made an appointment with a renowned Bulgarian politician, Professor Alexander Stanishev, whom he wanted to win over to their cause. And, indeed, he met with him and eloquently pleaded the case of the Bulgarian Jews.

The remaining Kyustendil delegates entered the Parliament building through the back entrance. Peshev had left orders to let them in. He met them in a hallway and immediately started introducing Suichmezov and Momchilov to his colleagues. "We started lively discussions with the [Members of Parliament] about the Jewish tragedy," Suichmezov wrote. He soon discovered, however, that it would not be an easy task. "Some of the Parliament Members didn't even want to listen to any arguments in favor of the Jews. They called them renegades, traitors. They accused us of defending those who suck our sweat."[36]

Others reacted differently. Very quickly a group of about ten members of Parliament gathered in Peshev's office.

Peshev went to see Filov, to arrange a meeting, but the prime minister refused to receive the delegation. Momchilov, a member of the Kyustendil delegation, disappointedly left the building.[37] Peshev and his friends decided, therefore, to meet again with Interior Minister Gabrovski, hoping "the minister would be impressed by the mood of the Parliament members, as well as by the degree of their discontent and their objection to the [deportation] measures."[38]

Gabrovski received them immediately. Suichmezov participated in the first part of that meeting.[39] As soon as they entered Gabrovski's office, the minister turned to Mikhalev: "Mikhalev, why are you so worried there in Kyustendil?"[40]

Mikhalev described the scenes he had witnessed in his hometown, the preparations for the arrest of the Jews, and the activities of the agents sent from Sofia, as well as the protest of the population against the planned deportation.

"I don't know anything about that," Gabrovski said.[41]

Peshev, speaking in the name of the entire group, succinctly summed up the information they had gathered. He spoke of their fears and firmly warned Gabrovski that they could not approve of the measures taken or accept any responsibility for them. Then he demanded that the deportation plans be canceled.

Gabrovski again stated that no new measures against the Jews were planned. He agreed, however, to ask for additional information and to see what he could do. Peshev wrote later:

I had the impression that the minister was confused and nervous, and although the full information in my possession contradicted his assertion that nothing new and unusual against the Jews was about to happen, I couldn't believe he was scheming to mislead us. I thought [his denial] was more of a formula, to get out of an embarrassing situation, and in any case he was going to abandon the [deportation] plan. For the moment that gave me satisfaction—after all the immediate goal of our initiative was to prevent these people to be sent out of Bulgaria.[42]

Gabrovski continued to insist he didn't know anything, until the members of the delegation mentioned the Belev-Dannecker agreement. Then Gabrovski seemed to be at a loss. He apparently realized the futility of making such a claim, when his guests knew of the top-secret agreement with the Germans.[43]

Mikhalev said: "Mr. Minister, the telephone is on your desk. Why don't you phone the district Governor of Kyustendil right away?"[44] Reluctantly Gabrovski made the call, and the information he heard over the telephone confirmed everything Mikhalev and Peshev had said.

Mikhalev was more critical of Gabrovski. "He understood that the secret about the deportation, which had been kept until yesterday, was now exposed, therefore he feigned surprise. He again repeated that he didn't know about the Kyustendil events, and he hadn't given orders for the deportation of the Jews."[45]

The Parliament members, even though unconvinced of Gabrovski's sincerity, seized the opportunity and insisted that he cancel the deportation orders immediately. If measures had been taken without his knowledge, they pointed out, he should cancel them right away. They made clear to Gabrovski that they were not going to leave his office before their demands were satisfied. It was late afternoon already, and the plenary session of Parliament was about to start. As the sun was setting, they couldn't help thinking of all the cities throughout the country where the police were waiting for darkness to fall in order to round up the Jews marked for deportation.

Finally Gabrovski gave in. He went to the other room, picked up the telephone, and made a few calls.[46] He called the governor of the Kyustendil region, Gerdjikov. He instructed him to stop preparations for deporting the local Jews, immediately, and to send back to Sofia the agents of the Commissariat for Jewish Questions dispatched to Kyustendil for that purpose. This order was to be immediately conveyed to the local authorities.

Gabrovski then said to Mikhalev: "Now you can calm down the people of Kyustendil."[47]

Picking up Gabrovski's telephone Peshev personally called Kyustendil's district governor, Miltenov, and informed him that the deportation was canceled.[48] Ikonomov called Dupnitza. Gabrovski ordered his secretary to send telegrams to all the other Bulgarian cities and instruct the local authorities to cancel the operation.

It was about 5:30 P.M. when the delegation left Gabrovski's office. Suichmezov was waiting in one of the hallways. Peshev hurried toward him. "Suichmezov, let's shake hands, the deportation is canceled, pass the news to Kyustendil!"[49]

Mikhalev himself hurried to call his brother so that the news would reach the Kyustendil Jews as soon as possible; he afterward met with Jacob Baruch and Colonel Tadjer and announced the good news.

As he left the Parliament building, Suichmezov was met by a large group of Jews, who welcomed him with boundless joy. A young Jew, Buko Leonov, burst into tears, repeating: "God bless you, Mr. Assen!"[50]

Suichmezov entered a liquor store to call the fire brigade in Kyustendil and ask them to spread the news. Telephones were rare in Kyustendil, and the fire brigade chief was a good friend. He would gladly broadcast the good news. While he was on the phone, Suichmezov noticed that two men had followed him into the store. The older one asked for Assen Suichmezov.

"It's me," Suichmezov said.

The man grabbed his hand. "I came to shake your hand. I am colonel Tadjer. Bravo for your courage!"[51]

Suichmezov needed his courage. When he later got in touch with his family, he learned that local Fascists had attacked his leather coat workshop and his home, as well as the homes of Peshev, Momchilov, and Mikhalev, and broken all the windows. The Fascists threw a large stone through Suichmezov's window; it lay on his bed amidst broken glass.[52] They painted *Bulgarian kike* and *traitor* on his walls.[53]

On the walls of Momchilov's home, local Fascists had painted the similar words. The front windows were shattered by stones. The rooms were filled with broken glass.

"I don't know how the Jews learned about the stone-throwing," his son said. "After all, it had happened after the curfew. But the curfew for the Jews ended at 6:00 A.M., and at 6:05 two Jews were at our house and replaced the broken windows."[54]

• • •

The cancellation orders didn't reach all of Bulgaria's cities on time. In several cases, the local authorities were instructed by telephone that the orders to round up the Jews had been repealed. But in several cities, the new orders were dispatched by telegram and reached their destination in the late morning of the following day.

On March 10, at 3:00 A.M., the police rounded up several hundred of the most eminent Jews in Plovdiv, the second largest city in Bulgaria. (The exact number of the people arrested that night is not known. According to one KEV list, there were 616; another mentions 497; while Metropolitan Kyril speaks of 1,500–1,600.)[55] They were the community leaders, the most influential, outspoken, and affluent Jews. The KEV report qualified them as "fanatic Jews . . . inspirers of the community and incorrigible anglophiles . . . ideological supporters of communism . . . disturbers of the public peace."[56]

Tragic scenes, similar to those that had taken place a few days before throughout Thrace, took place again, this time on Bulgarian soil. Again, the streets were sealed by armed police and military forces. Again, uniformed officers pounded on the doors in the dark of night and ordered the terrified Jews to pack a bag and be ready to go. Again, the desperate Jews, crying and appealing for help, were herded through the dark streets to schools and other public buildings. Yet, there was a difference. They were not beaten or roughed up by the police, and no degrading searches took place. Most of the Jews were assembled in a large school.

In the early morning, the news reached the head of the local church, Metropolitan Kyril. Strong-willed, ambitious, passionate, and courageous, Kyril fearlessly and repeatedly had criticized the government's policy toward the Jews. Back in 1938, he had written a brochure called "Faith and Resolution," condemning anti-Semitism.[57] A born leader and an independent man, he was among the leaders of the Bulgarian church's opposition to the anti-Jewish policy; but in addition to signing the Saint Synod statements, he also issued his own letters of condemnation against that policy.

He now acted immediately. He sent a telegram to King Boris, asking him to show mercy toward the Jews.[58] He then went out into the streets. At the railway station a special train was to pick up the Jews. According to certain sources, Kyril threatened that if a train loaded with Jews tried to leave the city, he would lie across the railroad tracks.[59] Another report tells of his coming to the school where the Jewish leaders were kept and asking to come in, to talk to them.

Kyril was stopped by the police officers on guard.

"You cannot enter, Father," an officer said, barring his way.

"I cannot enter?" the Metropolitan echoed. "Try to stop me!" Defying the guards, he climbed the fence, jumped into the schoolyard, and addressed the Jews who flocked around him. "Wherever you go—I'll go," he said.[60]

The Jews who had converted to Christianity went to his office to ask for his protection. He calmed them and said that if they felt they were in danger, they could take refuge in his private home. "Let them try to take you from my home," he said, thinking of the example of the ancient Christians who not only protected their own but also collected funds to buy Christians of other nationalities out of slavery.[61]

The fiery cleric asked to speak to the Plovdiv chief of police but was told that he was out of reach. He then tried to contact the district police chief but was told that he, too, was unavailable. Kyril then summoned the police chief's assistant and asked him to immediately send a message to the government. He stated that he had always been loyal to the government's policy, but that would no longer be the case. He was assuming freedom of his actions and would conduct himself according to his conscience as a prelate of the Church.[62]

This rebellion by one of the heads of the Church caused great concern in Sofia. This was the first time in Bulgarian history that a prince of the Church had announced his refusal to obey the laws of the country.

In Sliven, at the same time, the local prelate, Evlogi, was awakened by a Jewish citizen. The man was in tears. He told the cleric that all the Jewish men between the ages of seventeen and seventy were about to be arrested and sent to an unknown destination. They were all frightened and expected that after them the women and the children would be rounded up as well. Shortly afterward, a delegation of five Christian women came to see the cleric and ask that the Church intervene in favor of the Jewish women and children. Evlogi immediately sent his assistant to the chief of police.

It was 7:00 A.M., in Pazardjik, when three very frightened Jews knocked on the door of Parliament member Georgi Kenderov. The police had ordered the Jewish community to be ready for evacuation at 10:00 A.M. that morning, they said. Many of the Jews had already been assembled in the courtyard of the Jewish school. Kenderov hurried to the office of the district governor and informed him that he was leaving right away for Sofia. "As long as I am away," he said, "you are not to evacuate the Pazardjik Jews."[63]

Similar events took place in many other cities, like Samokov, Haskovo, and Shumen. The terrified Jews, huddled around their bags in school yards and tobacco warehouses, felt that their death warrant had been issued. In a few hours, perhaps less, they would be taken to the train station, and then—to be murdered.

But around noon word came from Sofia. The Jews in Plovdiv, Pazardjik, Sliven, and all the other towns were released immediately and sent to their homes. Crying, hugging their families, thanking the local leaders that had taken their side, the Jews were to remember this March 10, 1943, as the day of their utter despair—but also as the day of their salvation.

• • •

It was clear to everyone concerned that on the evening of March 9, Gabrovski had not decided on his own or on the spur of the moment to cancel the deportation that had been approved and meticulously prepared by the cabinet. In fact, a report sent by the German embassy in Sofia to the Main Imperial Security Office in Berlin stressed the reason for the cancellation. The report stated that "the Interior Minister had received instructions from the highest place "to stop the planned deportation of Jews from within the old boundaries of Bulgaria.[64]

The "highest place" meant, of course, King Boris III.

The senior officials of the KEV also learned, on March 10, that the king himself had intervened.[65] The officials reacted with rage and frustration. The king had acted at the eleventh hour, and the deportation had been thwarted.

But when did the king intervene? There is no evidence that Gabrovski or Filov had consulted the king in the late afternoon or on the evening of March 9. For years, scholars have debated when and how his instruction, mentioned in the German report, had been given.

To find the answer, we should first clarify several facts. The reports claiming that Gabrovski left the Parliament building late at night, apparently to visit the king, are mistaken. We know for sure that the deportation was canceled in the late afternoon or early evening.

Therefore, the royal instruction must have come before the early evening.

Other reports say that the meeting between Peshev's delegation and Gabrovski was interrupted so that Gabrovski could confer with Filov, and probably with the king. This assumption is erroneous as well. None of the testimonies of the participants in the meeting mention any such interruption.

Therefore, Gabrovski must have received the cancellation orders before the meeting.

The evidence points to a very simple answer: The royal intervention could have taken place much earlier in the day. We believe that Gabrovski alerted Filov and the king in the late morning of March 9, after his first conversation with Peshev.

Gabrovski had his own doubts about the deportation. He had reluctantly agreed to Belev's proposal to deport several thousand Jews from the country, but he had insisted on absolute secrecy. His lack of enthusiasm for the project was not the result of moral or humane considerations; openly anti-Semitic, Gabrovski was the tutor and patron of Belev. His reluctance stemmed from apprehensions about the scope of the popular reaction to the deportation, not from any love or sympathy for the Jews. That was why he had insisted on absolute secrecy. He must have been stunned when on the morning of March 9 he found out that Peshev knew of the deportation, that other members of Parliament were trying to prevent it, and that a delegation from Kyustendil had arrived in Sofia!

The secret was a vital component of the deportation plan. Gabrovski probably couldn't wait for the conversation with Peshev to end so that he could report it in detail to the prime minister. This was an urgent and crucial piece of information: The most closely guarded secret had leaked. The public was bound to react, and an open confrontation with major political and public figures, including some of the most respected leaders of the parliamentary majority, could be disastrous.

Filov probably heard from Gabrovski quite early in the day that the secret of the deportation had been exposed, and he therefore had to report this to the king. There was no way he could decide what to do next, without the king's backing. The fact that the secret was out had upset Filov to the point that, in the early afternoon, he refused to receive a high-ranking delegation of Parliament members, led by Peshev, who wanted to talk to him about the deportation.

But when the delegation walked into Gabrovski's office, shortly after 3:00 P.M., the decision had already been made: The deportation would be canceled. Apparently, in the late morning or around noon, Filov and Gabrovski had contacted Boris III. (The royal palace is located barely a few hundred yards from the Parliament building. They might have gone to meet the king or spoken to him over the telephone.) There is no doubt that in the afternoon, when the delegation came to see him, Gabrovski knew he had the full backing of the king and the prime minister; after falsely pretending he didn't know that the deportation was imminent, he picked up the phone and gave the cancellation orders. This sequence of events is corroborated by Peshev's deposition before the People's Tribunal, in which he speaks of "two meetings" with Gabrovski.[66]

Thus, Boris III changed his position and reversed the policy of Bulgaria.

# CHAPTER TEN

# TRAINS

On the evening of March 9, Gabrovski called Belev and informed him that the deportation from the old boundaries of Bulgaria had been canceled. Lily Panitza was at the office and witnessed Belev's explosion of anger and frustration.[1] The following morning Belev submitted his resignation.

He secluded himself in his office, refusing to see anybody but his close friends. "He yelled like a madman at the slightest pretext," wrote Maria Pavlova, "and none of us dared to cross his steps on the staircase, or enter his room."[2]

The KEV senior staff seethed with fury and indignation. "Gioshev, Velkov, Lukov, and Kalitzin fiercely protested against the violation of the agreement," wrote Maria Pavlova.[3] "Dannecker came to Belev's office."

Dannecker bluntly told Belev: "You didn't fulfill our agreement."

Belev mentioned the twelve thousand Jews from Thrace and Macedonia whose deportation hadn't been canceled, to which Dannecker retorted that the Germans could have taken these twelve thousand without the Bulgarians' cooperation, as "they belong to them anyway."[4] Dannecker flew to Germany for a few days, to report the failed plan and ask for further instructions.[5]

On March 9 Kalitzin returned from his mission in Thrace and the following morning went to see Belev. He was in a good mood, after having accomplished his task. "What are you smiling about?" Lily Panitza snapped at him. "What is so funny?" She angrily told him that the Bulgarian operation had been canceled by the "Kyustendil Jews," that "Gabrovski had been bought," and that Belev had submitted his resignation. But Gabrovski had refused to accept the Commissar's resignation. She added that everything already had been prepared for the deportation. Even the lists of the Sofia Jews to be deported in this first operation had been delivered for execution to the chief of police, Chavdarov.[6]

Maria Pavlova spoke to Lily Panitza, whom she disliked, and wondered "if she was expressing her own opinion, or repeating Belev's words like a parrot." She quoted Lily Panitza as saying that "by the violation of the agreement the government had discredited itself vis a vis Germany. Belev had been compromised most of all, as he was in charge of the fulfillment of that agreement and had personally vouched to Dannecker to implement it at all costs; now he couldn't cope with that shame."[7]

Panitza added that all of Belev's friends, who belonged to the Ratnik organization, begged him to cancel his resignation, saying that without him the KEV would be lost and unable to carry out its assignments. They also said, according to Lily Panitza, "that [the deportation] that couldn't be carried out right now, might be accomplished later and only Belev could carry it through."[8]

Pavlova didn't suspect, of course, that the same Lily Panitza who now "repeated Belev's words like a parrot" and urged him not to resign had secretly played a major role in canceling the deportation.

●　●　●

Belev angrily claimed that if the order to cancel the deportation had been given only four hours later, the operation would have been carried out successfully. Everybody at the KEV knew that the order to cancel the deportation from old Bulgaria had come from the king. According to Pavlova, Belev had been summoned to the palace "one Thursday," and there he was informed of the decision.[9] However, this is not accurate. It was Gabrovski and his assistants who informed Belev of the cancellation; the minister of the Interior had apparently mentioned the order from the royal palace. Still, the top officials at the KEV agreed that the deportation had failed because the secret had leaked, enabling powerful forces to organize and thwart the project.

Belev told Kalitzin that the Kyustendil Jews had raised tremendous sums of money—Panitza mentioned 100 million leva—and had bribed members of Parliament and ministers.[10] This was an outright lie. The Kyustendil Jews had raised barely 900,000 leva, (less than $11,000), and none of this money had ever been paid to Parliament members or ministers.

Dr. Ivan Popov, general inspector of the KEV, blamed Borislav Tasev for exposing the details of the deportation. Tasev was the KEV employee who had been sent to prepare the deportation of Kyustendil's Jews.

Tasev tried to defend himself against Popov's accusations in a "confidential" report addressed to Popov. He claimed that on March 6, he was in the Kyustendil town hall, to pick up lists of enlisted Jewish doctors, pharmacists, and others.[11] In the presence of the deputy mayor, Mr. Prokopiev, and another official, the secretary of the municipality asked Tasev point blank: "When are we going to round up the Jews and how many kilos of personal baggage can they take?"

Tasev said that he didn't know about such a thing and that such rumors shouldn't be spread. Prokopiev then turned to him and said: "Mr. Tasev, this is not a secret anymore. We received official notice [about this], and the date of the deportation has been fixed." He added that a Jewish pharmacist who worked in town had told him that he heard the news from the district governor.

Two days later, in the office of the district governor, Tasev met Parliament member Mikhalev, who asked him if all the Jews were going to be deported. In the late afternoon Tasev learned that a delegation was leaving for Sofia, to try to cancel the deportation. He sent an agent to the train station to learn the names of the delegation members.

At a public meeting that evening the mayor was asked what would happen to the Jews. He answered that on Wednesday, March 10, they would be assembled in a camp. Now that the secret had become public, the Jews hastened to the market to buy luggage and sell furniture to Bulgarian acquaintances. People even came from other cities to get good bargains on Jewish property. At the train station Tasev's people seized thirty-two suitcases filled with clothes and goods that Bulgarians from Sofia had bought from Kyustendil Jews.

Tasev was the last to be informed of the cancellation. On March 10, he went to the synagogue, to get more equipment for the Radomir camp. He was stunned when the community president, Comforty, told him "that their question had been solved, they would not be rounded up, and the curfew had been canceled." Tasev met a few other Jews who were leaving for Sofia with permits from the mayor. He finally called the KEV and was ordered to return to Sofia.

Tasev claimed that the deportation had been thwarted because the secret had leaked. He concluded his report by listing the causes of the leaks.

> The reasons for the cancellation of the operation are the following:
> 1. The order of the regional governor in Dupnitza [to place the Jews in house arrest].
> 2. The fact that Kyustendil is close to Skopje and Thrace.
> 3. The collection of equipment for the Radomir camp [which he himself had initiated].
> 4. The forewarning of the mayor and the regional governor of the forthcoming action.[12]

•  •  •

Eventually, Belev withdrew his resignation. His German friends pressured him to stay. After all, he was the RSHA's most reliable agent in the Bulgarian government. The same Dannecker who angrily confronted him after the cancellation of the March 10 operation knew well that without Belev the deportation from the old boundaries would never take place. On his return from Germany, he joined the efforts to convince Belev to cancel his resignation.

The second reason for Belev's change of mind was the deportation that was underway in Thrace and Macedonia. Belev knew well that he couldn't leave his position while the Jews of Thrace were about to be shipped to Vienna and while the Jews of Macedonia were being rounded up. His ferocious hatred of the Jews was stronger than his resentment against his superiors. Therefore he decided to pursue his diabolical scheme to the very end.

In the night of March 11, one day after the failed deportation from old Bulgaria, the next stage of the deportation began. At 2:00 A.M., during a blizzard, the army surrounded the city of Skopje, in Macedonia, and sealed the Jewish quarter. By the same methods already tested in Thrace, the 3,493 Jews of Skopje were arrested, taken to the Monopole tobacco warehouse, searched, undressed, and beaten. "With our own eyes," wrote Berta and Miko Noach,[13] two of the deportees, "we saw how they removed people's shoes, if they were to their liking."

Security was tightened: The transit camp was surrounded by machine gun positions, and armed police officers patrolled around the fences. Even the patrols along the Albanian border were reinforced, to prevent Jews from escaping into Italian-held territory.

Along with the Skopje Jews, 3,342 more Jews were brought by train from Bitola. Albert Sarfati, who later succeeded to escape, painted a horror picture of the Skopje camp.[14] "The worst was the deputy commander of the police, a sadist, who mercilessly beat young and old, women and children. . . . If somebody raised his voice or didn't display his Jewish star he'd draw him to the cellar where he'd beat him until he fainted. He beat the women with a three feet long rubber baton. We called him the bloody Tartar." The camp commander himself told the Jews that they were being taken to the old boundaries of Bulgaria, nobody believed him.

The last to reach the Skopje camp were 546 Jews from the picturesque city of Shtip, nestled in the steep Macedonian Mountains on both sides of a deep ravine. Liubomir Panev, the former director of the Bulgarian National Bank in Shtip, witnessed their deportation. He was badly shaken by the sight of "men, women, old people, and children, sick people and babies in arms being loaded like cattle in boxcars on this cold day, torn from their homes and their land, sent somewhere, perhaps never to return."[15]

In Skopie, police officers and agents brutally searched the Shtip rabbi, and after tormenting him, they ripped his black coat from the shoulders to the waist and told him he had sewn his money into the seam. The rabbi stepped aside, to his family, and burst in tears, while the police officers laughed.[16] "They took the young girls to the offices," Sarfati wrote. "I don't know what they did to them. They came back crying and shivering. I asked the girls what they did to them. They didn't dare to talk. A young girl named Janna told me they had raped her."

In a separate operation, that same night, the KEV raiders seized 158 Jews from Pirot. Rich Jews were forced to dig up their courtyards, where gold treasures were supposed to have been buried; others were taken, at night, to non-Jewish merchants, to raise ransom money. A Jew who tried to escape was caught and brought back to the local school that served as a detention camp. The KEV delegate, Christo Bakerdjiev, and a group of policemen brandished their revolvers and threatened to shoot anyone who attempted to escape.[17]

Joseph Levi, a Sofia Jew, was submitted to harsh beatings and searches, in which all of his family's valuables were robbed. Being of Bulgarian citizenship, he was finally released, only to find his house in shambles. "I went to the regional governor's office, to sign, under police threats, a statement [prepared by the KEV and saying that no property of mine was missing]. Outside, I saw the plush tablecloth of my dining table spread in the open car of Dr. Popov, the KEV official, and my brown hat on the head of his secretary, Nikolov."[18]

But their earthly goods were the least concern of the incarcerated Jews. The 11,343 Jews of Thrace and Macedonia were held in

schools and tobacco warehouses throughout Bulgaria, where they
waited to be sent to their deaths.

•  •  •

That same day, the Swiss chargé d'affaires in Sofia, Charles-Arthur
Redard, requested an audience with Prime Minister Filov. He
already knew that about twelve thousand Thracian and Macedonian
Jews had been brutally arrested and incarcerated in camps throughout Bulgaria.[19] He asked the prime minister to allow the children of
the deportees to be assembled in Sofia and sent to Palestine, as the
British government was ready to accept a number of Bulgarian Jews
there. He appealed to his humanity, to prevent sending those Jews
to Poland.

Redard asked to start with one hundred children that the
Ministry of Interior had agreed to let go and offered to send a
telegram requesting that they be accepted in Palestine.[20] Redard
didn't know that the interior ministry never intended to allow the
departure of even one child to Palestine and that the "agreement"
was only a smoke screen, intended to delay the British and Swiss
efforts.

Filov answered that it was too late, that the Jews were leaving
for Poland in a few days.[21]

"That means, they are going to their death," Redard said.

This was farfetched, Filov replied. The Jews would be used as
workers.

"The Jews are being treated inhumanly," Redard countered.

"How can you speak of humanity these days," Filov sharply
said, "when the peaceful population of the large cities is being mercilessly massacred?"[22]

Redard was shocked by Filov's fury. He had never before seen
the prime minister so angry, "although Mr. Filov is a very polite and
smiling person."[23]

According to Redard, Filov said:

> The measures that the Bulgarian government was
> forced to take and which it has no intention to cancel now,
> have been dictated by the circumstances.[24] We are forced
> to wage a total war. We'll either win or die. Germany and
> Bulgaria itself need workers. We'll take them where we
> find them. By their behavior, the Jews are harmful to the
> interests of the state. They might turn into a great danger,
> if Bulgaria became a theater of military operations. . . . We
> have to take our precautions. That is why, to my regret, I
> cannot satisfy your request: the Jews, evacuated from
> Thrace and Macedonia, will be sent to Poland, where they
> will work either in factories, or in the Todt organization.*
>
> As of now, the government hasn't made a decision yet
> about the Jews living in old Bulgaria, but I cannot assure
> you that such a decision would never be taken. We shall
> designate the Jews who will be allowed to depart for
> Palestine, those who will stay here, and those who will be
> sent to the General Government. The Jews who will stay in
> Bulgaria will be mobilized and will work in organizations,
> similar to the German Todt organization. You know how we
> tried, until now, to leave everybody free . . . I am the first
> to regret certain decisions we have to make, but I declare
> that our treatment of the Bulgarian Jews is more humane
> than that of bombing civilians, who live peacefully in non-
> military areas.

Filov added that other nations, like Croatia, Slovakia, and
Romania, had adopted the same measures toward the Jews and that

---

* The Todt organization, named after her founder, built roads and fortifications for
the Reich during World War II, using local and slave labor. It was well known that
young people from the Nazi sphere of influence, as well as prisoners, were used as
manpower for the large construction projects of the Todt organization. Therefore,
Filov's argument that the deported Jews might be used as a workforce for Todt
could seem logical.

only Italy and Hungary had decided to find a different solution to the Jewish problem.

"As far as I know," Redard intervened, "Romania has also can celled her decision to send Jews to Poland."

Filov said he had been informed, at the end of the previous year, that there were almost no more Jews in Romania. In answer to another question of Redard's, he assured him that no other foreigners living in Macedonia, except the Jews, would be deported.

Redard stated that at the end of the meeting "the benevolent smile" appeared again on Filov's face.[25]

Four days later, Filov met for two hours with King Boris and noted in his diary: "We spoke mainly on the Jewish question, on which the King insists on a firm attitude."[26] But this is a rather strange entry. Only six days before, the king had decided not to deport the Jews from the old boundaries. It is difficult to understand what Filov meant by "firm attitude," except that perhaps he wanted to leave the impression, in his diary, that Boris III agreed fully with his policy.

•   •   •

On March 18 and 19, two special trains took all the Jews from the camps at Dupnitza, Gorna Djumaya, and Pirot and drove them to Lom, a small river port on the Danube. At one railroad barrier an appalled man stepped out of his car and watched with horror as the boxcars carrying the deportees passed by. He was Metropolitan Stefan, the head of the Sofia church, who happened to be on his way to the Rila monastery.

What he witnessed "exceeded the notions of horror and the term of inhumanity," he wrote.[27]

> In cattle cars, old and young, healthy and cripple, mothers with newborn babies and expecting women, packed like sardines, standing and exhausted, are letting

a desperate cry for mercy, for help, for water, for air, for the smallest dose of humanity. The train is guarded by Nazis, the boxcars sealed, the routing is toward the Danube and Poland. Deeply distressed by what I heard, as I reached the holy cloister I sent a telegram to the Head of State, asking him to take action so that the Jews expelled from Thrace could travel across Bulgaria as human beings, and not like animals; and to relieve their unbearable conditions, with the wish that they not be sent to Poland, that has a sinister ring even in the ears of the babies.

The royal palace answered that everything possible and legal would be done.[28] In another exchange of messages, King Boris insisted that he had done all that he could, "in spite of the fact that [the deportees] were exiles from Hitler's military command."[29]

The Jews of Bulgaria could never forget the horrendous image of the trains carrying their people, driving their brothers and sisters like cattle to the slaughter. From a hill overlooking the railway, a young Jew, member of a labor gang, watched the trains making their way to a terrible fate. His name was Simcho Isakov. He was the most admired Jewish poet and was to become one of Bulgaria's greatest writers. In a powerful emotional outburst, that day, he wrote his famous poem "Trains."

> *The faces are yellow and scarring,*
> *Tortured birds are the eyes.*
> *Where's the laughter to light up their mouths*
> *What are your eyes seeing—children!*
>
> *The dresses are worn and threadbare*
> *Frostbitten they are and their shoulders are bare*
> *Wet are the cheeks, the eyelashes,*
> *What are your eyes seeing—women!*

*Like strings are the sinews tautened*
*Ready to burst and break open*
*No will have they left, and no power*
*What are your eyes seeing—men!*

*. . . And a car to a car is chained*
*and together they heavily move,*
*your eyes to the horizon are glued*
*What are your eyes seeing—pogrom!*

\* \* \*

*. . . In their eyes you saw it still reflected,*
*the Macedonia land—its forests and its mounts.*
*You heard the sound of rifles pounding on the gates,*
*startled out of slumber in the heart of night . . .*

*. . . The doors were broken. Fear and horror!*
*Like cattle the policemen herded them in the street.*
*"No questions asked! Walk to the Town Square!*
*One coat only! And you can take no more!"*

*They went. Women implored the heavens' mercy . . .*
*Where, where?—the children cried.*
*And like open eyes, seized by utter madness*
*the windows of their homes at the people stared.*

*. . . The city is asleep. The city is so silent.*
*Even the train, with its strident roar of pain*
*Could not wake it from its pleasant dream*
*And it is still asleep, until the end.*

*. . . The station her long trains dispatched*
*and in their bosom rain and winds were cast*
*And what these poor Jews thought at that departing*
    *moment?*
*When will the journey end—and where—the devil*
    *knows . . .*

\* \* \*

*And if you forgot*
*May your eyes rot*
*That saw that sight*
*When trains dark of sorrow*
*Dragged Jews to their death!*

*And if you forgot*
*May your right hand dry*
*That gave a chunk of bread*
*To little hands toward you stretched*
*And like arrows tearing your despairing flesh!*

*And if you forgot*
*May your heart stop,*
*That from love or from fury*
*On a moving train you wanted to throw*
*That was a moving hell on the land of men.*

*And if you forgot*
*May your tongue cleave*
*That screamed with fright and rage*
*"My brothers I did love, as much as hated I*
*the fascist scum, and their defiled hearts."*[30]

•  •  •

At Lom railway station, where the trains arrived on March 19 and 20, the suffocating Jews screamed for water. The long trip in the crowded cars, and the dried, salted meat they were given on departure, drove them crazy with thirst.

A local nurse, Nadejda Vasileva, filled a bucket of water and rushed to the trains. The police officers who were on guard ordered her to go back, but she kept trying, disregarding their threats. Some of them said they would shoot her, but she ignored them. She finally was able to approach the boxcars and began distributing water to the deportees.

Suddenly Slavi Puntev, the KEV representative in Lom, arrived with a squad of German and Bulgarian guards. He was also the local chief of the Red Cross and a cousin of Belev. He was furious.

"Go back!" he yelled at Nadejda. "I'll have you arrested!"[31]

She was not impressed.

Puntev turned to the police officers: "Disperse the crowds! Arrest all Jews! Arrest this woman too!" He turned to the nurse: "Don't you know who I am?"

"I know that you are Slavi Puntev," she retorted, "and you are the President of the Merchants Association and of the Red Cross. Don't you know me? I am a nurse and I am doing my duty."

The policemen moved toward her, and she went away, while they dispersed the crowd of Bulgarians, Jews, and Gypsies that had gathered around her. But soon she was back, now carrying items collected by the Jewish community of Lom—apples, yogurt, lemons, cigarettes, candles, and matches. Puntev reluctantly allowed her to distribute the items, after having checked them for concealed messages. A few Gypsies helped her distribute the food and the cigarettes.

They also picked up the heavy pails, full with urine and excrement, that the deportees handed them through holes or small windows in the boxcar walls. A railroad employee hosed down the boxcars and the pails and returned them to the deportees to use for drinking water. The smells from the cars were nauseating. Beside the foul odor from the pails, a sickening stench came from the body of a passenger who had died in the car and was decomposing.

But all the generous work of Nadejda and other good samaritans couldn't alter the grim fate of the deportees. On March 20 and 21, 4,219 Jews sailed to Vienna on board the ships *Kara Georgi, Voivoda Mashil, Saturnus,* and *Tzar Dushan.* Several of them died on the way, in the trains and on the boats. From the port control tower, Belev watched the last ship of deported Jews sail away.

The trip to Vienna lasted between five and ten days. A Bulgarian physician, Dr. Ivan Mendizov, accompanied one of the boats to Vienna. The Germans who waited for the transport expressed their disappointment in "the bad human material" that arrived from Thrace and asked about the Sofia Jews. Mendizov answered tartly and was arrested on the spot. Only after the zealous SS officers had forced him to drop his pants—to show that he was not Jewish—did they agree to let him go.[32]

From Vienna, 4,075 Jews were taken to Katowicz and then to the Treblinka extermination camp, in Poland. Less than a hundred Thracian Jews returned after the war.

The fate of the Macedonian Jews was not better. Belev arrived in Skopje, escorted by several German officers, and inspected the deportees. The following day the first train arrived, a locomotive and forty boxcars. The Jews called it "the train of death."[33] On March 22, March 25, and March 29, the Jews were herded into boxcars in Skopje railway station. The trains then traveled to the east. Of the 7,160 Jews from Macedonia and 158 from Pirot, who undertook the journey to Treblinka, 196 returned after the war.[34]

The liquidation by the KEV of the deportees' property, as well as the money and valuables seized in the searches, yielded 56.5 million leva, the equivalent of $700,000. The cost of the deportation was $257,000. The operation, after all, was profitable.

# CHAPTER ELEVEN

# FORTY-THREE SIGNATURES

Peshev had won a battle, but he hadn't won the war. When he learned about the agreement between Belev and Dannecker, he was revolted:

> This agreement had been concluded by an incompetent official and was contradictory to the constitution, to the regular laws and to the basic morality and humanity. It couldn't have any binding power as it didn't have any legal value; it was not an international agreement but a brutal transgression.[1]
>
> For me a question arose: what should I do? I could not stay silent or idle . . . the silence was contrary to my sense of responsibility as a Member of Parliament and as a human being. [Such silence] would make me passively responsible for what could happen . . . [The deportation] had been stopped, perhaps temporarily; in my mind it was a grave crime, both from a constitutional-political and from a moral, humane point of view.[2]

Meanwhile, the Jews of Bulgaria, stunned by the sight of their doomed brothers from Thrace and Macedonia passing through their cities on their way to Poland, feared that very soon they would follow them. Peshev knew he had very little time. "I had grounds to believe that the deportation measures had been only temporarily suspended, and could be revived, especially under pressure from the Germans, who wouldn't like a final cancellation of something they considered as agreed upon."[3]

Peshev learned that after March 9 several other groups and leaders had intervened at the royal palace on behalf of the Jews. Dimiter Stankov, a prominent citizen of Plovdiv, rushed to Sofia. Stilyan Chilingirov, the president of the Writers Union, and Trifon Kunev, a famous writer, also visited the royal palace.[4]

But this was not enough. Peshev thought of launching "some general action that would prevent any possibility of future surprises, because I knew that the Commissariat for Jewish Questions was furious about my intervention."[5]

What kind of action? Peshev decided that his initiative should involve a group of Parliament members, all of the governing majority. "Inaction of the majority in this matter would make it an accessory . . . to the mass murder of thousands of people."[6]

After consulting several of his colleagues, he decided to write a letter to the prime minister. The goal of this letter would be to forestall any future anti-Jewish measures that could politically and morally expose our country and our people and deny us the moral positions on which we always stood as a small nation."[7]

Peshev knew he had to be very cautious. Prime Minister Filov had held a grudge against him for a long time. When King Boris had appointed Filov prime minister, Peshev had openly vented his criticism of the king's "personal regime."[8] Neither Filov, nor the king, forgot Peshev's sharp attack. Peshev was also a marked man in the eyes of the Commissar for Jewish Questions and of his patron, the interior minister. They couldn't forgive him for having thwarted the deportation plans on March 9. He therefore decided to proceed very carefully in order not to expose himself to irrelevant criticism. He wanted to avoid any accusation that his goal was mounting an attack on the government's general policy or provoking a parliamentary crisis in order to satisfy the ministerial ambitions of certain politicians.[9]

His idea was to convince a large group of members of Parliament to sign the letter opposing the delivery of Bulgarian citizens to a foreign country. They would state their position in the letter but would not accuse the government directly, as it had never officially confirmed its intentions to deport the Jews.

Finally, he decided to have the letter signed only by members of the majority so that nobody could accuse him of acting against the government and promoting an anti-German policy. The letter had to be presented as a purely internal affair of the majority. The signatories should all be loyal supporters of the government's policy. Peshev, therefore, refused to ask the opposition leaders to sign the letter. He made two exceptions to that rule, however, by accepting the signatures of two right-wing opposition members, Alexander Kojukharov and former Prime Minister Alexander Tzankov. These two politicians could not be suspected of supporting an anti-German policy, as they were known as staunch supporters of the alliance with the Third Reich.[10]

Peshev wrote the letter on March 17. He secretly read it to his Jewish friend Jacob Baruch and got his approval.[11] He then began walking the hallways of Parliament, collecting the signatures of his colleagues. Dimiter Ikonomov, the member from Dupnitza, willingly assisted him in this endeavor.[12]

The response was very impressive. In less than two days, forty-two members of the majority signed the letter. Many signed with relief, feeling that by doing so they dissociated themselves from the attempt to deport Bulgaria's Jews. Alexander Simov, from the Breznik district, signed with a flourish and said to Peshev: "Bulgaria's honor is saved!"[13]

Professor Petko Staynov, an eminent leader of the opposition, who was not asked to sign the petition, sent a note to the deputy speaker:

> Dear Peshev:
> If my signature as a member of the opposition and a declared foe of the Law for the Defense of the Nation

wouldn't harm the impact of the letter and if you believe my signature can help, I am ready to give it.[14]

Former Prime Minister Nikola Mushanov, another opposition leader, also volunteered his signature, but Peshev politely declined.

On March 18, Peshev brought an unsigned copy of his letter to the Speaker of the House, Christo Kalfov. He didn't want Kalfov to suspect that something was being done behind his back; therefore he decided to inform him of his initiative. He gave the letter to the Speaker and explained its motives and its goals. Kalfov read the letter and replied: "This matter is embarrassing." Peshev left his office.[15]

Kalfov immediately rushed to Prime Minister Filov, who read the letter and became very upset. He instructed Kalfov to persuade Peshev not to send it.[16] The House Speaker called Peshev back to his office. The prime minister, Kalfov said, was asking that Peshev delay the official delivery of the letter and wait till the meeting of the majority, where all the questions raised in the letter would be explained. Peshev listened in silence, then turned and left the Speaker's office.[17]

As he walked along the halls of Parliament, he thought about Filov's request. He suspected that the prime minister wanted to thwart his initiative by pressuring the members of Parliament to not sign the petition or to withdraw their signatures. "I assumed that more pressure and persuasion would be applied from one place or another, even on me personally, in order to avoid the public impact of our initiative, that was unwanted by the government." Peshev had to act without delay.

Back in his office, he felt the "fury and confusion" his letter had caused in government circles, when Interior Minister Gabrovski, sick in bed, called from his home and asked Peshev to send him a copy of the letter right away.

Peshev decided to finish the signature collection that evening. He knew that many members of Parliament were expected back in Sofia the following morning and several of them undoubtedly would sign the letter. A friend of his, Spas Ganev,[18] had promised to come to his office the following morning, to sign the letter. But Peshev preferred to send the letter before Filov could begin a counteraction.[19]

On March 19, the letter was on Filov's desk, signed by forty-three members of Parliament. More than a third of the majority members had joined Peshev in his initiative.

The heart of the letter contained the following passage:

> Lately certain moves made by the authorities indicate that new measures are being considered and undertaken against the persons of Jewish origin. What exactly these measures are, on what grounds are they being undertaken, what do they intend to achieve and what are their reasons—[on these questions] there are no credible explanations from the responsible echelons. Even the Minister of the Interior, in a conversation with several Members of Parliament, has confirmed that no extraordinary measures will be taken against the Jews of the old boundaries, which will affect them as a whole. Indeed, following that conversation all the instructions of this nature were canceled . . .
>
> Our request is that when undertaking any measures only the real needs of the State and the people would be taken into account, without ignoring, however, the considerations of the prestige and the moral principles of our people.
>
> We cannot oppose measures, imposed by security needs . . . [We agree that] those who directly or indirectly hamper the supreme efforts of the State and the people should be disabled . . .

Nevertheless, the letter warned the government,

> . . . not to cross the necessary limits of the real needs and fall into excesses, which may be qualified as gratuitous cruelty. That's how any measures that would affect women, children and old people would be qualified, if no individual guilt can be established for each and everyone of them.

We cannot believe that the deportation of these people out of Bulgaria has been envisaged; this intention has been ascribed by a malicious rumor to the Bulgarian government. Such a measure is unthinkable, not only because these people, who have not been deprived of their Bulgarian citizenship, cannot be expelled out of Bulgaria, but because it would be a destructive measure, carrying grave political consequences. It would brand Bulgaria with an undeserved stain, that not only would burden her morally, but also would void all her moral standing.

Small nations cannot afford the freedom to ignore these [moral] arguments, which . . . would always remain . . . the strongest weapon in their hands . . .

What Bulgarian government would assume such a responsibility for the future?

The small number of Jews in Bulgaria, [and] the strength of the State make the disabling of any dangerous and harmful element . . . so certain, that . . . it is absolutely needless to recur to . . . utterly cruel measures which might lead to an accusation of mass murder.

That would burden the Cabinet above all, but certainly would transcend it and fall on Bulgaria's head . . .

For this we cannot share any responsibility . . .

The honor of Bulgaria and her people . . . is above all an element of her policy. It is a political asset of the greatest value, therefore nobody has the right to waste it without the approval of the entire nation.

•   •   •

Filov was furious. This was a rebellion. This was the first time that an important group of Parliament members from his own party openly dared to defy the government. These were not the usual troublemakers from the opposition, who had no real power. This time Filov was opposed by more than a third of the pro-government majority. Such an expression of independent criticism was unheard of. Besides, the prime minister was convinced that Peshev was aiming much higher than the cabinet's Jewish policy. "He intended to hurt the government, and if he failed to bring to its downfall, he at least would expose it."[20]

"This is a considerable demonstration," Filov wrote angrily in his diary, "and it will have consequences. Now I see indeed how strong is the influence of the Jews and how harmful they are."[21]

Utterly enraged by the letter, Filov decided to crush Peshev.

For the following week, the prime minister acted as if obsessed by the rebellion of the deputy speaker and kept devising ways to destroy him. He told some members of Parliament, who opposed the letter, that "the question is very important, he would call for a majority meeting and draw all the consequences."[22]

The following morning he conferred with the king's adviser, Iordan Sevov. He then spent most of the cabinet meeting discussing Peshev's letter. He decided to remove Peshev from his position of deputy speaker and to expel all the signatories of the letter from the majority. In his fury, the prime minister was ready to call for new elections: "It is a convenient moment, because we are at the end of the Chamber session, and the Jewish question is a convenient campaign subject, if there are new elections."[23]

That same day he began pressuring Peshev's cosignatories to withdraw their signatures from the letter. One member, P. Kiosseivanov, left Filov a letter in which he withdrew his signature. Another member, Spas Marinov, withdrew orally, but Filov insisted on a written statement.

On March 23 Filov spoke to the king about the letter. Perhaps Filov had cooled down in the meantime or the king reacted more cautiously, but the question of new elections was never raised again. "The King agrees," Filov wrote in his diary, "that we should censure Peshev at the majority [meeting] in order to disable him once and forever."[24]

• • •

The majority meeting took place on Wednesday, March 24. Out of 115 members of the majority, 114 participated. The only one who didn't attend was P. Kiosseivanov.

Prime Minister Filov came with all his cabinet ministers. He was tense and angry. He read Peshev's letter aloud. He apparently didn't want a debate on the Jewish policy of his government. Instead, he attacked the letter as a blow to the majority's discipline, its relationship with the cabinet, and the credibility of the cabinet's policy. "[He qualified it] as something like a revolt, although he didn't use this word," Peshev noted.[25]

Filov asked for a confidence vote, and the 114 members present unanimously voted full confidence in the government and its overall policy. Filov noted that in his diary, adding that this vote also meant a cancellation of the letter and approval of his Jewish policy.[26] In reality, though, it was a formal vote that had no importance whatsoever. Peshev and his friends, who staunchly opposed the government's position on the Jewish question, readily raised their hands in another vote, one that expressed full support for Filov's policy as a whole.

But in a separate vote, the members had to decide if Peshev should be censored and removed from his position of deputy speaker. "The voting began," Peshev wrote. "Actually it was a painful procedure, an inquisition, a brutal pressure . . . One after the other, the name of every MP was called; each had to get up and answer the questions, and the Prime minister took notes with a pencil in his hand. I had never assisted at such a scene before . . ."[27]

This was, actually, the real vote of confidence. In the end, according to Filov, sixty-six members voted for the censure of Peshev and his removal from his position; but thirty-three voted against and eleven abstained. Four members left the meeting before the vote. Most of those who voted against the motion and some of those who abstained had signed Peshev's letter. Peshev himself said of those who voted against the motion: "They remained faithful to their signature."[28]

Filov himself admitted later in his diary that the voting in favor of Peshev contradicted the unanimous vote of confidence in the government. Indeed, Filov had stated that the government saw in the vote for the removal of Peshev a vote of confidence as well. "But I didn't want to insist; in the second vote it was a question of saving face, and Peshev's comrades who had signed the letter couldn't abandon him."[29]

Peshev and Filov clashed again when Peshev assumed total responsibility for the letter but refused to resign from his position as deputy speaker. He wanted a showdown on the floor of Parliament. The majority could decide to remove him, but the official decision had to be made by the full chamber.

"You will be sorry for your action," he threw at the prime minister, leaving the room in silence, his comrades avoiding his eyes.

Filov theatrically threw back at him, in French, a phrase from a famous Moliere play: *Tu l'as voulu, Dandin* (You asked for it, Dandin).[30]

●  ●  ●

The final act, one that Moliere did not write, took place two days later, in the plenary session of Parliament.

It was a shameful session. Once again the entire cabinet, led by Filov, was present. The Parliament Speaker, breaking every paragraph in the regulations, invited a majority member, Dr. Ivan Popov, to read a motion to remove Peshev from his position.

Peshev jumped on his feet: "I request to have the floor, in order to submit my resignation to the Parliament."

The Speaker disregarded him, as well as the demands of other members, mostly from the opposition, who requested the floor. Several former ministers and prime ministers asked for a debate; one of them warned that the entire procedure was illegal. Peshev kept shouting that he had the right to submit his resignation. The Speaker ignored the protests. The chamber exploded in banging on desks and loud yelling: "Shame!" and "This is illegal!" Such a stormy exchange was very unusual. But Speaker Kalfov hastily brought the matter to a vote and announced: "Majority. The motion is adopted."[31]

Prime Minister Filov didn't hide his satisfaction with the outcome of the vote; but his sense of victory was soon to evaporate, when several opposition leaders managed to raise once again the subject of Peshev and the Jewish question.

Indeed, some eminent members of the opposition used their right to speak on other matters on the agenda and eloquently defended Peshev and his letter. They candidly criticized the deportation of the Jews from the new territories. Petko Stainov described the terrible suffering of the Jews deported from Thrace and Macedonia, then saluted the forty-odd signatories of Peshev's letter: "They've signed it in the name of humanity, in protest against the inhuman, illegal, unconstitutional treatment of some weak Bulgarian citizens, whom nobody else wanted to defend."

Todor Kojukharov made a powerful appeal for morality and against deportation of human beings:

> The only moral capital of a small nation is to be a righteous nation . . . Every Bulgarian should be proud of the phrase in our Constitution, stating: "Every slave becomes a free man the moments he steps on Bulgarian soil."
>
> This is the proudest statement in the Bulgarian Constitution, this is our moral capital . . . Only a righteous Bulgaria can demand that her rights be respected by stronger nations . . .[32]

●  ●  ●

After Peshev's dismissal, the nervous government hurriedly sent the Parliament into an early recess.[33] Peshev's letter had hurt Filov's government much more seriously than it was ready to admit.

But the man responsible for the disruption of Filov's government, Dimiter Peshev, left the Parliament meeting a broken man. He
was still a member, an elected position they couldn't take away from
him. But the ugly session during which he had been removed as
deputy speaker was for him "a tragedy."[34] He was also deeply hurt
by some of his colleagues who said that he had been bribed to write
the letter. Similar rumors circulated in Sofia and Kyustendil, fed by
Peshev's rivals. He would later testify:

> The rumors said I had received millions from the
> Jews. This dirty and vile insinuation, intended to compro-
> mise the pure and idealistic motives of [my] political
> action, spread throughout Bulgaria . . . I have to emphasize
> that in our Parliament a moral terror reigned, as far as the
> Jewish question was concerned. The rumors said that the
> Jews had collected many millions in order to buy support
> for their cause. That forced many to keep silent, to avoid
> the suspicions that they had been bought.[35]

Nine months later, Peshev seized an opportunity to set the
record straight. During a debate on the budget, in a plenary session
of Parliament, he made a speech harshly criticizing the procedure of
his removal and read his entire letter, in order to have it entered into
the Parliament minutes.[36]

But this partial success couldn't restore Peshev's position as
deputy speaker. This brave and gallant man had taken a step that no
sane politician would ordinarily take. By rebelling against Filov's
policy, he had not acted in his own best interests. For a member of
the pro-Fascist majority in the autocratic Bulgarian regime, success
was achieved through blind obedience to cabinet policy, not by insti-
gating an uprising against the prime minister.

CHAPTER TWELVE

# THE BLUFF

On March 28, the German ambassador visited the royal palace and handed King Boris an invitation to visit the Führer at the Eagle's Nest, his Bavarian mountain retreat in Berchtesgaden. As usual, Hitler sent for the king in one of his private planes. The invitation also included the chief of staff of the Bulgarian army. That worried the king. He feared the Führer would pressure him to send the Bulgarian army to the Russian front. "The king doesn't want to go this time," Filov notes. "He goes without heart, he believes the German cause is doomed."[1]

But there was no way the king could reject Hitler's invitation: It was actually a summons. The following day the king reviewed with Filov the main topics that might arise in his conversations with Hitler. Assuming Hitler might want to discuss the postwar order in Europe, they updated their positions on Greece, Serbia, and Turkey. The Jewish question wasn't mentioned, and nobody saw any connection between the urgent invitation from the Führer and the latest political storm at the Parliament.

On March 31 the king flew to Salzburg. He reached Berchtesgaden the same night. The following day, April 1, the king arrived at the Eagle's Nest. Hitler, who held Boris in high esteem, welcomed him warmly. Their talks touched upon a variety of subjects, and Boris's fears were dispelled—He was not asked to send the Bulgarian army to the Russian front. And Hitler didn't say a word about the failed deportation of Bulgaria's Jews.

But Ribbentrop did.

Joachim von Ribbentrop, the foreign minister of the Reich, was perfectly aware of the events in Bulgaria during the month of March. Beckerle had been informed as early as March 10 of Gabrovski's order to cancel the deportations[2] from the old borders of Bulgaria.*
On March 23 Beckerle had learned of Peshev's letter and had reported the information to Berlin.[3][†] The subject was on Ribbentrop's mind when he met with the king for a private conversation, in which Hitler didn't participate.

King Boris strongly disliked Ribbentrop. He defined his influence on Hitler as "especially harmful" and regarded the foreign minister as a "merchant-adventurer."[4] "De Ribbi," as the king mockingly referred to him, had a detailed conversation with Boris III on the Jewish question. Ribbentrop inquired about the deportation, and the king replied that so far he had agreed to deport to the East only the Jews from Macedonia and Thrace. As far as the Jews inside the old Bulgarian boundaries were concerned, he intended to deport "only a small number of bolshevik-communist elements." He would intern the remaining twenty-five thousand in concentration camps in the interior of the country, because he needed them for road construction.[‡]

Ribbentrop replied:[5] "By our understanding of the Jewish question the only right solution is the radical solution."

---

* "Exactly as I thought," Beckerle wrote. "My suggestion to deport only the Jews from the occupied regions would have been better and more effective." We have no prior knowledge of such a "suggestion" by Beckerle.

† He claimed that an extreme right-wing member of Parliament, Tzankov, had told a German journalist that he had signed the letter because of the inhumanity of the deportation procedure and his fear that Germany would be blamed.

‡ The figure of twenty-five thousand quoted by Ribbentrop seems rather strange, as we had no indication at any moment that the king intended to deport half of Bulgaria's Jews as "bolshevik-communist elements." The king may not have known the exact number of Jews in the kingdom and, therefore, just "threw out" the number twenty-five thousand.

(COURTESY OF BULGARIAN STATE ARCHIVES)

*Boris on hunting trip with Reichsmarshall Hermann Goering in Germany.*

The king tried to explain to Ribbentrop that the Bulgarian Jews were Sephardic Jews. Boris III used the term *Shpanioli* ("Spanish") and stressed that they absolutely did not play the same role as Jews in other countries. He probably meant that his country's Jews were more assimilated into the Bulgarian society and were not regarded as aliens; they were also poorer than Jews in other countries and not involved in banking, big business, and media.

Ribbentrop was not convinced. "Jews always remain Jews," he snapped.[6]

In retrospect, there is no doubt that the political storm in Bulgaria concerning the deportation of the Jews had been one of the main reasons for the summons of the king to Germany. It also seems likely that Hitler, unwilling to confront the king directly on the Jewish question, had chosen to charge Ribbentrop with that responsibility.

The doubts of the Nazi leadership about Bulgaria's intentions toward her Jewish population were well founded. In his reply to Ribbentrop the king actually implemented for the first time his new Jewish policy, which had resulted from the events of March 9, 1943.

• • •

On his return to Bulgaria, after his subdued confrontation with Ribbentrop, the king took another step toward a new Jewish policy. On April 13, in the royal palace, the king met with Filov and Gabrovski to discuss the Jewish question. He told his ministers that "we must mobilize the able [Jewish] men in labor units and thus avoid the deportation of the Jews from the old boundaries to Poland."[7]

This was a major decision. Already at the end of the previous year, Filov and Gabrovski had spoken with German representatives about their intention to use the Jewish men in labor units. They had done so after early consultations with the king. Now, the "road-building" was becoming the king's basic policy.

It is possible that the mobilization of the Jewish men for road construction, two years before, had begun as a genuine effort to use that free manpower for public works. The mobilized Jews worked hard, in rough conditions. Life in the labor camps was not easy, people suffered from diseases and malnutrition, and many Jews were brutally treated by vicious officers. But King Boris turned the forced labor into a scheme to protect the Jews from a much worse fate. The Jews and the road construction became King Boris's biggest bluff during the war.

Boris's decision was immediately carried out. In a few weeks, at the beginning of May, able Jewish men would be called again to special labor camps.[8] This clearly meant that King Boris stuck to his position even after the pressure von Ribbentrop had brought to bear upon him.

Filov and Gabrovski didn't protest the king's decision, nor did they take action against his breaking the agreement with Germany. In fact, their subsequent actions suggest that they didn't discern the profound change in Boris's policy. It is also possible that they didn't take the change too seriously because they knew that Boris tended to vacillate between alternating views.

But could their king, indeed, withstand the pressure for a long period of time?

• • •

On April 4, 1943, Ribbentrop sent a laconic account of his conversation with King Boris to the German diplomatic representatives in Sofia. Immediately upon receiving his telegram, the Gestapo attaché Hoffman wrote a long report to the Main Imperial Security Office, intended to appease Berlin, and to prove that the deportation was at least a partial success. It also stressed that despite the March 9 setback, the deportation was certainly going to continue. The report, countersigned by Beckerle, was dispatched the following day, April 5.

"We can already report," Hoffman cheerfully began, "that 11,343 Jews were deported. Out of those 4,221 Thracian Jews by boat from Lom to Vienna, and 7,122 Macedonian Jews by train from Skopje."[9]

After describing the negotiations with Gabrovski and Belev, and the decision to deport twenty thousand Jews, Hoffman pointed out:

> Whoever is familiar with the local situation, should have assumed that with the date of the evacuation approaching, difficulties would arise. They arose in connection with the deportation of the Jews from Bulgaria's old boundaries. The Commissar of Jewish affairs Belev, expecting those difficulties, had already assembled the most influential Jews in camps in Plovdiv, Kyustendil, Russe and Varna.* He had planned the same for Sofia, for March 13, 1943. The fact that the Jews of Bulgaria's old boundaries had to be included in the deportation became known in the meantime.

---

* This is not correct. Only the Jews of Plovdiv and some other towns were assembled on the evening of March 9 and were not immediately released because the telegram canceling the deportation arrived in their city only the following day. As we know, the Jews of Kyustendil were not rounded up.

After describing Peshev's intervention and the instruction "from the highest place" to stop the Bulgarian Jews' deportation, Hoffman noted that "the release of the Jews on March 10, 1943, created a significant uncertainty among the police chiefs in the aforementioned cities."

Hoffman rejected certain rumors coming from RSHA circles in Berlin, rumors suggesting that Gabrovski had backed away from his promises. "It would be wrong to assume that the Bulgarian government, and especially the Interior Minister Gabrovski, have seriously wanted to sabotage the anti-Jewish action."

Hoffman pointed out that the German ambassador, by his frequent visits to Filov, had obtained the prime minister's firm assurance that all the Jews would be deported. Hoffman then described the main reason for the Bulgarian reluctance to deport the Jews, which confirmed King Boris's words to Ribbentrop:

> To truly understand the position of the Bulgarian government, one should know that a Jewish question doesn't exist in Bulgaria in the form that it has existed in the Reich. In Bulgaria there are indeed Jews, who have reached key positions in the country's economy. Their number, however, is small. The ideological and racial reasons for presenting the Jewish question to the Bulgarian people as urgent and needing a solution, as it was the case in the Reich—do not exist here. By the deportation of the Jews the Bulgarian government pursues mostly material interests, consisting in handing to trustworthy Bulgarians the property of the deported Jews, thereby satisfying them, and simultaneously replacing the restive Jews in the newly acquired lands with reliable Bulgarians.

The Bulgarian government was ready to deport all the Jews. However, it "wants to avoid the Jewish question in Bulgaria being reported in the world press." That fear of exposure, Hoffman said, explained why the Bulgarian government had promised the Swiss chargé d'affaires to allow the immigration of a few thousand Jewish children to Palestine, while confidentially informing the German ambassador that the plan would be aborted. Still, he added, "our ambassador must, once in a while, use pressure [on the Bulgarians] in order to move the deportation process forward."

Hoffman's report also proved that Filov submitted to the Germans written notes or detailed verbal reports of any important diplomatic meeting. "Filov declared to the Swiss charge in Sofia . . . that the government was firm in its determination to carry out the deportation, as this solution is anyway more humane than the bombing of civilian areas." These were, almost exactly, Filov's words to the Swiss chargé d'affaires, as recorded in his diary. Hoffman quoted a few more phrases of Filov, that indicate, without any doubt, that he had got a full and detailed report of the prime minister's meeting with Charles-Arthur Redard. Filov was acting as a subservient German agent.

Hoffman stuck to his optimistic forecast:

> Considering that in Italy, Hungary, Spain etc. the Jewish question has not been even raised yet, and the deportation of the Jews has not yet started, I have to state, in conclusion, that the Bulgarian government works actively toward the solution of the Jewish question in Bulgaria . . .
>
> When we take these circumstances in account, the present result of the deportation of 11,343 Jews must be judged as satisfying. Out of an agreed number of 20,000, 56% was achieved.
>
> For tactical considerations, the ambassador will act now cautiously on the question of the deportation from the old boundaries of Bulgaria . . . He will intervene again, when he feels [his steps] would be effective and when that would fit into the general political context.

In the meantime SS Haupsturmfuhrer Dannecker maintains a permanent contact with the Commissar for Jewish Questions Belev, so that they would submit acceptable projects for further deportation to the Interior Minister.

We shall assume, therefore, that the deportation from Bulgaria will resume in the near future.[10]

# CHAPTER THIRTEEN

# THE
# METROPOLITANS

Metropolitan Stefan of Sofia was the most colorful person in the Bulgarian church, and perhaps in all of Bulgaria. Six feet tall, a large, handsome man, with a grizzled beard, a deep, powerful voice and eyes twinkling with intelligence and humor, Stefan was considered "the least saintlike of all those of the Saint-Synod."[1] He was extremely bright, cultured, and fiercely independent. Grandson of a daring revolutionary—who fought the Turkish occupiers by bombing their military factories—son of another freedom fighter and Pravoslav (Orthodox) priest (in the Pravoslav faith, priests are allowed to marry and have families), he was born Stoian Shokov in a Rhodope mountain village in 1878. He studied at a teachers academy and got a job in his native town. But the rebel in him soon emerged when Stoian organized the citizen resistance to the tax authorities and was accused of incitement to rebellion against the State. Thanks to his good connections, the charges against him were dropped, and he was able to pursue his activities in the Macedonian-Odrin revolutionary movement.

He completed four years of stimulating study at the Spiritual Academy in Kiev, where he became a great friend of the Russians and embraced the idea of "unity of the Slavs." But on his return, instead of taking the vows, he surprised the Holy Synod by applying to the officers' academy, where he graduated as a lieutenant.

He then was sent by Exarch Joseph, the head of the Bulgarian church, to work for three years as a teacher in Istanbul. In 1910, at the age of thirty-two, he was finally ordained as Stefan.

Four years later, following his patron Exarch Joseph, he rebelled against King Ferdinand because of "his fatal policy"—fighting on the side of the Germans in World War I. To protect him, the old Exarch Joseph sent his maverick protégé to Switzerland, where Stefan obtained a Ph.D. degree from Geneva University.

A doctor of philosophy, he returned to Sofia only after the abdication of Ferdinand. He rose in the ranks of the church with lightning speed. Three years later Stefan was elected as the primate of Sofia's church.

Very soon, he became one of the most eminent and controversial figures in Sofia society. Eloquent, highly cultured, fluent in foreign languages, the illustrious prelate was a charming, witty man of the world. "He was the delight of Sofia's anticlerical cartoonists," Stephane Groueff wrote, "who claimed that when traveling abroad the good metropolitan donned his civilian clothes to frequent unholy places in Paris and Vienna. If recognized . . . he would argue that it was the duty of the good pastor to have first-hand knowledge of vice in order  better to combat it."[2] Sofia's favorite rumors described the Metropolitan's amorous adventures, and the good life he enjoyed; some spoke of his manicured nails and dyed mustache.[3] Perhaps he thought of these sins when he wrote in his diary: "My weaknesses are not a result of insufficient creed . . . but an expression of my human feebleness, which I couldn't always overcome."[4]

Stefan's "human feebleness" did not interfere with his outstanding qualities as a man of the church, who was respected and admired by all his peers. He was deeply religious, and in his mind the presence of God and His teachings were tangible and relevant. He miraculously survived the Sveta Nedelya bombing, when the roof collapsed in the middle of his sermon, killing and wounding hundreds of people.

Stefan also devised a genial solution to one of King Boris's problems. Boris married Princess Giovanna, the king of Italy's daughter, in a Catholic ceremony in Italy; but Bulgaria's Orthodox church demanded an Orthodox wedding in Sofia. Metropolitan Stefan shrewdly devised a procedure that avoided a second marriage. When King Boris and his bride returned to Bulgaria, a prelate met them at the entrance of the Alexander Nevski Church, said a prayer, blessed them, and offered them Holy Communion. That was not, technically, a second marriage, but merely a sanctioning of the Catholic wedding, and it satisfied the Bulgarians. "The Metropolitan deserves the Grand Cordon!"—one of the

(COURTESY OF BULGARIAN STATE ARCHIVES)

*Metropolitan Stefan, Queen Giovanna, Princess Maria Louisa.*

highest decorations in the kingdom—King Boris said contentedly.[5] Years later, Stefan also baptized the king's children.

As the Metropolitan of the capital, he was present at every important ceremony and celebration and was almost in daily contact with the king, his ministers, and the senior officials of the kingdom. He was also well connected with the foreign diplomats and visitors to Sofia. This unique position allowed him to play a political role, and he did so with delight.

As World War II broke out, Stefan became the most outspoken enemy of the alliance with the Reich. "Only madmen," he wrote in his diary in April 1942,[6] "can fall into the hysterics that have taken control of the miserable Führer. But where is the culture, the great civilization of the German people, if it lets itself to be commanded by its insane Führer? Isn't this culture just a false façade of the barbarian rage of the Teutonic race?" Stefan didn't miss an opportunity to express his scathing criticism of the Nazis in articles he published in the press. The government censor, who was in charge of preventing antigovernment propaganda from being printed in the newspapers, often suppressed the essays of the independent cleric. Stefan was the last to be surprised.[7]

The Metropolitan, however, indignantly protested against the suppression of his articles when he met the censor and a group of German diplomats at a party in Sofia. "It isn't true that I am anti-German," the head of the Sofia church said to the censor, an amused twinkle in his eyes. "I am an admirer of many Germans, like Stefan Zweig, Thomas Mann, and Albert Wasserman."[8] He stared fixedly at his pro-Fascist interlocutor, to make sure that he had registered the names of the famous Jewish and liberal German writers.

He paid a heavy price for his courage. The radio and the pro-government newspapers didn't stop attacking and vilifying him;[9] the government propaganda organizations even printed threatening fly-ers against him and distributed them throughout the country. Brannik and other Fascist organizations made him a target of their attacks. Stefan was several times officially warned that he might be indicted for anti-State activity.

In the late fall of 1940 Stefan had been the main initiator of the church's bold statement against the Law of the Defense of the Nation (see Chapter Three). In early February he had complained to the police that the Brannik Fascist organization was harrassing and per-secuting Jews in the streets, tearing off their Jewish stars, and then beating them for not wearing them. With the assistance of Mrs. Ekaterina Karavelova, the widow of one of Bulgaria's most eminent statesmen, he was able to force the police to intervene and put an end to the Brannik activities.[10]

In September 1942, he stirred angry reactions in governmental and pro-Fascist circles by openly preaching against anti-Semitism. In his Sunday sermon he said that God had already punished the Jews for rejecting Jesus Christ and that man therefore had no right to persecute them. He said that Jews, especially those who had been christened, should be regarded by the Bulgarians as brothers.[11]

On February 28, 1943, when on a visit to Dupnitza, he met with a Jewish friend and a delegation of local Christians, who complained about the house arrest imposed on the town Jews.[12] They didn't know yet that the house arrest was supposed to serve two purposes: to prepare the town for the arrival of the Thracian Jews and to ready the Dupnitza Jews for their own deportation. Stefan contacted the local authorities and was able to put an end to that situation—on March 2 the Dupnitza Jews were allowed to leave their homes during the daylight hours.[13] In March 1943, shaken by the sight of the deportation convoys, Stefan tried, alone, to alert the king to the inhumane treatment of the Thracian and Macedonian deportees.

After the deportation of the Bulgarian Jews was postponed on March 9, Stefan took action within the church hierarchy, in order to get the entire Bulgarian church to oppose any further measures against the Jews. He didn't have to try hard, as the Bulgarian church wholeheartedly supported his views on the Jewish question. The fiery Metropolitan Kyril of Plovdiv and the deeply respected Neofit of Vidin, who also was the acting president of the Saint Synod, were among the staunchest opponents of the anti-Jewish measures. Neofit of Vidin even requested a meeting with the prime minister, after the deportations, and strongly urged him "to show mercy and humanity toward the suffering Jewish minority." He also requested special treatment of the Jews who converted to Christianity.

Filov responded with his routine answer: "Millions of people are being massacred on the battlefields," he said, "and that is the Jews' fault." Although he was more conciliatory about the converted Jews,[14] Neofit was not satisfied with Filov's answer.

On March 15, Colonel Tadjer and the president of the Jewish Community, Joseph Geron, came to the seat of the Saint Synod and asked again for the help of the church.[15] Neofit was sympathetic to their request, and following Stefan's initiative, he summoned his peers to Sofia.

•  •  •

On April 2, 1943, the leaders of the Saint Synod of Bulgaria's church met in Sofia. Only one of the prelates, Filaret of Lovech, couldn't attend. Ten heads of the Bulgarian church, from all over the country, came to the extraordinary meeting, whose main subject was the government's policy against the Jews. They assembled at the Central Siege of the Church in the capital, dressed in their long black robes and their tall black hats, their heavy crosses hanging on silver chains on their chests.

The Jewish question was one of the most frequently debated topics in the Saint Synod's meetings. In 1940 this supreme authority of the Bulgarian church had severely condemned the Law for the Defense of the Nation and demanded its cancellation. In 1941 the Saint Synod strongly protested against the ZZN decrees that forbade marriage between Bulgarians and converted Jews.[16] In 1942 the Church again asked the government to cancel or modify the ZZN— to alleviate the restrictions on converted Jews and stop persecuting the Jews as a whole.[17] The April 1943 meeting, however, was a direct result of the March 10 deportation attempt.

Neofit of Vidin opened the meeting. After reporting his conversation with the prime minister, he told the other Metropolitans about the deportation of the Thracian Jews and the attempt to deport the Jews of Bulgaria. Kyril of Plovdiv described the dramatic events in his city on March 10, when the police had rounded up the Jews for immediate deportation; he told his audience about the warning he had addressed to the government—even though he had been a loyal citizen in the past, he would cease to obey the government's orders, and reserve his freedom of action.

Stefan was clear and determined:

> The Jews know well, that there is nobody to speak for them with authority, but the Bulgarian church, and that if she acts more forcefully, her voice will be heard. Our help is especially needed by the converted, who must feel that they are treated as real children of the Holy Church.

He returned to the persecution of the Jews:

> Unfortunately, the Law for the Defense of the Nation
> is being implemented by a man [Belev] who, I am told, is
> not fully in equilibrium on these questions. And if our
> Church doesn't intervene to defend these wretched people,
> we should expect even worse outrages and acts of cruelty,
> for which one day our goodhearted people is going to feel
> shame, and perhaps other misfortunes.

One after the other, the princes of the Bulgarian church spoke
against the treatment of the Jews. Paissi of Vratza stressed that the
outlawing of a minority was against the Christian teachings and the
Christian morality; he asked his peers to forcefully oppose the plans
to deport the Jews out of Bulgaria's territory.

Joseph of Varna admitted his past errors. In the past, he said,
he had been the only one among the leaders of the Church to support the idea of a Law for the Defense of the Nation, hoping that it
would prevent foreigners from enslaving the Bulgarian people. He
admitted:

> Now I see things differently. It turns out that the Law
> for the Defense of the Nation was created only and exclu-
> sively against the Jews, and in order to take away the
> Jewish property. . . . This law is being implemented with
> cruelty and even with barbarity. All these things that are
> happening with the Jewish minority, and especially the last
> cruelties, concerning their deportation out of the country,
> have seriously distressed me, and today I am correcting
> my former position. . . . We have to tell the Bulgarian gov-
> ernment, that with this law, instead of defending the
> nation, it shames the good name of the Bulgarian people.

Klement of Stara Zagora accused the government "of creating a tendency in our country to establish a new morality—one of hatred and of persecution, one that wants us to bare our teeth and our nails."

Evlogi of Sliven stated: "The great majority of our people doesn't approve of the government's actions toward the Jewish minority."

Sofroni of Turnovo confirmed: "The feeling of the Bulgarian people is for the defense of the Jewish minority."

Other prelates spoke in the same spirit. And Stefan summed up the debate: "When we ask the state authorities what the Jews of our country are guilty of, they have nothing to say. They took everything away from the Jews, but when they reached to take away their life, the Jews asked for the defense of the Church. We cannot refuse it. They are subjected to inhuman suffering."[18]

•  •  •

The acting president proposed that the Church express her feelings about the Jewish question in a letter to the prime minister, with a copy to the king. The letter was indeed written and dispatched right away. It contained the following passages:

> The Pravoslav Bulgarian Church . . . cannot accept ideas like the racist idea, by which people can be inspired with hatred, and acts of oppression and cruelty may be committed. . . . Our Holy Church has been asked by the Jews for help, while Bulgarian Christians have asked us to act for the improvement of the fate of the Jews.
>
> Therefore the Saint Synod decided to ask the following from Your honor:
>
> 1. Not to deprive the Christians of Jewish origin and the Jews in general of their elementary rights as human beings

and citizens, and not to deprive them of the right to live in our country and to work here to assure a fair human living.

2. To ease the restrictions that have been imposed on the Jews and not to implement them firmly and cruelly.

3. To cancel the unjustified rule that Christians of Jewish origin should wear both a Christian cross and a Jewish star, and pay taxes to the Jewish consistory.

The Church cannot avoid reminding [you of] God's word: "With the measure you use, it will be measured back to you." (Matthew 7:2).[19]

Another letter, asking for a meeting with the heads of the Church, was dispatched to the king himself. Neofit described the Saint Synod meeting and bluntly said: "There was a general apprehension [among the prelates] that because of the extraordinary measures which are taken and implemented sometimes with unscrupulous harshness against the Jews in general, and in particular against the Pravoslav Christian-Jews . . . God's wrath against our people may be provoked." Neofit bitterly complained that the government, and even the king, do not listen to the voice of the Church.[20]

•  •  •

Both letters were delivered to King Boris soon after his return from Germany. He was offended and infuriated. Neofit's letter was written "in a very sharp tone," Filov noted.[21] Boris immediately agreed to meet the Church leaders. The night before the meeting, he had a long conversation with Filov about it, but mostly on the second item on the agenda of the meeting [besides the Jewish question], which concerned the election of a new head of the Church.[22] It also seemed that the king and Filov were upset by the fact that the strong criticism by the Church was put on paper and, thus, might become known to the public and the body politic.[23]

On April 15, the heads of the Church were invited to the king's palace in Vrana. He received them in the company of Filov. The king and Filov were very upset at the beginning of the meeting. Only a half hour before the meeting started, resistance fighters had assassinated a member of Parliament, Sotir Ianev, who was known for his support of the government. Still, in the sometimes absurd and contradictory direction of Bulgarian politics, the same Sotir Ianev had signed Peshev's letter of protest about the Jews. Two months before, another right-wing extremist, the Legionnaire leader, General Lukov, had been assassinated by a group of partisans that included a young Jewish woman, Violeta Yakova (no Jews participated in the assassination of Ianev).

As the meeting with the Saint Synod started, the king looked bitter and hurt. "If I didn't know His Eminence closely," he said to Acting President Neofit, who had signed the letter, "it is possible that this letter would have pained me."[24] He announced then that he would say "a few words" on the Jewish question.

"These 'few words' lasted more than half an hour," Neofit sarcastically reported.[25]

But they were harsh words, the harshest the king had ever used against the Jews. He sounded as if he were reading a propaganda flyer. He knew well the Jewry and its profiteering spirit, the king said.

> This profiteering spirit of the Jewry has been inflicting heavy damage on humanity for centuries. This [Jewish] spirit has been creating everywhere hatred, loss of faith, moral degradation, and treason. This spirit of profiteering and negation has created and creates, in peoples and societies, unrest, divisions, conflicts, wars, and troubles. The present world cataclysm has been, to a large extent, caused by this spirit. It is true, that some of the large nations make good use of the Jewish wealth, amassed by this profiteering spirit. But other European nations have been convinced that the Jewish profiteering is a fatal

obstacle to their spiritual and economic development. They believe that the sooner they are freed of the influence and the exploitation of the Jewry, the more their national feeling and their patriotism would be reinforced. And that can be obtained, if by law the various economic, financial, commercial, and industrial enterprises are taken from the Jewish hands. All throughout Europe legislation in this sense is being introduced. That has been done in our country as well—the Law for the Defense of the Nation. Our Pravoslav Church, known for her patriotism, can hardly have a different opinion.

. . . It must be stated, however, that while taking measures against the damage that the Jewry, by propaganda and profiteering, is creating in our country, the Supreme state authority is making all the efforts, so that in Bulgaria, if possible less, or none at all, of those [Jews] would suffer.

The king also promised to examine the complaints about possible excesses directed toward the christened Jews.

The king, feeling attacked and criticized by the Church, chose to quote the official anti-Jewish propaganda. He didn't say a word, though, about the cancellation of the deportation of the Jews from Bulgaria. Neither did he tell the prelates that two weeks ago he had rejected Ribbentrop's request to deport Bulgaria's Jews to Poland. He also refrained from mentioning that only two days before he had decided to mobilize all the Jews into labor units, "in order to avoid the sending of the Jews from the old boundaries to Poland."[26]

This was classic King Boris maneuvering. Externally, he would politely but firmly reject the Nazi request to deport Bulgaria's Jews. Internally, he would adopt a firm defense of the anti-Jewish measures. He feared that easing the restrictions against the Jews would expose him not only to the anger of the Germans but also to the intrigues of the extreme right-wing elements in Bulgaria. He also knew by now that his prime minister regularly reported inside information to the Germans about Bulgaria's domestic policy. He wanted to reassure Filov, and through him his German masters, that his policy wasn't going to change. In the meeting, he sat at the head of an oblong table, opposite Filov, who sat on the other end, with the prelates seated on both sides. He spoke directly to Filov, and Filov liked what he said.

Yet, if the king thought that by reciting anti-Jewish propaganda to the Saint Synod he would make them change their minds, and end their criticism, he was greatly mistaken. The prelates answered with utmost politeness and respect but didn't budge from their positions. They apologized for hurting the king's feelings. They assured him that they had not intended to break the Law for the Defense of the Nation.

Nevertheless, they clearly repeated:

> The Law for the Defense of the Nation most painfully hurt the Jewish inhabitants of our country. As soon as its implementation started, immediately were heard desperate complaints, appeals and calls for mercy and protection. . . . Especially moving were the appeals by the Jews who had accepted the holy Christening and become children of the Pravoslav church. . . . The same deplorable situation of the Jews was created also in the provinces. . . . While applying the Law for the Defense of the Nation, the attitude toward the Jews at general should be one of justice and humanity—a virtue that for centuries is inherent in the soul of the Bulgarian people.

The last to speak for the church was Stefan who dwelled on his "misunderstanding" with Filov about the treatment of the christened Jews. But he didn't forget to stress again: "I strongly intercede with the Supreme state authority to listen to the voice and the request of the Church and give instructions for the easing of the Law for the Defense of the Nation, and for its implementation with good will, humanity and justice."[27]

Prime Minister Filov, who spoke for the government, angrily pointed out that "the Parliament is against the Jews, and that the full powers that it had given the government [on the Jewish question] have been given specially with the directive to aggravate the Jewish situation." He also noted that written statements should be avoided.

As a whole, Filov was very pleased with the meeting.

> The king made a very good and detailed statement on the Jewish question, and stressed that it was not only ours, but all-European. . . . I pointed at the enormous propaganda done by the Jews, and that one shouldn't act on the force of rumors. At general, on the Jewish question, we were attacking and the prelates mostly had to defend themselves.

Summing up the meeting, Filov said: "The prelates were very meek and didn't use many arguments we had expected."

He was wrong. The prelates were meek, indeed, and called the meeting "a historic one." Still, Neofit concluded his report about it by saying: "If there is going to be any positive result of this meeting? That remains to be seen."[28]

●  ●  ●

The meeting didn't result in the expected relief for the Jews, and the struggle of the Church against the government's Jewish policy soon resumed. In their meetings, the Metropolitans dismissed most of the king's and the prime minister's arguments against the Jews and adopted an even stronger position against the ZZN and the deportation. In the following months the Saint Synod's leaders sharply criticized the anti-Jewish restrictions, over and over again, and dispatched letters and statements to Filov, stirring his anger.

# CHAPTER FOURTEEN

# BELEV'S DEVIOUS PLAN

hough he had failed to deport eight thousand Bulgarian Jews, Belev had not given up. In fact, he now set a bigger goal: to deport all the fifty thousand Jews living in the kingdom.

Subtly, deviously, he began preliminary preparations. He asked that every Jew in Bulgaria submit a detailed "Family card" so that his assistants could draw complete lists of the Jews in the country, including their addresses and the number of dependents in each family.[1] He then carried out a full census of Sofia's Jews—under the pretext that it was for statistical purposes—in order to update the addresses of the Jewish population.[2] He obtained, through Gabrovski, a budget for the acquisition of wooden huts—to lodge twenty-five hundred people—in order to build in a short period of time a transit site or a concentration camp "for people of Jewish origin."[3] He also met secretly with German embassy officials out of Sofia, to quietly prepare the new operation.[4] He was confident that this time the deportation would take place.

Lily Panitza, who continued to secretly meet with Buko Levi, tried to warn him. "You shouldn't fall asleep on your laurels," she said. "Your successes [in thwarting the March 10 deportation] shouldn't make you think that your struggle is over. On the contrary, Belev has plans to carry on his battle against the Jews, and won't stay put."[5]

Still, Belev didn't suspect that the king's policy toward the Jews had shifted.

He was not the only one to make that mistake. Filov, who was much closer to the king, also misjudged Boris's intentions. Filov didn't realize that the king had made a clear distinction between the deportation from Bulgaria's old boundaries, which he had canceled, and the deportation from Thrace and Macedonia, which, in a message to Metropolitan Stefan, he defined as "deportation from Hitler's military command."[6*]

Oddly enough, the prime minister was less impressed by the king's refusal to grant Ribbentrop's request to deport the Jews[7] than by his anti-Jewish remarks in his recent conference with the heads of the Holy Synod.[8] Filov even ignored the clearest statement of Boris's position on April 13, when the king had instructed him and Interior Minister Gabrovski to mobilize the able Jewish men in labor units, thus avoiding the deportation of Bulgaria's Jews to Poland.[9]

In April even the top officials at the German embassy realized that the deportation had become much more complicated. "The solution of the Jewish problem," Hoffman and Dannecker reported to Ambassador Beckerle, "as far as the deportation is concerned, has become much more difficult, since the Jews have been included in the building of roads."[10]

The "road building" triggered an outburst of discontent in the Sicherheitsdienst headquarters in Berlin and apparently reached the Reichsfuhrer SS Himmler himself.[11] His assistant, Bosshammer, called Counselor Von Thadden, a high official at the Ministry of Foreign Affairs in Berlin, and asked him to convey a message from the S.D. (Sicherheitsdienst) to Ambassador Beckerle in Sofia. Three days later, a letter repeating the major points Bosshammer had made over the phone was dispatched to Von Thadden by an SS officer named

---

* It is more than curious that while officially the king and his government claimed that Thrace and Macedonia had been returned to Bulgaria, he secretly admitted that they were under Hitler's military occupation, thus accepting the German version that these territories were only administered by the Bulgarians at that time.

Gunther. Its style and contents reveal the impatience of Himmler with his Bulgarian allies.

After the deportation to the East of 11,500 Jews from the new territories occupied by Bulgaria, there remain in the boundaries of old Bulgaria 51,000 Jews who constitute a danger for the German defense forces' rear, in the south-east area.

As a main reason against their deportation to the East, King Boris pointed out . . . among others, that these Jews are needed . . . for work in Bulgaria and cannot be ceded.

So far, 6,000 Jews [men] have been mobilized. Probably 8,000 more will report to work soon. This means, that in the near future the entire able Jewish population will be included in the Bulgarian work effort.

By this the entire Jewish population in Bulgaria will be secured. The separation of families isn't wanted, and doesn't serve the main problem of the final solution.

The efficiency of the Jewish work in road and railroad building has been minimal so far. For instance: in the Stara region 2,000 Jews have been assigned under the command of a Bulgarian crew lacking political training, so that they work a few hours a day and can have a very pleasant life. . . . Near the Jewish camp there is a Greek camp. Unlike the Jews the Greeks must work up to 12 hours a day.

The Commissar of Jewish questions himself believes that the mobilization of Jews in work units has not achieved a good result. . . . It must be stressed that the inclusion of Jews in the work effort [is used] by the Bulgarian government [as] the overall reason against the German demand for their deportation to the East, in order to prevent its execution on time.*

---

* In many cases, the Jews worked hard and were harshly treated. In many camps, though, the regime was mild, good relations were established between the

Because of the interest of the Reichsfuhrer SS [Himmler] in an immediate application of the final solution, the recent assassination in Sofia should be used during the German-Bulgarian talks on the deportation to the East, [to obtain] the deportation of all the Bulgarian Jews.[12]

The assassination Himmler was alluding to had taken place a few days before. The victim was a radio operator, Kulcho Yanakiev, who also was a German agent. (Actually, it was only an assassination attempt, as Kulcho Yanakiev survived the attack.) It was the last in a series of political coups carried by Communist underground fighters. In February a team of partisans, including the Jewess Violeta Yakova, had killed General Lukov, leader of the right-wing Legionnaires and a former minister of war. In April, another young man, Nikola Draganov, assassinated Parliament member Sotir Yanev, a staunch anti-Communist supporter of the government. In May, Colonel Atanas Pantev, the former police chief, who had ordered the beating and torture of many Communists, was also assassinated. None of the partisans were captured for a long while.

This time, however, Yanakiev's aggressor was apprehended. He was a Jew, Menahem Papo, who was subsequently tried and executed. The SS immediately requested that the murder be used for propaganda purposes, to prepare public opinion for the deportation of the Jews from Bulgaria.

On May 10, even before Gunther's letter to Von Thadden, Dannecker came to Beckerle and requested that he renew the effort for the deportation of the Jews, following the capture of the Jewish terrorist. Beckerle said they should wait, as the Bulgarians themselves might now speed the process.[13]

He was right. On May 15, Gabrovski revealed to the press that Yanakiev's assailant was a Sofia Jew. Furthermore, he said that a

---

Bulgarian officers and the Jews, and they posed smilingly together for the nearest city photographers. The author's father spent long months in a labor camp but quite often got furloughs or simply escaped for a few days, which he spent with his family. Nobody punished him for that.

group of seven terrorists were captured in the Danube port of Russe. Six of them, he stressed, were Jewish.[14]

By making that statement, Gabrovski was fulfilling the German expectations. He was preparing the terrain for a new deportation attempt. Like Filov, he apparently had failed to understand King Boris's real intention. Otherwise, this fanatic, but cautious man, wouldn't have authorized his subordinate Belev to prepare a much more ambitious and radical plan for the deportation of Bulgaria's Jews.

*A German soldier directing traffic in the center of Sofia.*

Belev submitted his new plan to Gabrovski in early May 1943. The plan was clear and thorough.[15] It was based on secrecy, deceit, and speed. It outlined a fiendish plan with surgical precision.

Belev began by defining the plan's purpose: "the deportation of all Jews out of the kingdom." There were a few exceptions—Jews who were foreign nationals, Jews married to non-Jews, Jews mobilized for vital government tasks, and Jews suffering from infectious diseases.

The Bulgarian Jews were to be deported to the Eastern regions of Germany (the term used for Poland), by September 30, 1943. The plan projected the deportation of 25,000 Jews from Sofia and another 23,000 from the provinces. The Jews would be handed to the Germans in the Danube ports, mainly Lom and Somovit. The rate would be 16,000 a month, starting May 30. By that date, all the Bulgarian Jews would already be concentrated in transit camps. They would be shipped by rail from their hometowns to those camps and from the camps to the Danube ports. Boats under Bulgarian guard would take the deportees to Vienna.

The plan specified the number of Jews to be taken from each city in the provinces, besides the 25,000 Sofia Jews. It devised a method to convince the Jews that the deportation was only from Sofia to the provinces. In the first stage the Sofia Jews would be taken by train to provincial cities, where they would be lodged in schools or Jewish houses. They would be told that the deportation stops there. The local authorities would be informed twenty-four hours before the arrival of the trains, in order to prepare the schools. Then, at a date chosen in advance, the local Jews would be rounded up as well, their homes would be sealed, and they too would be transferred to transit camps. The same day, together with the Sofia Jews, their transport to Lom and Somovit would begin.

The trains would be able to transport 10,000 Jews a week. In Lom, Somovit, Tziber, and a few other places the Jews would be lodged in camps for a short period, then board the boats on their way to Poland.

Belev detailed every aspect of the deportation, including food, health services, police control, and transportation. He also prepared instructions to the train authority, circulars to the KEV clerks, and reports to Gabrovski and the government, taking all possibilities into account.

In the middle of May 1943, it seemed that Belev had won. His plan had been accepted by Gabrovski, the organization was in place, and the deportation was scheduled for the last week of the month. In a few days Sofia's Jews would leave their homes and head for the deportation trains.

CHAPTER FIFTEEN

# DESPAIR

On May 18, 1943, Liliana Panitza met again with Dr. Nissim (Buko) Levi. This time, she informed him that Commissar Belev had completed his plan to deport all of Bulgaria's Jews to Poland. The first to go would be the Sofia Jews. Buko Levi immediately alerted the leaders of the Jewish community, who met on May 19 in the office of Leon Farhi, a renowned Sofia lawyer. Nobody had any doubt that the deportation meant certain death.

The Jewish leaders understood they had only a few days left. The countdown had begun. Early in the morning of May 20 the Jewish leaders learned that the expulsion papers of Sofia's Jews were already being printed. The resourceful Leon Farhi contacted a worker in the government printing office and procured the form containing the expulsion orders. The form stated that the deportees should be ready to leave the capital in three days.[1]

That afternoon the Jewish leaders learned that a large part of the Sofia Police Criminal Investigation Department was put under Belev's direct orders. Telephone calls to the KEV were not answered. Important police forces were deployed around the building, a four-story gray house on Boulevard Dondukov.[2]

That same evening Liliana Panitza again met Buko Levi. She informed him that all the employees at the KEV had been ordered not to leave their offices, and everybody was busy filling out the forms with the names of the Sofia Jews.[3]

Wild rumors spread like fire in the Jewish community: A cur-few was about to be announced; a pogrom was imminent; a police raid on the Jewish homes would start at midnight; boats were wait-ing at the Danube ports to pick up the Jews; transit camps outside the ports were being built.

Many Sofia Jews barricaded themselves in their homes, behind closed shutters and locked doors. The leaders of the Jewish commu-nity tried to keep their cool, meeting at different cafés and later in private homes, to decide what to do.

At 6:00 A.M. on May 21, the Jews living in some Sofia suburbs began receiving the expulsion orders. They were instructed to be ready to leave Sofia in three days, with only "the most essential bag-gage." They had to make a detailed list of the furniture and the per-sonal effects they were leaving behind, and remit it, together with the keys to their homes, to the KEV representatives. The names of the family members were listed, and precise instructions were given for the date, the time, the train number, and the destination of their trip. In an unconscious expression of black humor, the Jews were informed that they would be traveling "for free" to their destination.

The destinations printed on the orders stirred a new wave of panic. Vidin. Lom. Russe. These were Danube ports. Other destina-tions were Pleven, Razgrad, Vratza, Shumen, towns in the north of the country, directly connected by rail to one of the Danube ports. Finally, a large number of destinations were border cities, like Kyustendil. Everything led to the conclusion that they would be taken out of the country.

Desperate Jews gathered by the Jewish community offices. Someone brought his expulsion order carrying the number 2000, another one had the number 2600. The numbers were rising, and this meant that everybody would be included in the deportation. Many rushed to the stores, to buy suitcases and backpacks. Chaos and frus-tration spread through the poor Jewish neighborhood of Yuch Bunar. People were crying in the streets, bidding farewell to Jewish and Bulgarian friends. Families were split, as the elderly parents received expulsion orders to one city, while their grown children were sent elsewhere. A feeling of helplessness pervaded the younger people, who desperately wanted to defend themselves. Around noon the news of the first suicide spread throughout the crowds.

In the afternoon the community leaders were ordered by the KEV to form a committee that would receive from the deported families the keys to their homes and the lists of their belongings. But many Jews began selling their home furnishings, to avoid delivering them to the authorities. Peasants from neighboring villages descended upon the Jewish neighborhoods, gleefully loading on their carts furniture, clothes, and kitchenware they bought for pennies. Jewish women, crying aloud, piled outside their homes their most precious belongings, now for sale.

In hectic meetings the community leaders tried to establish a plan of action. The panic and despair that had swept through the community affected them as well. Whom should they ask for help? Peshev and his friends had been crushed. Bulgarian friends promised help, but Filov and Gabrovski were inaccessible. The leadership decided to dispatch Dr. Buko Levi and Jack Pardo to establish contact with powerful palace figures. Colonel Tadjer was sent to the leaders of the Saint Synod of the Church.[4] Several women undertook the mission of meeting with Ekaterina Karavelova, the eighty-year-old widow of legendary Prime Minister Karavelov, a woman of immense prestige and influence, also known as "Mother of the Royal Court." She had been the leader of Bulgaria's women for years. Her daughter had been married to a Jew, who was later assassinated. Mrs. Karavelova freely visited the royal palace and was deeply respected by the king. Others were instructed to meet with the wife of the Macedonian revolutionary organization's leader, and several influential Bulgarian women—writers and public figures.

Braving the curfew, the emissaries left the meeting late at night. They spread through the city, on their way to the homes of eminent Bulgarians, moving like shadows through dark alleys and connecting courtyards to avoid the police patrols.[5]

On May 22 alarming news arrived from Lom. Several schools had been commandeered and prepared to accommodate great numbers of people. The governor had bought great quantities of food. A large number of ships had arrived at the port. Later in the day, similar news came from Russe and Vidin.

In Sofia, the KEV made clear that there would be no exception to the deportation. War invalids and families of Jews working at labor camps received expulsion orders just like everybody else. Several families were able to obtain a delay of twenty-four to forty-eight hours by bribing KEV employees. Other desperate Jews hurriedly converted to Christianity, hoping to save their lives.[6]

Jewish leaders still rushed throughout Sofia, trying to raise support. Benyamin Arditi and a friend met with the Papal Nunzio, who promised to speak to Queen Giovanna.

The queen felt deeply for the suffering of the Jewish population and had several times discreetly intervened on behalf of some individual Jews. At the opening of an Italian exhibition in Sofia, the previous year, she had furtively whispered to the Italian ambassador, Count Magistrati, that she urgently needed Italian passports for some Jewish people. The Italian diplomat hesitated, as Jews were not allowed to move to Italy, but Giovanna was firm, promising that they would only pass through Italy on their way to Argentina. The passports were delivered, with transit visas to Argentina, and the lives of these people were saved.[7] The queen had also contributed a large quantity of woolen clothing to a charity distribution, organized by Boris's sister, Princess Evdokia, because she had told Giovanna it was for Bulgarian Jews.[8]

Filov's wife, the cynical, presumptuous and pro-German Evdokia Filova, sarcastically noted in her diary some instances in which the queen had shown her sympathy for the Jews. In February 1942, Queen Giovanna had been invited to visit a German exhibit, organized by the propaganda ministry of the Reich. Frau Beckerle, the German ambassador's wife, escorted the queen and Evdokia Filova and tried to show the queen a display of anti-Semitic books. The queen cut her with a remark: *"Das interessiert mich nicht"* ("I am not interested in this.")[9]

In March 1943, Filova wrote, three former ministers' wives had informed the queen "that the Jews from the new territories have been sent to Poland with utmost cruelty, and the queen had cried a lot." Mrs. Filova cynically added that these three women went to speak about this cruel treatment of the Jews not so much out of empathy but out of frustration and opposition to the government.[10]

The Jews believed that the king was also staunchly opposed to the Nazi measures. They knew he was not an anti-Semite. Like the queen, he had taken discreet action on behalf of Jews in danger. The KEV employees knew of several cases in which the king had intervened on behalf of individual Jews and families.[11] Some Jews, who had close ties to the palace, had even been helped to escape and received support when they were abroad.[12] Yet, the king had not acted publicly on behalf of the entire Jewish community.

While hoping that the palace would help at this desperate moment, Jewish leaders also met with foreign diplomats, writers, and politicians. Promises of support came from all over, but nothing changed, and the countdown continued.

After another night of despair and secret meetings, a bit of good news finally reached the Jewish leaders on May 23. Colonel Damian Velchev had called for a large meeting at his home to discuss ways of opposing the deportation. Velchev was an eminent political leader (who had been sentenced to death in 1936 and obtained the king's grace, partly thanks to the justice minister at the time—Dimiter Peshev). That day he had invited an impressive array of personalities: several former prime ministers and ministers, professors, writers, clerics, and other public figures. They wrote a somber letter to the king, describing the expulsion of Jews from Sofia that might lead to an expulsion from the country. "This inhuman measure, which doesn't become the spirit of our peace-loving people, can be cancelled only by Your Majesty, because Your Majesty is the government. Otherwise the full responsibility will fall on Your Majesty."[13]

Twenty-three people signed the letter. In the following days Velchev and his friends collected another forty signatures.[14]

Several other letters were sent to the king that day. Communist party activists surreptitiously distributed flyers calling the Bulgarian population to oppose the deportation.[15] Communist and allied radio stations broadcast appeals and warnings to Bulgaria.

News came from the royal palace. Dr. Khandjiev, the king's adviser, "wasn't pessimistic." Encouraging news came from the Saint Synod as well. Sofia's Metropolitan Stefan announced that the Church would strongly oppose the deportation.

But all this was to no avail. Joseph Geron, the president of Sofia's Jewish community, accompanied by a friend, was admitted to Alexander Belev's office. He begged the commissar to cancel or delay at least the deportation of families whose male members were in labor camps.

Belev was sharp and aggressive as always: "There will be no exception," he said. "Not a single Jew will remain in Sofia." Then he added, staring at Geron: "You too are on the list!"

"I'll share the fate of my people," Geron answered, "but I'll be the last to leave Sofia, after all her Jews are gone."[16]

That same day, in a friend's house, Belev announced: "The fate of Bulgaria's Jews is sealed!"[17] Filov, too, informed his friends that the decision to deport the Jews was final.

And the king was nowhere to be found. He had vanished from his palace.

That afternoon, a long line of Jews formed before Sofia's central synagogue, where the lists of furniture and household goods were deposited. Later, during a prayer service, somebody spread the news that the following day a huge Jewish protest was planned.

The mass prayer ended in an atmosphere of impending doom. Benyamin Arditi, one of the most active leaders of the community, walked home depressed and dejected. He wrote:

> Maybe that is our last prayer together. It is a wonderful May evening in Sofia. The sun spreads its last beams, which sneak into the almost abandoned houses, as if they want to caress and cheer the moving shadows . . . Not far from the city rises Mount Vitosha, its hulk becoming gray in the twilight . . . Then it becomes black, obscure, silent. Like a sphinx it hovers over the city, as if guessing the fate of the doomed people. Night is falling over the city . . . One more day, then the deportation starts.[18]

May 24 was a glorious, sunny day. Ironically, it was also an important Bulgarian holiday—Saints Kyril and Methodius day, named after the two priests who invented the Cyrillic alphabet. It was a popular celebration of learning and culture. Traditionally, thousands of students gathered at Alexander Nevski Square, where the sixth century St. Sofia basilica and the magnificent Alexander Nevski cathedral dominate the entire city. A ceremony was held in the vast square, then a public prayer followed by an address by the head of the Sofia church, the Metropolitan Stefan. The prime minister and his cabinet participated at the celebration. After the ceremony the students and the youth organizations formed a parade; it marched to the royal palace. There the king would welcome the parade and make a short speech.

The day before, the community leaders had discussed a mass protest in Sofia's streets. This morning, they met at 7:00 A.M. at the home of Vitali Haimov and decided to cancel the protest. They feared that a noisy protest in the streets might interfere with the discreet efforts to obtain a cancellation of the orders. They also feared that the Jewish protest might clash with the official parade, in which the Fascist youth organization Brannik and other anti-Semitic elements took part. Belev might use the protest, some pointed out, as a pretext to unleash his hoods against the Jews.

Therefore, they decided to lock the gates of the central synagogue, where thousands of Jews were to assemble, and to tell them to disperse and go home. This decision, however, was not conveyed to the second Sofia rabbi, Daniel Tzion.

Rabbi Daniel Tzion was a strange figure. He was a squat elderly man with a short grizzled beard. A fearless, fiery scholar, he was a mystic and an expert on comparative theology. Rabbi Tzion was a passionate student of other religions and religious sects and had close connections with the leaders of the Dunovist sect.[10] It was said that the king himself was influenced by that sect and might have been a secret member.

Many Jewish leaders treated Rabbi Tzion with suspicion because of his mysticism and his connections with the Dunovists. Their reticence toward him had grown a year ago, when he announced that he had heard a message from God, warning the Bulgarian leaders against persecuting the Jews. He wrote down the message, made several copies, and brought them to the king and several government ministers, members of Parliament, and the chief of police.

Most of the recipients of "God's message" treated Tzion with respect. Metropolitan Stefan told the rabbi he was sure the message came from God indeed. Rabbi Tzion went to the royal palace and told the king's chancellor that he had come to warn King Boris not to stir God's wrath against him and the entire land. The chancellor took the message to the monarch; a few days later he informed the rabbi that Boris had assured him the Jews wouldn't be sent out of Bulgaria's territory.[20]

Others, though, had not liked the rabbi's unorthodox activities, and the leaders of the Jewish community had been summoned to police headquarters, to explain the behavior of Daniel Tzion. In an effort to placate the authorities, the Jewish leaders officially fired the rabbi from his position on the religious court, but this didn't cool his ardent activities against the government's policy.

After the distribution of the expulsion orders, Rabbi Tzion had met his friend Lulchev. The king's advisor had agreed that the situation was grave and suggested that the Jews organize a huge protest and declare May 24 as a day of fast and prayer. Rabbi Tzion had brought Lulchev's suggestion to the Jewish community leaders, and they had initially accepted it.[21]

On May 24, at 5:00 A.M., the rabbi, escorted by Menahem Moshonov, met Lulchev at the Dunovist praying ground in Eastern Sofia. The king's adviser encouraged Daniel Tzion to go ahead with the planned demonstration.

But when the rabbi reached the central Sofia synagogue, he found the gates locked. A throng of Jews was waiting outside, blocking the street. The janitor refused to open the synagogue, saying he had received orders not to do so. Tzion didn't want to openly confront the leadership of the community. Thus, he led the huge crowd, which had assembled by the synagogue, to a smaller synagogue in Yuch Bunar, a few blocks away. Tzion led the crowd in a prayer and was joined by Sofia's chief rabbi, Asher Hananel.

Rabbi Hananel also supported the idea of a demonstration that would march to the king's palace and beg for mercy. He was surprised to find the gates of the central synagogue locked.[22] Both rabbis spoke to the congregation. People were crying. "Put your trust in God!" Rabbi Tzion said.[23] And Hananel added: "Why do you cry? You are the descendants of the Maccabees . . . I know what awaits us. I declare that Sofia's cemetery is more beautiful than any other cemetery. You know what you have to do. Let the trains leave empty, we shall stay here, we shall not go to the slaughter."[24] Rabbi Hananel probably expected the Jews to resist getting on the trains, even if they were killed in the process.

As the prayer ended, Rabbi Hananel and Rabbi Tzion were told that a few Jews had met with Metropolitan Stefan, who had promised to help them. Hananel and Tzion decided to turn to him as well and organized a small delegation that went to Stefan's home.

Shortly before, the Metropolitan had left his residence, on his way to Alexander Nevski Square. He already was dressed in his gold-embroidered vestments, which he would wear at the Kyril and Methodius ceremony. In the street, a large crowd of Jews, wearing yellow stars, surrounded him. They told him of cruel raids against the Jews, of persecutions and arrests since the early morning. Stefan was shocked and immediately agreed to receive a delegation. The celebration could wait. He went back to his home, and a few minutes later the rabbis arrived.[25]

He warmly greeted his guests and invited them in. Rabbi Hananel said to him: "We are not leaving the country. We are ready to die. Please tell His Majesty that we are ready to give our blood, but here, in Bulgaria, not outside the country."

The Metropolitan was distressed. "The bitterness and the fear, painted on the faces of my visitors because of this cruel persecution, happening on the brightest day for our homeland, revered and celebrated by the Jews and the Bulgarians alike, brought tears to my eyes."[26] He addressed the two rabbis. "The situation is critical," he agreed. "But what shall we do if His Majesty doesn't come to the parade today?"[27]

He immediately got in touch with the palace, "in order to protest against this cruelty and appeal for immediate intervention" (apparently Metropolitan Stefan telephoned the palace but didn't go there, as some historians have written). He was told that the king had left Sofia. He then asked to speak with the head of the royal chancellery, Pavel Gruev. He informed him that a delegation of Jews was in his house, that the courtyard and the street also were full of Jews, who had come to ask for the protection of the Church, and that they came to ask for mercy and justice. Stefan continued:

> I decided to ask His Majesty to say His powerful and decisive word: Enough! This absolutely unjustified persecution throws a stain on the bright outlook of our great holiday. The cries and the tears of the slighted Bulgarian citizens of Jewish origin are a lawful protest against the injustice done to them. It should be heard and complied with by the king of the Bulgarians. I ask the king now, more than ever, to show wisdom and statesmanlike foresight, in the defense of the rights of men to freedom and dignity, which the Bulgarian people has always cherished, by tradition and by spirit.[28]

Gruev promised to deliver Stefan's message and suggested that he speak to the prime minister at the holiday celebration. In that matter, he said, Filov was the most competent authority.[29]

Stefan turned to Ms. Lora Farhi, a young woman who was a member of the delegation. "My child," he said, "take your friends to Mrs. Karavelova, who is like a mother to King Boris. Tell her that I support your action."[30] He also suggested that the delegation met with the Catholic priest Romanov, the queen's spiritual father.[31]

The delegation immediately went to Mrs. Karavelova's house. "The Mother of the Royal Court" welcomed them and listened to Rabbi Hananel's plea. She burst into tears, took the rabbi by the hand, and led him to her study. "My son," she said, "here is a pen, here is ink. Please write down what you said to me, and I'll send it to the King."[32]

In his letter, Rabbi Hananel repeated that Bulgaria's Jews were ready to sacrifice their lives for Bulgaria, but within Bulgaria's borders, not outside them; he asked the king to cancel the deportation. Mrs. Karavelova, with a trembling hand, added a phrase to the king: "My son, you too are a father. Don't do wrong to anybody." She then countersigned the letter, which was immediately sent to the royal palace.[33]

Metropolitan Stefan now went to Alexander Nevski Church and walked out to the square. He was an impressive, dominant figure, as he stood on the podium facing the huge square—a large, bearded man, dressed in a resplendent clerical robe, exuding authority and spiritual leadership. Most of the government ministers were present at the ceremony. From the elevated podium, Stefan led the prayer. At its conclusion he spoke to the large crowd massed before the church. In past years, he said, Jewish students always participated at the Saints Kyril and Methodius celebration.

> This year our celebration is flawed by the persecution undertaken against the Jews. [This year our celebration] is not according to tradition, because the Jewish students are absent. I send from this high place an appeal to the state authorities to not enslave the freedom-loving, democratic and friendly Bulgarian spirit . . . to foreign indoctrination, influences, and orders.[34]

Stefan's criticism of the German hold on Bulgaria couldn't be clearer. Then, in spite of the angry stares of the ministers boring into his back, he strongly condemned the persecution of the Jews as contrary to the traditional spirit of the Bulgarian people. "In this holiday of our great teachers I beg those who steer the ship of our state, to remove any policy of estrangement, division and persecution."[35]

After the parade of the students, Stefan had a short conversation with Filov, but the prime minister bluntly rejected his demand and told him to stop interfering. "The law concerning Bulgaria's Jews," Filov formally said, "is a State necessity, and as such will not be cancelled and will be fully implemented."[36] When they parted,

Filov warned Stefan to stop bothering the king and the government with interventions concerning the law against the Jews.

Stefan didn't heed the warning. Later in the day, news reached him that the raids against the Jews were continuing, and many of those who had come to seek his protection that morning had been arrested and sent to jails before deportation to concentration camps and perhaps abroad. The rabbis were arrested too, he was told. Deeply disturbed, he wrote a detailed letter to the king, and asked him "to put an end to this act of vandalism, which is a real scandal for the Bulgarians who love peace and their fellow men." Stefan stressed that his appeal was based on the fundamental principles of Christianity, humanity, patriotism, and democracy. He asked the king "to stop the implementation of the anti-Jewish law and order its full cancellation . . . By this august act, Your Majesty, you would remove the suspicion that Bulgaria is a prisoner of Hitler's anti-Jewish policy."

The king was not in Sofia. Still, he sent an oral answer, which the head of his chancellery delivered to Stefan. (It is not clear whether the king's answer reached Metropolitan Stefan the same day or on the following day.) Boris III stressed that:

> after Stefan's first letter He had given the order to treat well the deportees from Thrace, in spite of the fact that they were deportees from Hitler's Military Command. Now His Majesty again will take Stefan's appeal into account, to relieve to the maximum the treatment of the Jews in the course of the implementation of the law concerning their fate and their rights in our country.

As far as the law itself was concerned, the king answered that it had been passed by the government and was a result of Bulgaria's commitment to her ally, Germany. The king hinted that he was not free to cancel the law by himself.[37]

The royal chancellery rushed Stefan's letter to Filov as well. The prime minister angrily warned Stefan to stop intervening on behalf of the Jews and let the Commissariat for Jewish Questions fulfill its duties. The Metropolitan was also informed that the attorney general was preparing to sue him for "anti-State activity."[38] He was not impressed. He sent a sharp protest to the king, but this time he got no answer. "This was the only case in my long relationship with the king," he noted, "that was marked by silence and haughtiness; nevertheless, the convoy [meaning Stefan's intervention in favor of the Jews] continued its progress on the road of its duty."[39]

(COURTESY OF BULGARIAN STATE ARCHIVES)

*Nikola Mushanov.*

• • •

Later that day two other brave Bulgarians went to see Filov. Former Prime Minister Nikola Mushanov and his friend and colleague Professor Petko Staynov demanded that Filov "cancel the cruel measures against the Jews." They said the action was "inhuman and unconstitutional," besides being damaging to the State. Filov wouldn't even listen and refused to delay the deportation.[40] Mushanov and Staynov left his office utterly disappointed and hurriedly dispatched a letter of protest to the king.[41]

But in the meantime, a much more powerful drama was taking place in the Jewish Quarter. At the end of the prayer in the Yuch Bunar synagogue, more than a thousand people stood in the courtyard and the street. Some were crying, others were speaking of opposing the deportation by force. A young man, Solomon (Gosho) Leviev, felt that something must be done. He jumped on a bench in the courtyard and made an impromptu speech. "Jewish brothers," he shouted, "we can't accept this situation. Let's go on the street and show that we are Bulgarian patriots!" The public cheered, several young men gathered around Leviev, and they advanced into the street. An aspiring writer, Jacques Melamed, also known as Dragomir Assenov, emerged with a national flag, and fell in step beside Gosho. The assembled Jews joined the demonstration, which turned into the wide Klementina Boulevard, heading for the royal palace.[42] It was a bitter, desperate march, a last attempt to oppose the government's actions, even if it was to end in bloodshed and loss of lives.

It also was exactly what the Jewish establishment feared. A delegation headed by three leaders of the community, Haimov, Finzi, and Arditi, hurried toward the crowd, trying to stop it. They failed. Members of the youth Zionist organizations, Maccabee and Betar, formed human chains and tried to contain the crowd.[43]

They failed as well. The front line of the protesters clashed with them at the street corner and continued their march. They advanced a few blocks to the corner of Opelchenska Street, when suddenly they were confronted by large forces of armed police, who had been waiting for them.[44] The police had been brought over in buses. They were soon joined by police on motorcycles and horse-mounted detachments. They hurled themselves on the crowd, beating the protesters with rifle butts, submachine guns, and whips. Wounded women and children fell in the middle of the street, KEV plainclothes agents threw men into covered vans, and police officers ran after the protesters who escaped into the smaller streets leading away from the melee. About 250 men were arrested on the spot, another 120 were taken away from their homes a few hours later, and orders for the arrest of the two chief rabbis and the leaders of the Jewish community were issued right away. By midnight, 412 Jews had been arrested.[45] That was the end of the spontaneous protest of May 24.

Actually, it had not been spontaneous. Most of the participants in the protest didn't know the full truth about it. Nor did the leaders of the Jewish community.

A few days before, a Jewish Communist woman, Nastia Isakova, came to see Betty Danon, the secretary of the Yuch Bunar Communist party branch. The Communist party had been banned, and its activists were in constant danger of arrest, torture, and death. Betty was Jewish as well, and wanted by the police for her Communist activities. Nastia was working with Communist leader Zola Dragoitcheva. She also was very close with Rabbi Daniel Tzion. She said to Betty: "Rabbi Daniel wants to hold a prayer for the rescue of the Jews. We want to bring people to the event."[46]

(COURTESY OF PEKO TABOV)

*Vulka Goranova, who directed the Communist's secret participation in the protest against Jewish deportation on May 24, 1943.*

Betty Danon tried to establish contact with Todor Jivkov, the future Communist president of Bulgaria, who was at the time the secretary of the Communist party third Sofia district. Jivkov was very sympathetic to the Jewish cause and had written the first Communist flyer against the persecution of the Jews. But Jivkov was nowhere to be found.

Betty then turned to Vulka Goranova, a member of the Sofia regional committee of the Communist party. Vulka was a legendary figure, carrying out her illegal party activities in spite of two death sentences hanging over her head. Vulka immediately realized the importance of the projected protest. "You must bring as many people as you can to the mass prayer," Vulka said. Vulka herself recruited quite a few non-Jews in the first and second districts of the party.[47]

Betty called three women—Betty Astruk, Matti Nehardea, and Stella Benvenisti—all of them members of her party branch. They spent the night of May 23 sneaking from house to house in Yuch

Bunar, knocking on doors and asking people to join the prayer and the protest the following day.

Neither Betty nor Vulka could participate at the protest, as the party did not allow them to appear in public, because of the danger for their lives. But many of their friends were there, including Gosho, the fiery speaker whose words triggered the protest. Gosho was a member of the RMS, the young Communist organization.[48]

The Communists saw the protest as their main effort in defense of the Jews. In future years all the official Communist historians would describe the protest as a tremendous success, while Jewish leaders and independent observers would stress that it was dispersed a few blocks from its starting point. Some claim that the same night, Commissar Belev came to see some of the arrested Jews, who were held in a school, and said mockingly: "You made it easy for me to complete my task."[49]

•  •  •

When the orders for the rabbis' arrests were issued, both Tzion and Hananel were not to be found. Rabbi Tzion had returned from the meeting with Stefan, said a few words to the people assembled at the synagogue, then returned home before the protest started. He was immediately arrested, driven in a police car to police headquarters, then sent with many other prisoners to the detention camp at Somovit, where they were treated very harshly.[50]

Rabbi Hananel had disappeared. He had not participated in the protest. But when he telephoned his wife she told him: "The police are looking for you. Don't come home."[51]

He sneaked through side streets and reached his mother's home. He was lucky. As he approached the house, he saw police officers leaving it. He spent the night at his mother's home, while police agents waited for him outside his apartment. Certain sources claim that he found shelter, at least for a while, in the home of Metropolitan Stefan.[52]

Early in the morning of May 25, Rabbi Hananel returned to his home and was arrested right away. His wife rushed to Metropolitan Stefan to beg for his help. The Metropolitan showed her a telegram he had just sent to the king: "Don't persecute, lest you be persecuted yourself. With the same measure you measure others, you'll be measured yourself. Know, Boris, that God is watching your acts from Heaven."[53]

After spending the whole day in police headquarters, Rabbi Asher Hananel was taken to the KEV. Liliana Panitza escorted him to Alexander Belev's office.

As the rabbi walked in, Belev started yelling at him:

> You, the Jews, why do you try to influence the Crown and the government? Don't you know that we are the Crown and the government? That we don't do anything without the Crown? You have asked for the intervention of Metropolitan Stefan. We don't respect this Metropolitan, we hate him! You, together with the Anglo-Saxons, are undermining the existence of our Fatherland!

Hananel couldn't restrain himself:

> Mr. Commissar, you have no right to insult us like that. I am a Bulgarian officer, I fought in the wars, I shed my blood for this Fatherland, I was wounded . . . I carry the Cross of Valor, and this Fatherland is mine as much as it is yours.

Belev was beside himself: "Your words are good for Metropolitan Stefan. They don't impress me."

Belev plunged into a long diatribe against the Jews and their activities on the black market. But he suddenly blurted his angriest and most significant words: "You have to be grateful that you have support, strong support. Otherwise I would have arrested you like all your community and priests, and sent you to Germany!"[54]

Reluctantly, Belev ended the conversation: "You are free, but I warn you. You're under house arrest, and you won't get in touch with the authorities except through me and my organization."

Hananel walked out of the KEV building and into the balmy Sofia night. He didn't immediately realize what Belev had actually told him, speaking of "the strong support" for which the Jews had to be "grateful."

On the morning of May 26, the deportation of Sofia's Jews begun. The well-oiled machinery of the KEV and the police operated efficiently. In twelve days—between May 26 and June 7—19,153 Jews were deported from Sofia to the provinces. They were lodged in schools or other public buildings or shared the homes of the local Jewish population. Their living conditions were poor and, in some cases, became deplorable, but they all managed to survive.

Out of the 5,856 Jews who remained in the city, 3,500 were actually already in forced labor camps outside of Sofia, and their deportation was deferred until their return. The remaining 2,300 were mostly foreign nationals, people working in vital government industries, or war heroes.[55] Rabbi Hananel was among the latter.

In the following days more letters and petitions were sent to the court. Rabbi Hananel himself went to the Swiss embassy and obtained promises for help. There is no record, though, of a Swiss intervention at that time. In addition to the appeal of Damian Velchev, signed by sixty-three public figures, other statements and petitions were delivered to the court and some government offices.

A few weeks later the Apostolic Nuncio in Istanbul, Monsignor Angelo Roncalli (the future Pope John XXIII), sent a letter to the king pleading for some Jewish families. His letter, although tainted by an anti-Semitic hint, was a noble humanitarian step, especially in those days when the Catholic church tried to ignore the sorry fate of the Jews.

> I know that it is only too true—according to what I read coming out of Bulgaria—that some of the sons of Judah are not without reproach. But alongside the guilty, there are also many who are innocent; and there are many

cases where some sign of clemency, over and above the great honor it would bring to the dignity of a Christian sovereign, would be a pledge of blessings in time of trial.

King Boris replied to the letter verbally, through the Vatican's representatives in Sofia. Roncalli wrote on the copy of the letter:

> Il Re ha fatto qualche cosa ("The king has done something") but he also has his own difficulties, which he asks us to understand. To deal with individual cases arouses the jealousy of others. But I repeat, he has acted.[56]

The Bulgarian lawyers union, which had already protested against the Law of the Defense of the Nation, in 1940, and against the March deportation,[57] now dispatched a letter to Interior Minister Gabrovski, demanding that he cancel the deportation that would "harm the supreme moral values of our country."[58]

A delegation of the Lawyers Union visited Gabrovski and handed him the letter. His answer was firm and tough:

> The measures are taken according to the government's decision of May 21, taking into account . . . the security, the order and the well being of the state, while observing the supreme moral values of the country and protecting and understanding Bulgaria's interests. In the application of these measures, the principles of humanity and fairness are observed."

Still, Gabrovski sternly attacked the Jews for their actions:

> I described to the delegation the behavior of the persons of Jewish origin, their efforts to organize a protest, the disturbance of the peace and the undermining of the measures taken by the authorities, as well as the atmosphere of propaganda that Bulgaria's enemies are trying to create in that matter.[59]

Only years later did the truth about these days come to light. The events of May—the protests, the letters, and the delegations—were a dramatic expression of the support many brave Bulgarians extended to the Jews. But they didn't change the government plans. Even before May 24, King Boris had decided not to send one single Jew out of Bulgarian territory.

# CHAPTER SIXTEEN

# THE KING
# HAS VANISHED

In Belev's deportation plan there is an odd sentence, long gone unnoticed. It concerns the temporary transit camp at Tziber, a stream close to the Danube port of Lom. "If the deportation is not decided upon, a permanent camp will be built at Tziber."[1]

This was the only hint that deportation out of the country might not take place. It came out of several secret discussions between Belev, Gabrovski, Dannecker, and Hoffman. Apparently, the Germans were much more realistic in their assessment of the situation than was Belev. Perhaps because they didn't hold him in high esteem, Beckerle reported to Berlin that "statements made by the Commissar of Jewish Questions shouldn't have been taken verbally. He belongs to one of the opposition groups that are in most extreme opposition to the government . . . I often regarded Belev's measures with the greatest doubt . . ."[2]

Dannecker and Hoffman, therefore, didn't fully share Belev's conviction that the deportation would take place. They feared the deportation plan would be rejected and believed that an alternate plan should be prepared, in order to save face and perhaps achieve at least a partial result. On Dannecker's suggestion, Belev prepared two plans for submission to the king. Plan A: The deportation of all the Bulgarian Jews to the Reich's Eastern regions for reasons of state security.

Plan B: (if plan A was rejected) The expulsion of the Sofia Jews into the provinces.

Both Belev and Dannecker believed that plan B could eventually lead to the later implementation of plan A, as it was easier to deport the Jews from the provinces than from Sofia.[3]

Gabrovski approved Belev's plans and told the Germans that he preferred plan A. He now asked for an audience with the king, in order to submit both plans for his decision. He was invited to come to the palace on May 20, 1943,[4] the same day that Belev requested the printing of the expulsion orders.

This meeting was crucial. It was going to determine the fate of fifty thousand Bulgarian Jews. The audience with the king was short. Gabrovski presented plan A and plan B, as his own plans. He asked for the king's decision. The king immediately rejected plan A.[5]

The deportation of the Jews from Bulgaria was ruled out, even before the first expulsion order reached a Jewish family. However, the king accepted plan B, the deportation of the Jews from Sofia.

Gabrovski left the palace without saying a word to anybody. Neither did the king disclose the results of their conversation. Even his closest advisers remained in the dark. Shortly thereafter, the king vanished from Sofia. (It is not known exactly on what day King Boris disappeared. However, he was absent at least on May 23 and 24.)

For years to come the king would be accused of fleeing Sofia on the eve of the deportation, thus giving control to Belev, Gabrovski, and their German cronies. Political and religious leaders who desperately tried to reach Boris couldn't find him. He even missed, for the first time in his life, the Saints Kyril and Methodius ceremony. The Communists accused him of fleeing Sofia, for fear of the people's wrath—though unwilling to cancel the deportation orders.

The truth is rather different. In 1993 a new testimony was published in a short book written by Sava Djevrev, the king's private driver.[6] Djevrev wasn't a sophisticated man, and his account includes some serious mistakes, based on hearsay and rumors. But it definitely gives us the facts behind Boris's disappearance.

"At that time," Djevrev wrote, "our intellectuals raised their voice in defense of the Jews—to let them stay in Bulgaria and not give them to Hitler."[7] The king didn't meet with the delegations that asked to see him. He called his driver, entered his car, and left Sofia. His valet, Svilen Nikolov, was the only other passenger in the car. They reached Cham-Koriya, a spa close to Rila Mountain, where the king had a palace. They left the car at the Tzarska Bistritza palace; Svilen stayed at the palace. A hunter joined the king and his driver and the three of them climbed to the royal chalet, Yastrebetz, at 2,400 meters (about 7,900 feet.) They stayed in the chalet for three days, without contact with the outside world, except for phone calls the king made by field telephone to Svilen in Tzarska Bistritza. (Some of the calls could have been relayed to the palace in Sofia, and that's how the king might have sent his message of May 24 to Metropolitan Stefan). The king hid in the chalet. He didn't even go hunting, for fear that the shots might attract attention and make his presence known.

After three days, the king, Djevrev, and Svilen returned to Sofia. There, Djevrev learned the true reason about the king's hiding. A very important German had come to Bulgaria on a special plane, Djevrev was told, to obtain the king's signature on a "document from Hitler," to deport the Jews out of Bulgaria. To avoid signing, Boris hid in the mountains.[8] The king, Djevrev stressed, didn't hide from the intellectuals who wanted to intercede for the Jews; he hid from Hitler's envoy.

Yet no German envoy came to Bulgaria in May of 1943. Actually Hitler didn't need such an envoy. If he wanted to pressure Boris to deport the Jews out of the country, a telegram or a telephone call would have been enough.

We believe that this, indeed, was Boris's main fear—to get a telegram or a phone call from Berlin, or to be subjected to any other form of internal or external pressure to change his decision and accept plan A. As he wasn't a strong man and had always tried to evade confrontations, he chose to hide during the fateful days, when a change in his decision might have brought death upon fifty thousand Bulgarian Jews.

• • •

The decision to deport the Jews only to the interior of the country was officially approved by the government in a meeting on May 21, 1943. The government "charges the Commissariat of Jewish Questions to deport the persons of Jewish origin living in Sofia . . . into inhabited areas in the interior of the country.

"This decree is not subject to publication in the State *Gazette*."[9]

Though it was made clear that the Jews would be deported only to the interior of the country, many Jewish and Christian leaders regarded it as a temporary measure, soon to be followed by deportation to Poland. Many took immediate steps, to thwart any new deportation.

Metropolitan Stefan, considered by the Filov government to be "public enemy number one," tried a new tactic: to christen all the Jews who so desired. By christening them, Stefan hoped their names would be removed from the lists of Jews subject to deportation. At first he had wanted to wait until Pentecost, in early June; but now he felt that every minute counted.

Some priests reported that soon lines of Jews formed outside some of Sofia's churches.[10] Belev was quickly informed that "a mass christening of Jews was under way" and that Stefan had instructed the parish priests to christen all the Jews who so desired. The chief of the Sofia criminal police brought to the commissariat several documents on that subject, including a secret letter from Stefan to the priests. He also reported that the Church authorities had issued many christening certificates that didn't bear any date, or even a post-date.[11]

Belev and Gabrovski hit back. On May 28, 1943, the director general of the Ministry of Religions, Mr. Sarafov, telephoned the Metropolitan. "The government," he said, "has decided not to recognize the christening certificates of the Jews who have converted in 1943. Therefore, they will be deported out of the country."[12]

Stefan answered that such a resolution by the government obstructs the mission of the Holy Church. "Therefore," Stefan said, "I shall send a circular letter to the parish priests, and ask them to inform all those who wish to be christened, that such a sort awaits them."

This answer was tantamount to a declaration of war. The government certainly didn't want the parish priests to know about the deportation and to spread the word from their pulpits. Something had to be done, right away, to stop Stefan. Gabrovski, apparently at a loss, and acting impulsively, made a far-reaching decision, unprecedented in the history of Bulgaria.

Less than an hour after his telephone conversation with Stefan, Sarafov called again. "The Interior Minister," he said, "has ordered to close for a while the Sofia churches, in order to prevent excesses in connection with the [mass] christening of the Jews."

Stefan, astounded, fired back. "I protest against this use of force, I shall not obey such an order, and I shall order the Sofia churches to hold services as usual."

Sarafov hung up. Stefan immediately wrote his circular letter and sent it to the parish priests.[13] A copy of it was conveyed to the prime minister by the attorney general. Stefan also alerted the Saint Synod, and Neofit officially notified the Ministry of Religions, that "the Church will not obey" its new order.[14]

Soon after, the order to close the churches was canceled.

Gabrovski retreated from his position, probably because he feared a confrontation with the Church. He knew well that if it came to an open conflict with the Church, the king wouldn't back him. A few weeks before, in a meeting with Filov and the king to discuss the question of the christened Jews, both the king and Filov had opposed Gabrovski's request that christened Jews be included in the Jewish community and therefore subjected to the Law for the Defense of the Nation.[15]

Yet, Gabrovski and Filov were in full agreement that the troublemaker Stefan should be stopped. The Saint Synod was informed that a meeting of judges and state attorneys had been urgently convened, to discuss the possibility of indicting the rebellious Stefan on charges of sabotaging the Law for the Defense of the Nation.[16] The Criminal police chief, Konstantinov, reported to senior KEV officials that government attorneys were preparing orders for the arrest and the punishment of Stefan. He also reported that the police had seized many church records, in which the names of the newly christened Jews were listed; they had also arrested a priest.[17] But Belev dismissed the idea. "There is no chance whatsoever that [Stefan] will be incriminated," he bitterly said to Kalitzin.[18]

He was right. In the end, the plan to indict the head of the Sofia church was dropped. In this last confrontation with the government, the indomitable Stefan had won again.

The last resort for Filov, Gabrovski, and their cronies was to malign Stefan. A new wave of defamatory flyers, full of allegations and insults directed at Stefan, swept through the country. They also hinted at Kyril's part in the various pro-Jewish activities. The flyers stirred anger and frustration in the Church and were discussed in a special meeting of the Saint Synod. Although refraining from naming the government as the source of the flyers, the Church leaders stressed that the government and the police didn't seem at all eager to take action against the hand that wrote, printed, and distributed the slanderous sheets. All the prelates declared they stood by Stefan, although some of them judged that he had gone too far by initiating the mass christening in Sofia. The final decision of the Saint Synod was the one the government feared most: to publish a press release on the Jewish question, and if it was to be censored by the government, to have it reprinted in circular letters to the parishes.[19]

Once again, the Church stood firm against the government's policy. There is no doubt that in the entire history of the Holocaust, the Bulgarian church stood high above any other Pravoslav, Protestant, or Catholic church, in her bold and unyielding struggle to rescue the Jews.

• • •

But the Church was not the only organization in Bulgaria to pursue the struggle. Even after May 24, various public figures and organizations continued to plead with King Boris for the cancellation of

*King Boris (second from left) with friends, including writer and national hero Ellin Pellin.*

any future deportation plans. The former Bulgarian diplomat, Dr. Ivan Strogov, sent the king a straightforward letter, in which he raised his voice "against the insanity of a policy that condemns Bulgarian Jewry to sure and senseless annihilation."[20] A few days later, Strogov was invited to meet with the royal adviser, Dr. Khandjiev, who informed him that the king fully agreed with him regarding the Jews. "The king will do everything in his power to alleviate the lot of our citizens of Jewish origin."[21]

A group of Jewish leaders—Buko Piti, Vitali Haimov, Benyamin Arditi, and Nissim Mevorach—visited Bulgaria's most famous and admired writer, Ellin Pellin, who was a personal friend of the king, and asked for his help.[22] Though Pellin had never before discussed political matters with the king,[23] he agreed that in this case he would do so. Pellin sent an urgent letter to the king, requesting a meeting. The king agreed immediately. A few days later, Pellin met with King Boris.*[24]

Pellin was indeed a close friend of the king. Boris was relaxed and open in his presence. The two friends had made up comical code words, which they used to communicate with one another, both orally and in writing. When out of Sofia, the king would send Pellin letters and postcards signed by names of folk tale heroes. They joked about Hitler, whom the king had nicknamed Verban, and about Filov, whom they referred to as "his Parrotlike eminence."[25]

Ellin Pellin was a big man in his early sixties, with a clear forehead, dreamy eyes, and a drooping, fluffy mustache. When he met with the king this time, Pellin reminded him that he had been one of the signatories of the writers letter against the Law of the Defense of the Nation. Now, he said, he had come to the king as a member of the Writers Union and was speaking in the name of some of his colleagues.

"What is being done with the Jews is not human and not dignified," he said. "These people must be kept in Bulgaria, at all cost, and not delivered to the Germans." He also described several "very bad cases" of Jews being mistreated. The cases had been reported to him by Jewish acquaintances. He asked the king to put an end to these persecutions.

The king listened to Pellin's words very attentively. He then went to another room, where Pellin heard him make a phone call. When he finally returned, he was very angry and blurted a single word: "Jackasses!"[26]

Pellin didn't ask who the king was referring to.

---

\* Pellin's version is different, although not necessarily contradictory. He claimed that he had asked to see the king, after being informed by his nephew, Zakhari Velkov, who worked at the KEV, that "there was a decision to send the Jews to Germany." This information, he says, had reached him about ten days before the deportation of the Jews. Still, Pellin testified in favor of his nephew, who was being tried for his anti-Jewish activities, and tried to prove that Velkov always had helped the Jews. Therefore, he might intentionally attributed the "early warning" to Velkov.

There is only one record of an angry conversation on the Jewish question between the king and a public official. Maria Pavlova, who was an official at the KEV, agreed to speak after more than fifty years of silence about an event "which she had kept secret all her life."[27]

One day in 1943 she was in Alexander Belev's office, waiting for him to sign several papers, when the door opened. His secretary, Liliana Panitza, walked in, "all thunder and lightning."

"Mister Commissar, the Royal Palace is on the line!" she announced dramatically.

Belev waited for Panitza to leave his office and picked up the phone. "Yes," he said. His tone changed immediately. "Yes, Your Majesty . . . Certainly, Your Majesty . . . Of course, Your Majesty . . . It will be executed as you say, Your Majesty." Pavlova noticed that he became as pale as a sheet.

When he hung up, he had a ferocious look in his eyes. He picked up a heavy paperweight made of marble and, in a fit of temper, smashed it on his desk, shattering the thick glass plate that covered it.

He raised his head and, noticing Pavlova, who was watching him, ordered her to return to her office.[28] Pavlova claimed that two hours later Commissar Belev summoned all the KEV senior officials and informed them that the deportation of the Jews was canceled by order of the royal palace. It had been established, however, that both in March and in May, it had been Gabrovski and his assistants who informed Belev of the decision not to deport the Bulgarian Jews. On the other hand, Pavlova's account of Belev's conversation with the king seems genuine. The conversation between the king and Belev took place, but we believe it had nothing to do with cancelling the deportation. We believe that after Ellin Pellin's intervention, the king called Belev and ordered him to put an end to the inhuman treatment of Sofia's Jews.

The king's meeting with Ellin Pellin passed largely unnoticed. But another audience the king granted at the beginning of June stirred a lot of interest in diplomatic circles. A delegation of the International Red Cross visited Bulgaria in late May and early June and met with government officials. The head of the delegation,

Dr. Edouard Chapuissa, met in private with the king on June 7. He was favorably impressed by Boris III, who said to him: "I am the crowned president of a democracy."[29]

Chapuissa then raised the Jewish question, and "recommended" that they not persecute the Jews on Bulgarian territory. The king assured him that "the Jews of Bulgarian origin will not be deported outside of the country borders." This decision didn't apply to Jews who were foreign citizens, however, like the Polish Jews who were sent to their country. The Bulgarian Jews were to be evacuated out of Sofia and concentrated in camps "around the city."[30]

The meeting between Chapuissa and Boris apparently alarmed the German embassy. In a report to Berlin, advising against any new pressure on Bulgaria regarding deportation of the Jews, Gestapo attaché Hoffman mentioned the meeting of King Boris with Chapuissa. "It can be assumed that they also discussed the Jewish question," Hoffman wrote, subtly hinting that the deportation, at least for now, was out of the question.[31]

# BELEV'S REVENGE

Still fresh in our minds is the memory of March 1943, of the manner in which were deported the Jews from Thrace and Macedonia . . . as well as of the manner in which were liberated the Jews from the old borders, already rounded up for deportation. [We also remember] the comedy in the National Assembly organized by the Judeo-plutocracy by means of Peter Kiosseivanov [a famous Bulgarian politician] and signed by 40 Parliament Members.

This was the opening paragraph of a bitter Ratnik flyer entitled "The deportation of the Sofia Jews into the provinces, or—The Judeo-activists unmasked." The flyer was printed in the end of May 1943, shortly after the failure of the second deportation attempt.[1] There can be no doubt that it was inspired by Belev or, at least, received his approval. In the hate-filled text, the Ratniks hurled accusations at the government, the Jews, and some eminent Bulgarians who again had thwarted the deportation plans.

The flyer sharply criticized the government for deporting the Jews from Sofia to the provinces and for rejecting Germany's offers to deport them to Poland. "Half of the Jews were already concentrated [in Sofia] and subjected to a very tight control. Now, that they would be dispersed in the provinces, who would be able to control them?" The flyer spoke of the Jews as assassins, lice, and a danger to Bulgaria. It fiercely assaulted the Jewish influence in Sofia:

> In these days, the Theater of the Arts allows itself to produce the operetta "Malinarka" by the Jew Leviev, Pancho Vladigerov [a famous Jewish composer and conductor] brings hysterics and kike influences to the official Bulgarian music, Dora Gabe [a celebrated Jewish writer] writes and is read by Bulgarian children . . . the Jewish labor camps have turned into vacation resorts.

The main assault was, naturally, directed against Metropolitan Stefan, who had been the major figure fighting the May 1943 deportation plans. The Ratniks attacked him as a "pseudo-Metropolitan," a "total traitor," a "spy of World War One," who consequently "sold Bulgaria" to the Yugoslavs, the Soviets, and the Anglo-Americans and, in May 1943, hid the chief rabbi of Sofia in the Metropolitan's residence. "The cup [of our patience] has overflown!"

The frustration of the Ratnik activists was understandable. Once again, the plans for the deportation of the Jews had failed at the last moment.

Belev, furious, vented his frustration on the Jewish leaders. In Sofia, 412 Jews, including eminent public figures and participants in the May 24 protest, were rounded up by the police, acting on KEV orders. One of the main figures in this group was Rabbi Daniel Tzion.[2]

Tzion was brutalized and humiliated. After he stood for ten hours with other detainees in the courtyard of the Sofia police headquarters, Belev appeared and hurled at him: "Because of you, these four hundred people will be sent to Poland now!"[3]

Dr. Buko Levi, expecting to be arrested, called Liliana Panitza, who told him: "Tonight you don't sleep at home." He quickly vanished, spending the following months in hiding.[4] Levi also warned Joseph Geron, the community president, who found refuge at the home of former Minister Dimo Kazasov.[5] Dr. Jacques Benaroya, a physician, was warned by an unknown woman, sent by Panitza, and also was able to escape.[6]

Many of those who had been arrested were taken in locked and sealed boxcars to an improvised detention camp at Somovit, by the Danube. Belev's goal was to remove from Sofia the leaders of the community and the instigators of the May 24 protest. He also wanted to spread panic throughout the Jewish community.[7]

The detainees spent several months in Somovit. The regime in the camp was cruel and degrading. Some of the officers and the guards beat up the prisoners, cursed and harassed them, and submitted them to harsh restrictions. Rabbi Tzion suffered humiliations, and at least once had his ears pulled by a young second lieutenant, because he didn't shout his name loud enough at a roll call.[8] The food was inedible and insufficient, the living conditions appalling. The prisoners expected to be put on boats at any moment and sent over the Danube and across German-occupied territories to Poland.[9] There is no doubt that this was Belev's original plan.

That didn't happen, however. The Sofia detainees were soon joined by Jews from other cities—Plovdiv, Dupnitza, Pazardjik, Russe. Some of them were accused of breaking the ZZN decrees, others had been arrested because of their central position in local leadership. Belev's second in command, Kalitzin, took revenge upon Kyustendil's Jews—for triggering the rescue operation in March—sending to Somovit as many of their leaders as he could find.[10] In the late summer the number of camp inmates reached five hundred. They were the private prisoners of the KEV, and the KEV decided who was going to be arrested and who was going to be released.[11]

After several weeks, the living conditions improved slightly, the restrictions were eased, the prisoners were allowed to receive food parcels from home, and some were set free. On September 24, 1943, the regional police chief visited the camp, comforted the Jews, and promised them that their conditions would improve.

By October most of the prisoners had been released. A group of about two hundred, though, were transferred to a camp outside Pleven, named "Kailuka." The conditions there were worse, mostly because of the brutal camp commander. On July 10, 1944, fire suddenly broke out in one of the detention huts, turning it into a death trap. Most of the prisoners escaped, but eleven were burned to death. No one was able to establish whether the fire was the result of arson.

# CHAPTER EIGHTEEN

# THE LAST EFFORT

O nce again, Belev refused to accept defeat.

On May 25, the very day when he admitted to Rabbi Hananel that he was unable to deport the Jews out of Bulgaria (see Chapter Fifteen), he secretly informed Theodore Dannecker that "the deportation of the Sofia Jews to the provinces was only an intermediate step to their deportation to the Eastern regions of the Reich."[1]

Germany's Ambassador Beckerle immediately reported the good news to Berlin, which was promptly relayed to Adolf Eichmann.[2] Belev also informed Dannecker that the final deportation would come in a matter of days, perhaps weeks.

Belev was so certain that the deportation would be carried out that he asked Dannecker to hold in the Bulgarian ports the six boats that had been prepared for the transfer of the Jews across the Danube. The boats could carry twenty-five thousand Jews in a single voyage; they should be ready to sail in the first half of June. Belev told Dannecker that he was even ready to pay the high costs of the boat maintenance (25,000 leva a day)—from the Bulgarian Jews' fund—in case the deportation was delayed or the boats were requested for other purposes.[3]

Berlin was more skeptical. After Beckerle's optimistic telegram, the foreign ministry began asking questions. Berlin wanted to know whether it would be useful to pressure the Bulgarian government into carrying out the next stage of the deportation right away. The S.D. (Sicherheitsdienst) and foreign ministry top officials were probably prompted to do so, in view of the forthcoming visit of King Boris to Germany.

On June 3, following exactly the same procedure as after the failed deportation of March 1943, an urgent invitation was extended to Boris, to be the Führer's guest at Berchtesgaden. Once again, Boris was invited at the last minute. Once again, the Führer's personal plane was sent to Sofia, and the king flew to Germany for a brief visit. It could be just a coincidence, but we believe the visit was connected to the king's second refusal to fulfill Germany's wishes. Still, the goal of that visit was not to openly confront the king on the Jewish question. That had been done in April, and the king had given a cautiously worded but essentially negative answer to von Ribbentrop. (German diplomats often quoted this negative answer in secret correspondence about Bulgaria's Jews.) The main reason for Boris's invitation to the Eagle's Nest was to confirm his continuing loyalty to Germany, as his refusal to deport the Jews on May 20 could indicate a wavering of his support. It appears that Germany looked upon Bulgaria's treatment of the Jews as a barometer of her loyalty. Hitler wanted to be reassured that Boris's protection of the Jews was not caused by his secret intention to change camps and sign a separate peace treaty with the Allies. Rumors about such a possibility abounded in Berlin.

Boris's visit to the Führer was very successful. Nothing concrete came out of his talks with Hitler, but they certainly dispelled all doubt of his loyalty.

But Berlin kept pressuring the German embassy in Sofia for results. Bulgaria's Jews should be deported, the Reich officials insisted, and the embassy should exert strong pressure on the Bulgarian government to comply. This pressure demanded a full response from the embassy.

The Gestapo attaché at the German embassy in Sofia, Karl Hoffmann, who was Dannecker's main communication channel, dispatched a long report to Berlin. The report described in detail the events of the last few weeks and stressed that the Bulgarians were determined to keep their promises.

Hoffman admitted that on April 5 he had forecast that the Jewish deportation would soon be carried through. "[But] during April the situation got worse, because the Bulgarian government openly sided with the King's view, that the Jews should be used as a labor force, and not deported."

Nevertheless, Hoffman pointed out, the labor project had fallen short of expectations. Besides, the Bulgarians were unable to build enough huts for the lodging of the Jewish workers. In the meantime "the 100% Jew" Papo carried out an assassination attempt against a radio engineer, Yanakiev; six out of the seven members of a Communist gang arrested in Russe, a Danube port, were also Jews. The result of all this was that "the Jewish question surfaced again." Therefore, Gabrovski prepared the public, with his press conference, for new measures against the Jews, while Belev proposed to him new deportation plans.

Hoffman made it clear that the idea of an alternative plan was Dannecker's. "Following Belev's communication to SS Hauptsturmfuhrer Dannecker, two possibilities were envisaged:

A) The deportation of all the Bulgarian Jews to the Eastern regions for reasons of the State's internal security.

B) The deportation of 25,000 Jews from Sofia to the province towns, if plan A could not be carried out."

Apparently trying to explain the failure of the May deportation, Hoffman presented a new theory about the difficulty in implementing plan A: "Lack of sufficient police forces to carry out the raids [on the Jews], without hurting the economic life." This theory was probably concocted by Belev, to excuse a possible failure.

Hoffman now tried to convince his superiors that the final deportation to Poland was imminent:

> Because of the large sums of money in the Jews' possession, there is no doubt that the prices of food will rise in the towns where Jews have been sent. . . . The existing anti-Jewish feelings in the provinces will be strengthened. From the point of view of internal policy, as well, the concentration of such numbers of Jews in towns unprepared

for that goal constitutes a certain danger. . . . It should be concluded, that it is clear to both the Bulgarian king and the cabinet, that the deportation of the Sofia Jews to the provinces represents only an interim measure, that necessarily would lead to the deportation of the Jews into the Eastern territories.

Hoffman repeated his conviction that Filov and Gabrovski were committed to the deportation. He commended "the faultless behaviour of Prime minister Filov," who reassured Ambassador Beckerle "that he was determined to deport all the Jews to the Eastern territories." Filov reportedly had declared to Parliament's majority group, after the murder of a pro-Fascist member, that "in any case, the deportation of the Jews out of the country's boundaries would continue."

Hoffman concluded: "The process is under way, and there is no turning back. . . . The promise of the Bulgarian government, and especially of Prime Minister Filov, will be kept."[4]

•   •   •

Ambassador Beckerle countersigned Hoffman's report but joined to it his own account, which was different in several points. Beckerle offered a more realistic assessment of the situation in Sofia. For him, the struggle was not yet over.

The first point in his report had to do with Dannecker's allegations (that also had been transmitted to Berlin by telephone) that the government had been disappointed by the Jewish labor project. Beckerle strongly denied this allegation, which probably had been whispered into Dannecker's ear by Belev. Jewish labor is an important factor in the Bulgarian economy, Beckerle wrote. "There have been no complaints about results in road and railway building by Jews," and the king, the prime minister, and other "competent leaders" have stressed the need to recruit Jewish labor groups.

Beckerle also fiercely criticized Commissar Belev, Dannecker's main source of information, using him as a means to express veiled skepticism about the "immediate deportation":

> We should not rely absolutely on the statements of the Bulgarian Commissar for Jewish Questions. The Commissar for Jewish Questions belongs to an opposition group, whose members sharply oppose the government policy, and adopt a double-faced behavior toward the Prime Minister and the government. I often viewed his actions with utter doubts, because he ignored several important assumptions. The evolution of the situation confirmed my assessment.

In this extraordinary report, Beckerle also dared to discuss some of the characteristics of the Bulgarian people, from which stemmed a distinctive attitude toward the Jewish population. This is one of the most important written admissions by German officials about the unique spirit of the Bulgarians, as well as about the image of the Bulgarian Jews.

Beckerle wrote:

> I am convinced that the Prime Minister and the entire Cabinet desire and aspire to a final and total solution of the Jewish question. But they are tied by the mentality of the Bulgarian people, that lacks the ideological enlightenment that we have. The Bulgarian, who was raised with Armenians, Greeks and Gypsies, doesn't see in the Jews any flaws justifying taking special measures against them.

Beckerle also played down the official anti-Semitic propaganda:

> As the majority of the Bulgarian Jews belong to the working class, and unlike other workers, are often more

diligent, the Bulgarian government in my view has the right
to tackle that question from a different point of view.[5]

Beckerle therefore dropped anti-Semitism as a motive for the
deportation of these Jews and suggested that if the Bulgarian government wanted to take action against them, it should do so for
other reasons: the participation of the Jews in sabotage, their acts
against the Axis powers, and their Communist activity. "The tech-
nical difficulties," he guardedly assessed, "connected with the
deportation from Sofia will bring perhaps a swift deportation to the
Eastern territories."

Still Beckerle warned his superiors not to exert any pressure on
Bulgaria. "Bringing strong pressure to bear will [result in] a tactical
setback, which will transfer the responsibility on us, and on the
other hand, in consideration of the Bulgarian mentality, will bring to
an opposite result of the one we desire."

Less than three weeks later, Hoffman sent another report to
Berlin. It started on a cheerful note: "The deportation of the Jews
from Sofia to the provinces is practically over. Twenty thousand Jews
have been evacuated." Hoffman stressed that his forecast of June 7
had been accurate. "The situation in the provinces has evolved to
the Jews disadvantage."

But very soon his tone turned grim and pessimistic:

> On the opinion of the German Embassy, no German
> pressure whatsoever can be presently exerted on the
> Bulgarian government concerning the deportation of the
> Jews to the Eastern regions. For general political reasons,
> and considering the Bulgarian mentality, the deportation of
> the Jews should be desired by the government itself and its
> execution should be carried out by it willingly. . . . For the
> time being, we should assume that the action under way
> for the final solution would be temporarily stopped."[6]

•  •  •

Summer came. In July the Allies landed in Sicily. The Americans were now in Europe. The Russians were advancing. Influential circles around the king began to whisper about a separate peace with the Anglo-Americans. Soon deportation of the Jews might become impossible.

In August 1943 Belev made his last effort, pleading with his German friends to pressure Bulgaria into surrendering her Jews. On August 15, 1943, on the very day when King Boris completed another visit to Germany, an angry telegram arrived at the embassy of the Reich in Sofia. Signed by Horst Wagner, it was personally addressed to Beckerle.[7] In the name of the (S.D.) Sicherheitsdienst, it demanded that he take "most insistent action" in his contacts with the Bulgarian government for "the solution of the Jewish problem by a deportation to the Eastern regions."

Wagner presented the reasons for the urgent demand:

> The deportation of the Jews in the provinces did not bring about the expected strengthening of the anti-Semitism, but enabled the Jews to extend the demoralizing propaganda throughout the entire country. The enemy espionage is being assisted by the Jewish network in the entire country.
>
> The Jewish influence on senior political and clerical circles is in a state of continuous growth, and makes the solution of the Jewish question more difficult.
>
> In the case of an enemy landing in the Balkans, the Jews would constitute a danger in the rear of the fighting armies. . . . For reasons of security the fastest settlement of the question is necessary. The S.D. believes that the Bulgarians will yield to the German pressure, because they agree to a solution by deportation, but they wish to be

subjected to German pressure in order to be covered vis-à-vis the Allies.

The fingerprints of Alexander Belev were all over the telegram. He knew that only by exerting pressure on the Bulgarian government could a positive result be achieved.

Beckerle acted immediately. He sent the military attaché at the embassy to meet with the senior officials at the Ministry of War. The Bulgarian officials expressed "their full agreement" with the German suggestions, but pointed out that the Ministry of War was not competent to deal with the Jewish deportation.

Beckerle met with several ministers and with the prime minister. For the first time Filov didn't repeat his promises for a swift deportation. Beckerle came out of the meeting feeling that "it was absolutely useless to suggest deportation at the present time."[8] The Bulgarian government, he assessed, sharply rejects any suggestion in that direction, "and wouldn't accept it even if our side exerts strong pressure."[9]

Four days later, Beckerle telegraphed back to Berlin: "Any effort to pressure the Bulgarian government would be of no use whatsoever."[10]

He detailed his arguments in a long report sent by diplomatic courier. After describing the reactions of Filov and the government to the S.D. suggestions, he explained why the Bulgarian government had changed its mind:

> The major reason is the determination of the Bulgarian government to avoid any internal political troubles because of the Jewish question, and avoid a needless sensation outside the borders, the more so as it had stalled until now, under various pretexts, the English offer to have Jewish children immigrate to Palestine.
>
> The same way that the Bulgarian government has prevented any publicity about the participation of Bulgarian fighter aircraft in the downing of American bombers dur-

ing the attack on Ploesti [in Romania],* the same way it had forbidden the anti-bolshevik propaganda, especially when the personality of Stalin was concerned, it refuses to allow any continuation of the activities concerning the Jewish question. Because of its panicky fear of air attacks, the Bulgarian government hopes that by this behavior, it will maintain among the enemy forces a false image of the internal political situation in Bulgaria. . . . [This will continue until the time] when a new activation of the German military leadership would remove the danger of terrorist attacks on Bulgaria.

There is no doubt that the Bulgarian government is a little surprised, that the Jewish question has not been brought to a solution in Hungary and Romania, as [the Bulgarian government] had been informed earlier. On the contrary, in many cases these countries had allowed immigration to Palestine, which had been avoided only by the refusal of Bulgaria to grant transit visas, following our intervention. The behavior of these countries, naturally, has an impact, as Bulgaria doesn't want to take upon herself the reputation of being the champion of the anti-Jewish hatred.

Beckerle frankly pointed at the conditions necessary to solve the Jewish problem: the resumption of German military successes and the failure of the "invading enemy offensive."

He concluded: "For the moment I maintain that any pressure on this question has no chances of success, and from a generally political point of view it will be even dangerous." He expressed his certainty that if the question was raised before the Bulgarian ambassador in Berlin, the result would be the same—a total refusal.[11]

---

* Perhaps the only military act of Bulgaria against the Allies was the participation of a few Bulgarian fighter planes in an attack on American bomber aircraft, on a mission against the oil fields in Ploesti, in Romania. Bulgaria imposed strict censorship on that sortie, and Germany concurred.

The foreign ministry in Berlin, in a long report to the S.D., repeated the main arguments of Beckerle's report.

This was the beginning of the end. Dannecker left for Italy, to deport her Jews, while Berlin stopped requesting the deportation of the Bulgarian Jews.

And in the end of August 1943 a dramatic event shook Bulgaria.

CHAPTER NINETEEN

# THE MYSTERIOUS DEATH OF BORIS III

O n August 9, 1943, Ambassador Beckerle requested an urgent audience with the king. As soon as he left, Boris called his junior secretary, Stanislav Balan. "Get ready," he said, "we are traveling on Friday." Hitler had invited him for a visit, the king added, and was sending his private plane to pick them up.[1]

Balan had begun his preparations, when the king appeared in his office. "Sorry, Balan, there is a change. I made a mistake. I did something foolish that I shouldn't have done, and now you must help me get out of it." He then explained: "I do not travel on Friday the Thirteenth!" He added, in French, "On Friday the Thirteenth, *je ne fonctionne pas!*" ("I don't function!")[2]

Balan was not surprised. As a member of the king's entourage, he was well aware that the Bulgarian monarch was a highly superstitious man and that even a summons by Adolf Hitler wouldn't make him take any risks on a Friday the Thirteenth. Balan rushed to the German embassy, walked into the ambassador's office, and under the pretext of "unforeseen political emergency" was able to push up the date of departure by one day, to August 14.

That Saturday Hitler's pilot, Hans Bauer, picked up the king and his small entourage at Vrajdebna Airfield, near Sofia, and flew to Germany. This time, however, Hitler didn't invite his guest to his

Eagle's Nest retreat in Bavaria, but instead to the Wolf's Lair, his military headquarters at Rastenburg, in East Prussia.

At the camouflaged airfield, Boris was greeted by Foreign Minister von Ribbentrop and the chief of staff, Field Marshall Wilhelm Keitel, then rushed to the huge maze of concrete underground bunkers where Hitler was waiting. The conversations with Hitler lasted most of the day, continuing through lunch and dinner. After dinner, Boris conferred again with Hitler, Keitel, and von Ribbentrop.

The negotiations resumed the following morning and ended with a lunch at Hitler's residential quarters. Hitler and Boris ate alone, with no aides present. When they emerged out of Hitler's quarters, they looked "tremendously upset—tense and angry."[3] The goodbyes were grim and cold.

When he returned to Sofia, the king told Filov that the Germans had asked him for two infantry divisions, to be positioned in northern Greece and eventually Albania. The king had cautiously replied that he was ready to place a division in readiness in Macedonia, but for that he needed the arms promised by Germany. He was assured the arms would arrive soon. "They were confident concerning the Russian front," the king told Filov. "However, they did not indicate in what manner they planned to deal with the situation."[4]

That was how the king described his meeting with the Führer to his prime minister, Bogdan Filov, whom he knew to be a fervent supporter of Germany. Yet, he blurted a single sentence that expressed a deep concern: "Today, during our flight back, I wished that enemy planes had shot our plane down, so it all would be over."[5]

This death wish resulted from a secret he carried with him from the *Wolfsschanze* but could not reveal to the pro-Nazi Filov.

To Filov, Boris said the meeting dealt mostly with the two divisions needed in Greece. But he gave a totally different account of the meetings to two people he could really trust. In an account dictated to his chief of cabinet, Pavel Gruev (the father of Stephane Groueff), he spoke of "an unusually stormy meeting during which Hitler insisted that Bulgaria join the war against Russia." Hitler angrily rejected Boris's worn-out arguments that it was in Bulgaria's and Germany's interest "that Bulgaria remained neutral in relation to the Soviet Union." The quarrel between the two men was not resolved, and the king was extremely upset at the end of the meeting.[*]

The following day, August 16, the king revealed the secret of his quarrel with Hitler to Strashimir Dobrovitch, his oldest adviser, who had been his father's chief of cabinet. Dobrovitch was dying of throat cancer, and the king visited him on his deathbed. "I have something to tell you that will make you happy," the king said. He spoke of a terrible fight he had had with the Germans at the Wolf's Lair, mainly with von Ribbentrop and the German generals. The Germans had demanded that Bulgaria declare war on Russia and send her army to fight, but the king had flatly refused. "The year 1918 won't happen again!" the king said to Dobrovitch, hinting at the fatal mistake of his father, who had sided with the Germans and the Austro-Hungarians in World War I and had been forced to abdicate. "Now my hands are free. I untied them just in time."

The king went on:

> But in order to achieve this I had to put up a terrible fight. Hitler went into a rage when I refused his demands about Russia. Screaming like a madman, he attacked me and Bulgaria in a torrent of accusations and threats. It was horrible! But I didn't give in one inch! He tried to frighten me, but instead, I calmly explained the situation, saying what I had to say, clearly and unequivocally, i.e. that I have decided that we should follow our own road. My hands are now free.

---

[*] The account itself was lost, but fourteen days later, Pavel Groueff, deeply disturbed, revealed its contents to his son, Stephane, who visited him at the royal palace.

"I saved you," concluded Boris, meaning that he saved Bulgaria from being drawn into war with Russia. "Even if I have to pay for it!"[6]*

This account, even if it seems vastly embellished, still confirms a major point: Hitler had asked Bulgaria to join Germany in the war against the Soviet Union, and King Boris had refused. That had certainly made Hitler and his entourage very suspicious of the Bulgarian king. Although Hitler liked Boris and admired his shrewdness, he had lately made some seething remarks about him. He had become quite irritated by Boris's refusal to get more actively involved in the war operations, while increasing his territorial demands. Even after recovering Dobrudja and occupying Thrace and Macedonia, Bulgaria's appetite had not been sated. In 1943, Boris had requested that parts of Greek Macedonia also be handed to Bulgaria. "The Bulgarians are now behaving," Hitler had said to some of his aides soon after, "as if the developments in the Balkans were all the results of their decisive action. In reality, Boris, caught between cupidity on the one side and his cowardice on the other, was so hesitant that the strongest intervention on our part was necessary to make him do anything at all."[7]

● ● ●

On August 23 the king was in his palace working with his chief of cabinet. At 7:30 P.M. he cut short their working session, claiming he felt ill. A few minutes later he was seized by violent spasms and vomiting. The palace doctors, Daskalov and Alexandrov, were

---

* The king's words were reported by Dobrovitch, two weeks later, to the king's sister, Princess Evdokia, who noted them in a handwritten letter to her nephew and niece, Simeon and Maria Louisa, marked "to be opened after my death." Evdokia died in 1985. Quoted in Stephane Groueff, *Crown of Thorns*, 360.

rushed to his bedside. They assumed he was having a gallbladder attack.

The following day the king's condition worsened, and his counselor, Khandjiev, was dispatched to meet with the German air attaché, Colonel Carl-August von Schoenebeck. Khandjiev made Schoenebeck swear he would keep the matter secret even from Ambassador Beckerle. The truth was that King Boris despised Beckerle.[8]

Khandjiev, who had been sent to the air attaché under the explicit orders of Boris, asked Schoenebeck to fly over from Berlin Dr. Rudolf Sajitz, who had treated the king for many years. Schoenebeck made the necessary arrangements, and Dr. Sajitz arrived the following day by a special plane. That very day, his clinic in Berlin had been hit by an Allied bomb, and a special unit of rescuers dug the doctor out of the ruins and rushed him to the plane in his rumpled clothes, still covered with dust and mortar.

In the following days, Sajitz was joined by two other well-known experts, Dr. Hans Eppinger and Dr. Maximilian de Crinis, from Vienna—also flown to Sofia by special planes. Their diagnosis, to which their Bulgarian colleagues concurred, was a heart attack.

The king wasn't known to suffer from a heart condition, but he had often complained of pains in his chest and predicted that he would die from heart disease. The immediate cause of the attack might have been emotional or physical stress, the doctors said. Both were possibilities. The king had undergone a traumatic experience in Hitler's headquarters, clashing for the first time with the most powerful and the most dangerous man in Europe. He also had behaved recklessly on his return, going on a climbing expedition on Mussalla Mountain, the highest peak of the Balkans, in spite of his physical fatigue. After the 2,923 meter climb (about 9,600 feet), he had complained to his brother, Prince Kyril, of "a sharp burning sensation in the area of his heart."[9]

The king's condition quickly deteriorated. All the doctors' expertise couldn't save him. On August 28, 1943, King Boris died.

• • •

Very soon after the king's death, strange rumors spread in Bulgaria and abroad. The king had been poisoned, the rumors said. The first to express a suspicion that he had been a victim of assassins was his sister Princess Evdokia. He was still alive when she said to Prince Kyril: "Could he have been poisoned? He has been *there*. [She meant in Germany]. Do you think *they* fixed him?"

Kyril had dismissed her suspicions, insisting their brother was suffering from a heart condition. Another rumor had originated with one of the king's Bulgarian doctors, Dr. Daskalov, who had hinted to the king's adviser, Iordan Sevov, that there might be another reason for the king's illness.[10] The rumors would have been cut short if they had not been fueled by the most authentic source: the German doctors themselves.

On August 27, when the king was still fighting for his life, the doctors secretly reported to Colonel Schoenebeck, the German air attaché. King Boris, who despised Beckerle and hated von Ribbentrop, had explicitly demanded that Schoenebeck be the one to bring over the doctors and to report about his illness to Hitler through Reichsmarshall Goering.[11] Schoenebeck asked the doctors about the nature of the king's ailment. He wrote down these words: "For the first time the doctor voiced the suspicion that the king could have been poisoned. This suspicion increased with the appearance of unusual signs of disintegration in the inner organs."

On August 28, shortly after the king's death, the doctors visited Schoenebeck again. He noted in his diary:

> The town, in its anguish, still cried and whined. I closed the windows, so we could talk undisturbed. What was the real cause of King Boris's death? I asked the doctors. My question floated in the air, but the answer was not forthcoming. Professor Sajitz lit a cigarette, deeply engrossed in his thoughts. Professor Eppinger scratched his head and said slowly: "I believe it is a poisoning! This irreproachable king

has fallen victim of a most common murder. That's my opinion. What do you think, dear colleague?"

Professor Sajitz nodded and said that the spots that had appeared on the body before death indicated an absorption of poison . . . Professor Eppinger added that, some time ago, he had been called to the sickbed of the Greek Prime Minister Metaxas, and had seen the same symptoms on his body. Metaxas had certainly been the victim of a poisoning. Eppinger spoke of the use of some Indian poison, which becomes effective only after a few months . . .

Because of the Byzantine intrigues in the German embassy and the fierce rivalry between Schoenebeck and Beckerle, the doctors had not been allowed to meet with the German ambassador. They finally visited his office on August 29. "Because of suspicions," Beckerle asked them if the death could have been due to some outside cause. He mentioned poison.

Beckerle wrote:

> The three doctors answered unanimously and immediately in the affirmative, invoking the similarity of the symptoms. Eppinger spoke of a *typical Balkan death*. But could they say more? Could they reliably attribute the death to such cause? This could not be said with certainty; an autopsy would have been necessary for that.

The real cause of death could be established only by an autopsy, and the doctors suggested at least a brain autopsy.[12] But the royal court refused to give its authorization.

Realizing that the doctors were "convinced of a violent death," Beckerle asked them to keep their opinions secret and, on their return to Germany, "restrict their statements to the general diagnosis of the illness." He explained that it was their duty, as citizens, to follow those directives.[13] More than twenty years later, Beckerle stuck to his firm belief that King Boris had been poisoned.[14]

Beckerle requested an urgent meeting with Filov and spoke to him "of the many rumors blaming the Germans for the death of the king. One rumor states that the stress involved in visiting the Führer's headquarters brought on a heart attack, another purports poisoning following refusal of German demands." Filov brushed aside the rumors of poisoning and called them "ridiculous." Still, Beckerle didn't regard the rumors as ridiculous at all. In an urgent report to von Ribbentrop, he suggested that Germany launch a strong counter-propaganda effort and blame Germany's enemies for Boris's death.[15]

The mystery of King Boris's death is still unsolved. The theory of a poisoning rests, practically, on the opinions of the doctors,

(COURTESY OF BULGARIAN STATE ARCHIVES)

*Peter Gabrovski departs from the Ministry of the Interior. Front row,*

expressed in a highly emotional state, and perhaps meant to clear them of accusations of faulty treatment. Still, Prince Kyril later changed his opinion and maintained that the Germans had assassinated his brother;[16] Queen Giovanna remained convinced that her husband had been assassinated and wrote this in her memoirs.[17] Other members of the family agree to the assassination theory but blame the Russians.[18] The man who could have solved the mystery was Dr. Hans Eppinger. But Dr. Eppinger spent the last part of the war carrying out inhuman experiments on inmates of the Nazi concentration camps. Accused of war crimes in 1946, he committed suicide before his trial in Nuremberg.[19] The most farfetched theory about the assassination was the one Hitler himself spread. Hitler

eventh from left, Alexander Belev, Gabrovski is eleventh from the left.

accused the Italian court of poisoning Boris, more precisely Princess Mafalda, Queen Giovanna's sister, whom he fiercely hated.[20] The story was not believed and faded quickly. Princess Mafalda, though, was arrested by the Nazis (for unrelated charges) and deported to the Buchenwald concentration camp, where she died on August 28, 1944, exactly a year after Boris.

If King Boris was indeed assassinated, it certainly was not as a punishment for his August 15 refusal to send the Bulgarian army to fight the Russians. The only logical reason might have been the fear in Germany that he intended to pull out of the war and sign a separate peace with the Allies. Persistent rumors about secret peace talks between Bulgaria and the Allies were circulating in RSHA circles in Berlin. At the beginning of August 1943, the king's adviser, Iordan Sevov, went on a mysterious trip to Ankara. The Germans believed that he had established contact there with Allied diplomats. Soon after, Bulgaria's ambassador to Berne, Georgi Kiosseivanov, returned to Sofia. Kiosseivanov, a former prime minister, had actually been exiled to Berne, because of his anti-German views. He was reported to have brought, on his return, a message for the king from Allen Dulles, the OSS representative in Europe. In this message, transmitted through a former League of Nations official, Rene Charron, Dulles had asked the king to indicate that he intended to withdraw from the Axis. He also recommended that the anti-Jewish measures be canceled.[21]

These political maneuvers, which were very closely watched by Berlin, could have been the reason for assassinating King Boris, in order to prevent his defection.

•  •  •

The king's death stirred a tremendous wave of grief and bereavement throughout Bulgaria. He had been extremely popular, and the Bulgarian people mourned him sincerely. But his death also put in motion several political moves.

Six-year old Prince Simeon was crowned as Simeon II, king of the Bulgarians. A regents council was formed, composed of Bogdan Filov, Prince Kyril, and General Nikola Mihov, the minister of war. All three appointments had been approved by the Germans.

A new prime minister was appointed. He was Dobri Bojilov. He replaced most of the ministers, including Interior Minister Gabrovski. Gabrovski was forced to resign, as Filov feared that he might form a group of opposition to his reign as regent. Gabrovski was replaced by one of his friends, another notorious anti-Semite, Docho Christov. Rumors spread that Belev, too, would soon be replaced. They didn't fire him right away, Belev claimed, because they feared that such a step would be interpreted abroad as a sharp reversal of Bulgaria's Jewish policy.[22]

Soon after the swearing in of the Bojilov government, Docho Christov, the new minister of interior, convened the regional directors of Bulgaria. "The Jewish question is becoming more and more difficult," he said. "This is a result of the fact, that we didn't succeed to deport them. To send them back is unthinkable. The question [for us] is how we can use their work; [how] to free the Bulgarian society from the influence of the Jews."

Christov informed the directors of his decision to give the Jews, discreetly, some relief, so they wouldn't be a burden on the State and on society. He would impose censorship on their letters and mailed parcels, but on the other hand he would devise a way to supply them with foodstuffs "in order to cut off their use of the black market." The Jews would be allowed to sell their movable property and use the money. Expropriated property wouldn't be sold. Confiscated Jewish property would be rented by the State.

"We shall not deport Jews anymore," Christov grimly said. "Wherever they are, there they shall remain."[23]

# CHAPTER TWENTY

# A BODY IN A DITCH

F ollowing King Boris's death important changes took place in the government. Officially, nothing had changed. Nevertheless, in the following weeks a new reality slowly began to emerge.

Two of the new ministers in Dobri Bojilov's cabinet, Ivan Beshkov and Ivan Vazov, had been among the forty-three members of Parliament who had signed Peshev's letter.

With Gabrovski's departure, a scandal exploded, involving the KEV and a corrupt physician, Dr. Iosif Vatev. Vatev had been the doctor who, for a bribe, would provide Jews with false certificates concerning their state of health. He had also informed Haim Rahamim in February 1943 about the projected deportation. Although Belev had nothing to do with the Vatev affair, he was asked to resign as well. He was replaced by Christo Stomanyakov, an assistant procurator in the Sofia appellate court, who was less extreme and anti-Semitic than his fanatic predecessor.[1]

On September 8, 1943, Italy officially surrendered. Although most of Italy was immediately conquered by Germany and Mussolini was restored to his position, the Italian collapse augured the approaching defeat of the Axis. Later in the fall of 1943 the first Allied bombardments of Sofia took place. The royal palace at Vrana and the Parliament building were hit, as well as many homes and public buildings. A disorderly exodus from Sofia began.

Defeat was in the air, and Bulgaria was changing her policy, pathetically striving to distance herself from Nazi Germany. One of the first steps taken by the Bojilov government had dramatic significance for the Jewish population. Bulgaria allowed Jews to immigrate to Palestine! True, the families allowed to leave were few and the other restrictions of the ZZN were not lifted, but it was still a beginning. In March 1944 a group of fifty children also left for Palestine and, in July 1944, another forty children.

The situation in the Balkans had been reversed. While Bulgaria was easing her treatment of the Jews, Hungary changed her policy for the worse. In March 1944 an extremely anti-Semitic government took power in Hungary, and large deportations began. In Romania, thousands of Jews were killed in massive pogroms in Iasi and over a hundred thousand in extermination camps operated by the Romanians themselves.[2] In Italy, where deportation attempts had been so virtuously opposed, the Jews were being rounded up and herded to the grim boxcars bound for the death camps. The operation was directed by Theodore Dannecker, who had left Sofia after all his efforts to deport the Bulgarian Jews had failed. Bulgaria remained the only country whose entire Jewish population had been spared.

On May 31, 1944, Bojilov's government resigned and was replaced by a cabinet headed by Ivan Bagrianov. Bagrianov initiated secret contacts with the Allies. He met with Filov, now one of King Simeon's regents. The same Filov who had so staunchly struggled for the deportation of the Jews now advised the new prime minister "to take the necessary measures concerning the Jews, but quietly, without noise . . ."[3]

Bagrianov didn't listen and took an unprecedented step to help the Jews. The new prime minister lived in a villa in Pavlovo, belonging to a Jew, Landau. He asked Landau to set up a meeting between him and some Jewish leaders. Three Jews came to the meeting, and Bagrianov told them:

> Gentlemen, the power is in our hands. From now on, a new policy will be in vigor in Bulgaria. The Jews will recover all the rights they had in the past, and again will enjoy their full citizen rights. But we can't do all of this in a single move, because the German army is still on our

soil, therefore we shall have to proceed by two steps forward and one backwards . . . First we shall replace the Commissar of Jewish Questions with somebody you'll choose, and you'll work in cooperation with him. Give me also the names of the Jews who should form your new Consistory, and we shall approve it right away.

The Jews proposed Justice Protich, a Sofia judge, as commissar. His appointment was immediately approved by the cabinet. Colonel Avraham Tadjer was appointed president of the new Consistory.[4]

The Jews were released from the labor camps only in September 1944. But earlier, on July 27, 1944, in his speech before the Sobranie, the prime minister cancelled the ZZN and its restrictions. Jews no longer were required to wear yellow stars, the signs on their homes were removed, and their freedom of movement was restored. The only action left to be taken was the restitution of the Jewish homes and businesses.[5]

Germany was in full retreat in the Balkans. On August 16, 1944, Bulgaria, trying to salvage what she could, declared her neutrality in the war. On September 2, Prime Minister Ivan Bagrianov was replaced by Konstantin Muraviev, who immediately initiated peace overtures with the Allies. The Soviet Union refused to negotiate with him. On September 5, 1944, the Soviet Union declared war on Bulgaria. The Red Army crossed the Danube and entered into Bulgaria. Bulgaria did not resist. On September 9 the former regime collapsed and a pro-Soviet government was established in Sofia. Soon after, the Bulgarian army joined the Soviets in the last stage of the war against Nazi Germany.

•  •  •

Lily Panitza stayed in the Commissariat for Jewish Questions after Belev left. She told the new commissar, Stomanyakov, that she was ready to resign, but he asked her to stay. In September 1943, though, after some acid remarks she made about Sofia's lawyers and their contacts with the commissar's office, Stomanyakov fired her.[6]

She then found a position in the Ministry of Evacuation. Yet, she continued to see Belev, who had now assumed a new job, as chief of the Central Directorate of Control in the Ministry of Interior. She had moved to the suburb of Pavlovo and rented a small room on Boyanski Vazhod Street. Across the street was a house, surrounded by a small courtyard. Alexander Belev lived on the second floor of this house. It seems very unlikely that they became neighbors by chance. From her window and her small balcony, Liliana had a clear view of her lover's windows. Whenever she was home, day or evening, she kept watching her lover's windows. In the evenings, when she would see light in the windows, she would often cross the street and knock on his door.[7]

She also viewed everyone who visited Belev. Once she saw her rival, Lily Stoika, with her mother, coming to stay with Belev. The two Lily's found themselves together with Belev in the air-raid shelter, when the alert was sounded. Fortunately, Lily Stoika's stay on Boyanski Vazhod Street was very short.

The acquaintances of Panitza and Belev knew well that the bond between them had not been severed when they left the KEV. Always discreet, Lily told her friend Ilya Dobrevski that she had just "happened to bump into Belev in the street a few times."[8] Other friends of Belev knew better. They would often ask Lily about him or even give her notes and messages for him. Belev would even meet some of his friends at Lily Panitza's home.[9]

Belev was no longer the fierce, confident Fascist she remembered. After his two failures to deport Bulgaria's Jews, he had become bitter, nervous, and depressed. He resented his former patron and mentor, Gabrovski,[10] who had betrayed him. He also reached the conclusion that the war was lost. "Germany has lost," he told Lily as early as September 1943, after the Allied landing in Italy. "I'll move to Germany. I'll disappear among all those people there, as the Jews [in Bulgaria] anyway will hold me responsible for everything. As for Gabrovski, he always finds a way to hang on."[11]

At the end of August 1944, seeing the light in his windows, she went to Belev's room. She hadn't seen him for about two weeks. He was in one of his dejected moods. They spoke of the German defeats. "The Germans deceived us," Belev said, "and now they are lying on the radio." Still, he said he was sending his mother to Germany. Lily asked why he didn't send his father as well, and Belev answered that the Germans admitted women only.

"Won't you try to get there yourself?" she asked.

"It isn't worth the effort. They'll find me anyway."

A few days later Lily Panitza went to see Belev's mother, cooked her a meal, and helped her clean her house. Belev also gave Lily some money for his father. In spite of what he had told Lily earlier, he apparently did plan his own escape.

On September 1, 1944, Lily Panitza was on her way home. Darkness was falling. As she passed by the villa where Alexander Belev lived, she heard a voice: "Panitza!" It was Belev, standing in the dark. "Wait," he said, "I must give you something." He went inside and came back, holding a package. "Keep this for me," he said. "You know what's going on."[12] She thought it was the manuscript of his book. When he was commissar of Jewish questions he often spoke to her about a book he was writing. "If something happens to me," he would say, "I'll be very sorry for the book." He meant that the book would not be completed.

For a couple of days Lily didn't open the package, but finally her curiosity prevailed. She untied the bulky bundle and found inside a thick file, containing documents from the KEV, letters from Gabrovski, papers concerning the deportation, and the original February 22 agreement between Belev and Dannecker.[13]

On the last day before the Red Army crossed the Danube, Lily saw Belev get out of a car, carrying suitcases, a backpack, and a blanket. She hurried down. "Where were you?" she asked.

"I was in Kyustendil, but couldn't get to Skopje." He didn't tell her why he was trying to cross the border. Then he suddenly asked her: "Will you have dinner with me?"

She felt "very embarrassed." She had never gone out with him alone, to a restaurant or a bar; besides, the political situation was very tense, and she assumed that he knew what awaited him.

"I am not hungry," she managed.

"You don't want to expose yourself?" he asked.

Her embarrassment growing, she countered: "This is not the reason, but if you think so, I'll come."

They had their first and last public meal together in a nearby restaurant.

The following day, September 9, the Red Army crossed the Danube and pro-Communist forces seized power in Sofia. After meeting Belev in the morning, Lily went to the center of Sofia, then came back to his room. The door was unlocked, but Belev wasn't there. His landlady didn't know where he was. Lily was worried; she knew that people, identified with the pro-Fascist regime, were being arrested all over Sofia.

Suddenly Belev walked in. "They arrested me in Kniajevo," (a Sofia suburb) he said. "They took my revolver and my two typewriters. They told me they didn't know if they had to detain me." He aimlessly paced around the room and all of a sudden blurted: "I'll go out. I'll try to find a place to sleep."

Lily Panitza never saw Belev again.

A couple of days later she heard that Belev had committed suicide in the Serdika Bank, the bank of the Ratnik organization, of which he was chairman. Lily rushed to the bank. The director told her that he had heard such a rumor, but it hadn't happened in the bank.

Lily returned to Belev's home. According to her testimony, she moved his clothes to her room, as she intended to give them to his father. It is possible, though, that because of their intimate relationship, Belev had spent some nights in her room, where he also had left some clothes.

Soon after, the People's Militia, the police of the Communist regime, came to her room and searched it. "Whose are these clothes?" they asked, seeing Belev's suits hanging in her wardrobe.

"My brother's," she lied, scared.

The police found the file Belev had left with her, and took it with them. They took Panitza to the police station, questioned her, and let her go. She hurriedly transferred Belev's clothes to her land-lady's apartment. A few days later they arrested her again. This time, they found in her handbag the only document she had removed from Belev's file.

It was the paper that had started it all: the original agreement on the deportation of twenty thousand Jews, signed between Belev and Dannecker.[14] For the first time the officers saw Dannecker's green-inked signature, and the black-ink lines that Belev had made to change the document's meaning, as he signed the infamous agreement.

Lily Panitza stayed in prison for more than six months. She was frequently interrogated, beaten, and tortured. She suffered much more than all the other KEV officials, who were arrested as well. She gave long and detailed depositions. But they were not enough. The Militia searched her personal affairs and discovered the draft of a love letter she had apparently written to Belev.[15] The letter was used in Lily's brutal interrogation. The torture and the beatings and the repeated interrogations were not attempts to force Lily Panitza speak of her work at the KEV. They were not even attempts to force her to give up the list of Ratnik members employed in the KEV (which she supplied willingly).[16] The Militia could just as easily get the Ratnik lists from other employees.

They wanted something else from Lily Panitza. They had only one question for her: Where is your lover? And Lily was unable to provide the People's Militia with the answer.

Belev was never found. He was tried in absentia by the People's Court and sentenced to death. Some believed he had escaped from Bulgaria and found a hiding place in Western Europe or South America, like a few of the leaders of the pro-Nazi regime. But he never emerged and was never accounted for.

Actually, Belev was dead long before his trial began. Future research was to establish that he had traveled to Kyustendil again, apparently hoping to cross the old border into Macedonia and from there make his way west, to Germany.

However, the same Kyustendil that had thwarted Belev's project now sought vengeance. The small town that had dared to revolt against Belev was waiting for him to show up, for the final reckoning.

Belev was recognized at Kyustendil railway station by a group of partisans.[17] They captured him and found a handbag full of money in his possession. They decided to send him to Sofia and charged a Jewish partisan to escort him. Some say the escort's war name was Belo.

When they got out of town, the Jew shot the man who had symbolized the persecution of the Jewish people.[18] He dumped Belev's body in a ditch, where he was left to rot.

# CHAPTER TWENTY-ONE

# THE HOUR OF RECKONING

After September 9, 1944, partisans, Communists, and members of the Agrarian party summarily executed large numbers of Fascists, known Branniks, Ratniks, and Legionnaires, activists, police agents, officers, and commanders who had led punitive actions against the resistance. Some say the number of people killed in these acts of vengeance amounted to many thousands.[1]

More than 130 young Jews who had joined the resistance units fell in the armed struggle against the Fascists. Among them were young men and women who became legendary heroes, like Annie Ventura from Russe, Mati Rubenova of Yambol, Violetta Yakova from Dupnitza, Emil Shekerdjiski, Menahem Papo, Leon Tadjer (Ben-David), and others.

A few weeks after September 9, the "Fatherland front" government that had taken power in Bulgaria, established a People's Court, to try the leaders of the former regime for war crimes. The People's Court sentenced former Prime Ministers Filov, Bozhilov, and Bagrianov to death. Peter Gabrovski and twenty-five other former ministers, King Simeon's regents Prince Kyril and General Mihov, the senior staff at the royal palace, and sixty-eight members of the twenty-fifth Sobranie were also sentenced to death. Many of these

Parliament members had signed Peshev's petition in March 1943. King Boris's head of the royal chancellery, the soft spoken Pavel Gruev "the Jewish consul", the Dunovist leader Liubomir Lulchev, and the Macedonian leader Vladimir Kurtev, all of them friends of the Jewish community, were also sentenced to death. All the sentences were carried out by firing squad within twenty-four hours (with the exception of Lulchev and Kurtev, who were executed at a later date).

The People's Court VII was established to try those who had persecuted the Jews. Sixty-four KEV senior officials, anti-Semitic writers and propagandists, commanders of detention camps and labor gangs, were brought to trial on March 7, 1945. The sentences were read on April 3, 1945.

Two people were sentenced to death in absentia—Alexander Belev and Kyril Dalakchiev, the police commander of Dupnitza during the deportation proceedings. Three others (including two in absentia, Borislav Tasev and Spas Stoianchevski) were sentenced to life in prison. Twenty-eight of the accused received sentences ranging from a year on probation to fifteen years of hard labor. Twenty-two of the accused were acquitted. Nine were not tried, for various reasons. Christo Stomanyakov, who had succeeded Alexander Belev as commissar for Jewish questions, was sentenced to only five years. Dr. Ivan Popov, one of the KEV most senior officials, who had been very active in the deportation of the Thracian and Macedonian Jews, was acquitted. Maria Pavlova, Peiu Peev, and other senior officials of the KEV were acquitted as well.

The prosecutor asked for a light sentence for Liliana Panitza, who he said was "the closest person to Belev, who even filled for him when he was absent."[2] She was acquitted, however, after the leaders of the Jewish community testified about her secret role in the rescue of the Jewish community. She was released from prison. She died a year later, possibly as a result of the beatings and the torture by the secret police.[3]

On September 9, 1944, Dimiter Peshev stayed at home, waiting to be arrested by the new regime's militia. When he went out to a restaurant for lunch, he dressed with care and left a note on the door, indicating where he could be found. He was finally arrested and jailed, as were the other Parliament members who had supported the pro-German governments.

Dimiter Peshev was tried but was spared the tragic fate of most of the majority Parliament members. The Jewish leaders intervened in his favor, testifying about his valiant actions. He was even defended by a Jewish lawyer. He was sentenced to fifteen years of hard labor but his sentence was reduced and he was released after less than a year in prison. He never practiced law again.

For the rest of his life, Peshev lived in his Sofia home at Neofit Rilski Street, with his two nieces, Kichka and Kaludka Kiradjiev.[4] He had been deeply affected by his imprisonment. He lost his sense of humor, his nieces say. In 1952 he suffered a heart attack, but recovered.

He never married. An introvert, he led a strict, rigid way of life: meals at certain hours, a late morning walk in the streets of Sofia, lunch, rest, and a lot of reading. He watched his diet and was always neatly dressed. A great admirer of the French Revolution, he read books of history, underlined the passages he liked, put folded sheets of paper, covered with handwritten reflections, between the pages of his beloved books. He also wrote, in a large number of copybooks, his memoirs, culminating with the stormy years of World War II.

After 1965, he received, until the day of his death, a small pension in U.S. dollars, from the Bulgarian Jews in Israel. This allowed him a more comfortable life, but as a proud Bulgarian he felt uneasy receiving foreign currency from abroad. A good friend, who didn't forget him, was Buko Lazarov. Lazarov often came from Israel to visit him, bringing him presents. They spent long hours reminiscing about the dramatic events of March 1943. Once, noticing that Peshev looked with interest at his colorful pullover, Lazarov spontaneously removed it, and gave it to his friend.[5] Dimiter Peshev died in 1973.

Buko Lazarov was also very active in obtaining pensions for two other members of the famous Kyustendil delegation, Assen Suichmezov and Peter Mikhalev. Assen Suichmezov's last years were bitter, marked by need and poor health. Lazarov continued to visit him and his other close friends, Peter and Parka Mikhalev in

Sofia. Most of the members of the Kyustendil delegation had a miserable life under the Communist regime (for various reasons unrelated to their action). Their contribution to the rescue of the Jews was not widely recognized. Ivan Momchilov was not bothered by the Communist regime. He died in 1966. Assen Suichmezov died in 1977. And Peter Mikhalev died in 1985.

At the end of the war, German Ambassador Beckerle was taken prisoner by the Red Army and spent eleven years in a Soviet forced labor camp, before returning to Germany. The Gestapo attaché, Karl Hoffman, allegedly tried to escape by car to Skopje. (It is possible that Belev tried to join up with Hoffman, when he twice traveled to Kyustendil [see Chapter Twenty.)] On the way the car was captured by freedom fighters, and its passengers were shot.[6] SS Haupsturmfuhrer Theodore Dannecker emerged in the war trials as one of the worst Nazi criminals, responsible for the death of seven hundred thousand Jews from Austria, France, Thrace, Macedonia, and Italy. He committed suicide on December 11, 1945. Because his body was identified only by his wife, and because Hoffman's body was never found, an indictment for mass murder against both of them was issued in June 1960 by the Supreme Regional Court of Frankfurt on Main.[7]

After the war, Metropolitan Stefan became the Exarch of the Bulgarians—the supreme head of the Bulgarian church. However, he was removed from this position by the Communist government two years later and exiled to a small village, where he remained until his death in 1957. After his dismissal, the supreme leadership of the Bulgarian church was bestowed upon the Metropolitan Kyril of Plovdiv, who had been Stefan's arch rival and bitter opponent. There was one endeavor, however, in which they both had fully cooperated: the struggle for the rescue of Bulgaria's Jews.

In his last will and testament, Stefan wrote:

> What a moral disaster was the insane anti-Jewish action! What a mental derangement of the Fascist Mafia, of the appointed parliament and of the indifference of the

society, who in order to please Hitler denied our people the sublime feeling of defending the oppressed, the persecuted minorities, of their peaceful and innocent Bulgarian citizens of foreign origin. Still today I recall with pain the persecution of the Jews.[8]

After their deaths, both Exarchs Kyril and Stefan were laid to rest side by side in the Bachkov monastery near Plovdiv.

King Simeon continued to reign over Bulgaria under the guidance of a new regents' council, which was formed by the "Fatherland Front" government. On September 8, 1946, a referendum was held in Bulgaria, and the kingdom was abolished. The nine-year-old king and his family were exiled to Cairo, and later moved to Europe. They were not allowed to return to Bulgaria until the early nineties, after the Communist regime had been abolished. Today, King Simeon lives with his wife and children in Madrid, his sister, Princess Maria Louisa, lives in the United States, and their mother, Queen Giovanna, lives in Portugal.

Nobody was rightly punished for the deportation of the Thracian and Macedonian Jews. The KEV officials and the police officers who carried out the raids on the Jewish communities in these countries either received ridiculously light sentences or were acquitted by the People's Court. Some were not even indicted.

This handful of anti-Semites and sadists didn't represent the Bulgarian people—far from it. But their monstrous deeds left a stain on Bulgaria, casting a dark shadow on the noble attitude of so many Bulgarians toward the Jews. Bulgaria, however, was too lenient toward these fanatics. Their crimes against the Thracian and the Macedonian Jews were discussed during the People's Court proceedings, but nobody really made an effort—like those who prosecuted Maurice Papon in France—to have them punished for so eagerly arresting, robbing, humiliating, and sending to their death 11,343 people. Still today, no one—no lawyer, no organization, no government—has been willing to undertake the tremendous challenge of righting this injustice.

(COURTESY OF BULGARIAN STATE ARCHIVES)

*The Bulgarian Army emerged from the alliance with Hitler unscathed. After the Soviets occupied Bulgaria, the Bulgarian Army joined the Allies in the final stage of the onslaught on Nazi Germany.*

The Macedonian and Thracian Jews died because no one interfered, no one stood up and fought for them. Thus, they became easy prey for the Holocaust machine. After their deaths, they became victims for a second time. Their martyrdom and suffering was submerged beneath the icy waves of indifference. Their memory was erased, as if they had never lived on the sunny shores of the Aegean Sea and in the green valleys of turbulent Macedonia.

In their lives and their deaths, they remain the orphans of the Balkans.

The dramatic protest of May 24, 1943, when many Sofia Jews attempted to march to the royal palace, had an astounding sequel, many years later.

On May 24, 1943, the Bulgarian Communist party was active in organizing the rally and the protest against the deportation. After the prayer in Yuch Bunar synagogue, a young Communist named Solomon Leviev (Gosho) jumped on a bench in the synagogue yard and called the crowd to protest in the streets. His short speech became the keystone for one of the greatest lies concerning the rescue of the Bulgarian Jews.

Thirty years later, in books, press articles, speeches, and a "documentary movie," a different story emerged. The Bulgarian Communist regime offered a new version of the events of that day. A young man was described as having jumped on the bench of Yuch Bunar, indeed, but now he had the face of a young Todor Jivkov—who meanwhile had, in fact, become the powerful president of Communist Bulgaria.

The official historians of the regime said that the young man whose speech had sparked the protest was not Gosho but Tosho (Todor Jivkov's nickname). They also said that Jivkov had been the one who organized the entire protest and, thus, had earned the eternal gratitude of the Jewish people. Vulka Goranova's part was completely erased. In the many books commemorating the rescue, her name and picture were left out. But these books contained large photographs of Todor Jivkov. Some of his aides even submitted his name as a candidate for the Nobel Peace Prize, for saving the Jews.

No sane Bulgarian dared contradict this version. Nobody wanted trouble with the authorities. David Elazar, the Jewish director of the Institute of Communist Party History, even forced Haim Oliver, a writer and a movie producer, to include the Jivkov version in his documentary film about the rescue.[9] Vulka Goranova and her family, who had suffered a great deal of humiliation, were forced to sit silently in the audience at huge public meetings where Jivkov was hailed for having accomplished what she had done. After the Communist regime collapsed, Vulka Goranova and Betty Danon signed a statement asserting that Todor Jivkov had not played a role in the protest.[10] In his article "Our Common Guilt,"[11] Solomon Leviev (Gosho) states openly that Jivkov had nothing to do with the events of May 24, 1943.

After interviewing Betty Danon and late Vulka Goranova's husband, Peko Takov,[12] I met with Todor Jivkov in Sofia.[13] Jivkov had never before spoken of his part in the famous protest of May 24,

1943. He told me he had organized it and directed it from behind the scenes. He couldn't risk being seen in the front lines of the protest, he said, therefore he held back and didn't march with the others. That was why nobody remembered seeing him. When I questioned him, though, he admitted that he hadn't met or seen Rabbi Daniel Tzion, that he hadn't participated at the prayer, that he hadn't been present at the Yuch Bunar synagogue, that he didn't remember where the protest started and where it ended. He only remembered that that same night the police came to arrest him, but he escaped from the house where he was staying.

President Jivkov spoke highly of Betty Danon. But when I confronted him with her testimony in favor of Vulka Goranova, he angrily said, "She had been manipulated."

In his memoirs, published a few months after our meeting, he claimed responsibility for "the direct leadership of the [communist party] campaign for the defense of the Bulgarian Jews."[14] He also claimed that the Central Committee of the party had charged him "to organize and direct the [May 24] demonstration."[15] I didn't find any evidence to support these claims.

All Jivkov could say about the protest itself is that it was led by "the capital rabbi."[16] This, of course, is absolutely untrue. No rabbi participated in the protest. Jivkov also claimed that the protest "scared the authorities . . . and they didn't dare to send Bulgarian Jews to the death camps in Poland."[17] The reader knows by now that the protest had nothing to do with the rescue of Bulgaria's Jews. My conclusion is that Todor Jivkov had nothing to do with the protest, although I have no doubt that he was a sincere friend of Bulgaria's Jews and tried to help them as part of his struggle against the pro-Fascist Bulgarian government.

The description of Jivkov's role is not the only distortion of the historical accounts concerning the fateful days of 1943. Obedient to the official policy, Bulgaria's historians for many years maintained that "the Bulgarian people" and "the Communist party" had saved the Jews from deportation. They completely or partly denied the role of the Church, of central figures of the establishment, and of King

Boris III. Even today, in their books or collections of documents about that period, these historians quote, as proof of the Communist's major role, the broadcasts from the Caucasus of the Soviet-sponsored radio station "Christo Botev," that very few Bulgarians listened to during the war years, or illegal Communist posters and flyers, which very few read.

But the Communists are not the only ones who have tried to rewrite history. In 1996, in a deplorable decision apparently stemming from hatred for the defunct Communist regime, the Bulgarian Supreme Court "rehabilitated" Bogdan Filov, Peter Gabrovski (and Prince Kyril). The grounds for the "rehabilitation"* were irregularities at the trial.[18]

This "rehabilitation," by a highly insensitive and irresponsible court, of Filov and Gabrovski, two of the worst and most despicable war criminals in Bulgarian history, is a repugnant act.

Almost all fifty thousand of Bulgaria's Jews immigrated to Israel when the Jewish State was proclaimed. This community, which many historians define as "the most Zionist in Europe," took the road en masse, to achieve its dream. Between the years 1948 and 1952, they settled mostly in Jaffa, Ramla, and Lod, in kibbutzim and moshavs (cooperative villages). Industrious, educated, and patriotic, the Bulgarian Jews became a success story in Israel, where they are regarded as one of the finest communities that immigrated to the Jewish State.

Speaking of their unique character, Nora Madjar of Plovdiv said: "There are four types of Jews: Orthodox, religious, secular, and Bulgarian."[19]

On October 21, 1996, the Jewish National Fund inaugurated a forest in the name of Bulgaria. In this forest, memorial plaques were dedicated to Dimiter Peshev, to the heads of the Bulgarian church, and to King Boris and Queen Giovanna, for having rescued the Jews of Bulgaria from the Holocaust. Another plaque was dedicated to the

---

* "Rehabilitation" was the term used in Bulgaria for clearing the record and the reputation of Filov and Gabrovski.

memory of the 11,343 Thracian and Macedonian Jews who were massacred in the death camps.

Every year, on March 9, Israel celebrates the rescue of the Bulgarian Jews from certain annihilation. The Bulgarian Jews in Israel hold a large rally, and many people come together, including the president, the prime minister, cabinet ministers, and members of the Knesset, the Israeli Parliament. A high-ranking delegation from Bulgaria is traditionally invited to participate in the celebration of its former citizens. The Bulgarian-born Israelis, their sons and daughters, thus express their deep gratitude to this small far-off nation that stood up and saved her Jewish citizens.

# EPILOGUE

German Ambassador Beckerle wrote, in 1943:

> The Bulgarian society doesn't understand the real
> meaning of the Jewish question. Beside the few rich Jews
> in Bulgaria there are many poor people, who make their
> living as workers and artisans. Partly raised together with
> Greeks, Armenians, Turks and Gypsies, the average
> Bulgarian doesn't understand the meaning of the struggle
> against the Jews, the more so as the racial question is
> totally foreign to him.[1]

He later added:

> I am convinced that the Prime Minister and the entire
> Cabinet desire and aspire to a final and total solution of
> the Jewish question. But they are tied by the mentality of
> the Bulgarian people, that lacks the ideological enlighten-
> ment that we have. The Bulgarian . . . doesn't see in the
> Jews any flaws justifying taking special measures against
> them . . . The majority of the Bulgarian Jews belong to the
> working class, and unlike other workers, are often more
> diligent . . .[2]

And the Gestapo attaché, Karl Hoffman, commented:

> The Jewish question doesn't exist in Bulgaria in the
> form that it has existed in the Reich . . . The ideological
> and racial reasons for presenting the Jewish question to
> the Bulgarian people as urgent and needing a solution, as
> it was the case in the Reich, do not exist here.[3]

"In Bulgaria there was no anti-Semitism in the conventional
sense of the word," German jurists noted after the war.[4] "My impression of the Bulgarians," said the former Swedish commercial attaché
Utgren, "is that anti-Semitism is foreign to them and they regard
deportation or [other] measures against anybody because of religious reasons as something absolutely illegal."[5]

The Bulgarians, indeed, were among the least anti-Semitic peoples in Europe. They never considered themselves superior because
of their religion or origins. They would be the first to ridicule any
idea of racial supremacy. Even before the Turkish conquest, they
had displayed a high degree of tolerance toward the Jews. Then, for
five centuries, they had lived with Jews, Greeks, and other minorities under Turkish rule, in an oppressed but highly egalitarian society. Modern Bulgaria remained faithful to this tradition.

Of course, there were anti-Semitic occurrences in Bulgaria
too—blood libels, books and articles against the Jews, cases of violence. There were staunch anti-Semites, and there still are. But most
of the Bulgarian anti-Semitism was either religious—tied to the old
accusation that the Jews had crucified Jesus—or imported from
abroad, from different societies and alien mentalities. It couldn't
spread and develop deep roots in Bulgaria. Even the anti-Semitism
of most pro-Fascist politicians and writers, before and during the
war, wasn't fanatical and cruel. The deep hatred for the Jews
infected only the lunatic fringe of the wartime society, the Ratniks,
Branniks, and Legionnaires and some sadistic police and army officers and KEV officials.

As Beckerle pointed out, it was difficult hating the Jews in
Bulgaria. A very large number of them were simple, modest workers,

living in the poorest Bulgarian neighborhoods, sharing with the Bulgarian working class their daily life, their joys, and their hunger. Very few of them were wealthy. Very few, if any, were bankers, moneylenders, or owners of large businesses who could be the object of hatred, suspicion, or envy. Very few could be depicted as "parasites, sucking the people's blood." The image of the Bulgarian Jew was totally different from that of the wealthy Jew painted by the Nazi and traditional anti-Semitic propaganda in Western Europe. "Our Jews are Spanish," King Boris told von Ribbentrop. "They absolutely don't play the same role as Jews in other countries."[6]

For many Bulgarians, the Jews "were like everybody else."[7] They didn't fit the image of the hated and feared alien, who dressed differently, lived differently, spoke a strange language, engaged in strange rites. Many Poles and Ukrainians hated the Jews instinctively, because they looked different, foreign. The Bulgarian Jews looked, dressed, and lived almost exactly like their Bulgarian neighbors. There were no Hassids among them; almost nobody wore hats or skullcaps; the only Jews with beards were the rabbis; side locks were never seen; some of the Jews ate kosher food (perhaps), but most of them didn't, and rather liked the taste of nonkosher meats and seafood; some of the older Jews prayed in the synagogue on Saturdays and High Holidays, but most of them didn't; many worked on Saturday; many studied in non-Jewish schools; many became poets, writers, composers, and were considered Bulgarian national artists; many spoke Bulgarian better than the Bulgarians themselves, sang their songs, felt a deep sense of belonging, passionately loved the country, and were ready to fight and die for it.

The Bulgarian Jews were very proud of their Judaism (although many didn't exactly know what it meant) and Zionism (although they were very comfortable in Bulgaria). But they were not preoccupied by their religion—as went the saying: "When Jehovah came to earth to visit His communities, He found the gates of Bulgaria locked."

The Bulgarian intellectual and political elite was even more tolerant. Most of the intellectuals and statesmen embraced, with fervent devotion, the goal of making the Bulgarian society one of the most enlightened in the world. They were extremely proud of their

Constitution, which guaranteed absolute equality of minorities. They regarded its humane principles with a very innocent, Bulgarian idealism, bordering on naïveté.

Other nations had, perhaps, a more enlightened heritage, like the French. That didn't prevent them from collaborating with the Nazis and brushing aside the immortal slogan of "Liberty, Equality, Fraternity," which the French Revolution had bequeathed to the world. Perhaps the French were too sophisticated, or too pragmatic, to take seriously such ideals at this time of bitter defeat. The Bulgarians differed from them. They cared about their country's honor and its image throughout the world. They took their Constitution seriously.

The intellectuals, the academics, the writers, the doctors, the lawyers, launched a fierce crusade against the Law for the Defense of the Nation and the deportation. It had no equal in any European country within the Nazi sphere of influence. The princes of the Church fought with total dedication against the anti-Jewish measures, confronting the government over and over again. The elder statesmen, the Communist party, the opposition members of Parliament, struggled with tenacity and courage against the anti-Jewish policy of the government.

Even pro-government members of Parliament, who owed their seats to their support of Prime Minister Filov, couldn't follow him in his Jewish policy. They stuck to the principles of their Constitution, even in the atmosphere of messianic intoxication surrounding the creation of Greater Bulgaria. Dobrudja, Thrace, and Macedonia had been liberated. Bulgaria's flag was waving over Skopje and Kavalla, over the Macedonian mountains and the golden shores of the Aegean. Bulgaria's German allies had made the realization of that dream possible. This was a new era, a new order, a new world. Who cared about a handful of Jews and their rights, compared with this momentous achievement? Weren't they expendable? Shouldn't they be sacrificed, to make this historic unification of Bulgaria possible?

The answer was no. Even at the height of their enthusiasm, when they were welcoming every speech of Filov with cheers, applause, and hurrahs, many members of Parliament revolted against the shameful treatment of the Jews; many signed Peshev's letter and by doing so joined the unique rebellion against the government policy, by government supporters, in wartime Bulgaria.

They stood up against the deportation, which would brand Bulgaria with an "undeserved stain." They stood up to defend "the honor of Bulgaria and her people," which they considered "a political asset of the greatest value."[8] They were not the majority, indeed, but they were a very large minority. Considering their almost total dependence on the Central Power, their initiative was an expression of courage and morality.

This was the social and political background to King Boris's actions.

•   •   •

Unlike the three-level hierarchy of Filov, Gabrovski, and Belev, Boris III was not an anti-Semite.[9] He didn't hate the Jews and didn't want to harm them. By character he was the opposite of a fanatic; he admired democracy, he resented violence, and he could find his natural place in the Allied camp. But he opted for the alliance with Nazi Germany, expecting it to fulfill his dream of Greater Bulgaria. This implied that the Jews had become pawns in the game for the recovery of Bulgaria's lost lands. "The Germans don't want to meddle in our internal affairs," reported Filov to the king, quoting a message from the Führer's secretary. "Germany," he said, "would support any government that is able to deal with the communists, with the Jews, for whom there is no place in the new Europe, and with the street [meaning—with the popular masses] . . ."[10]

Until March 9, 1943, Boris III carried out, willingly or unwillingly, an anti-Jewish policy, whose main stages were the adoption of the Law for the Defense of the Nation (the ZZN), the creation of the

Commissariat for Jewish Questions, and the Belev-Dannecker agreement for the deportation "at first" of twenty thousand Jews from old and new Bulgaria. Perhaps the king didn't mean to sacrifice his Jewish subjects on the altar of Dobrudja, Thrace, and Macedonia. Perhaps he hoped that by procrastinating, by passing anti-Jewish laws but not implementing them too zealously, he could gain time and spare his Jewish subjects a horrendous fate. And indeed, except for the unique tax on Jews, imposed by a new law in July 1941, the authorities were rather lenient in implementing the ZZN restrictions, to the point that some right-wing extremists mockingly started calling it "the Law for the Defense of the Jews."[11] Feeling, indeed, that the ZZN was not strictly enforced, Peshev and many other Parliament members didn't fight against the law after it was passed.[12]

However, the king was caught in his own game. He agreed to the Belev-Dannecker agreement, and by doing so he condoned a death sentence on twenty thousand Jews.

As far as the Jews of Macedonia and Thrace were concerned, Boris didn't believe he had the power or the authority to save them. In his message to Metropolitan Stefan, he called them "Jewish exiles from Hitler's High Command."[13] Alexander Belev, in his confidences to Liliana Panitza, and even Theodore Dannecker also regarded those Jews as "belonging to the Germans anyway."[14] In spite of the formal propaganda about the unification of Bulgaria's historic provinces and the laws passed to that effect, King Boris knew the truth: In Germany's eyes Bulgaria was only occupying and administering these territories, and their final status was not going to be decided before the end of the war. Boris thought he was powerless to take any step against the Germans.

When the Bulgarian Parliament passed the laws annexing the new territories, it refused to grant Bulgarian citizenship to the Thracian and Macedonian Jews. On the other hand, Bulgaria gave that citizenship to the Jews of Dobrudja. The argument was that Dobrudja's return to Bulgaria had been officially accepted by the Romanian government and recognized by the outside world.

Immediately after its annexation, Dobrudja became a full-fledged part of Bulgaria. Thrace and Macedonia, on the other hand, in spite of their title—"newly liberated lands" were treated by the Bulgarians "as an occupied area."[15] They were governed by civil servants and police officers dispatched from old Bulgaria and were not granted any kind of self-government or representation in the Parliament.

If Boris was more caring and courageous, he might have tried to save the Thracian and Macedonian Jews. But he was not. The truth is that many other eminent Bulgarians, who strongly intervened for the Jews of old Bulgaria, didn't do so for the Jews of Thrace and Macedonia, whom they regarded as aliens. Most of the Bulgarians were indifferent to the Thracian and Macedonian Jews. Even the Jews of Bulgaria, apparently too concerned with their own imminent annihilation, didn't try to prevent the tragedy of the Jews in Thrace and Macedonia. Actually, they couldn't have done anything, even if they had tried.

The deportation of these 11,343 wretched people, however, and the way it was carried out by Bulgarian officers, Bulgarian soldiers, and Bulgarian policemen, has left a dark, grim shadow over Bulgaria's past.

Yet, although the status of Thrace and Macedonia could be an excuse for Boris not to interfere with the deportation, he had no formal or informal excuse for agreeing to deport the eight thousand Jews of old Bulgaria. The king's unconditional supporters advance two arguments. The first argument is that the king didn't know that the Belev-Dannecker agreement included Jews from old Bulgaria. The plan, they say, was never submitted for his approval.

This argument is absurd. No major decision, like the deportation of eight thousand Bulgarian citizens, could be made in wartime Bulgaria without the king's knowledge. Gabrovski and Belev would have never dared to make such a decision without Filov's agreement and the King's approval. If they had done it on their own, they might have been severely punished by the king. They might have paid a heavy price for that "personal initiative," a price that could even exceed the loss of their political positions. They would have never taken such a risk. They were fanatics, but they were not madmen. There is no doubt that Filov informed the king, probably at their meeting of February 17, 1943, of the forthcoming agreement; and Boris didn't reject it. "He agreed with me," Filov wrote of the conversation (which also dealt with other subjects), "although he didn't seem very convinced by my arguments."[16] (Filov never mentioned the Belev-Dannecker agreement in his diary.) In February 1943 Belev informed his deputy that Filov had reported to the king and obtained his agreement to the deportation.[17]

The second argument of the king's defenders is that perhaps Boris had "invited" the public pressure so that he would have an excuse to cancel the deportation. He might have wanted the Church, the intellectual elite, and the public to protest, thereby pressuring him to stop the deportation of Bulgaria's Jews. That way he could explain his change of policy to his German allies, claiming he had to yield to the pressure.

This argument, too, cannot withstand a serious examination. If the king wanted indeed to trigger public pressure, he should have made sure that the public, the politicians, and the Church learned early enough about the deportation plans. But we know that the preparations for the deportation were carried out in utmost secrecy. Nobody was supposed to know about Belev's project. If everything had worked as planned, the secret would not have leaked. If the Kyustendil Jews had not learned about the plan to arrest them, if the Kyustendil delegation had not rushed to Sofia at the last moment and against all odds, and if Peshev hadn't launched his spontaneous rebellion, eight thousand Bulgarian Jews would have been sent to their deaths. Even the king of the Bulgarians couldn't have masterminded such a sequence of events, which was crowned with the cancellation of the "Aktzia." As Belev himself said, if the cancellation order had come only four hours later, the first deportation of the Bulgarian Jews would have been executed.

Peshev's eleventh-hour initiative, combined with the staunch struggle of the Church and the intellectual elites, had shaken the king

and made him come to his senses. It had torn him from his meek obedience to the Germans. It had showed him that the Bulgarian society,
and even his most loyal and devoted supporters in the Sobranie,
couldn't accept such treatment of the Jews. Peshev, the
Metropolitans, Ellin Pellin, had forced Boris to face his responsibility as the king of the Bulgarians. He could no longer afford the luxury of looking the other way, burying his head in the sand, or subtly
maneuvering in the dark and trying to gain time, as he had done for
the past three years. He had to make a choice—honor his agreement
with Germany and deport the Jews or refuse to deliver his Jews to the
Germans, even at the cost of a confrontation with the mighty Reich.

This confrontation, although in overtones and vague terms, took
place in the Eagle's Nest, when Boris III had to face von Ribbentrop.
King Boris stood his ground. He had decided to reverse his policy,
and he stuck by his decision. For a weak man like him, haunted by
fears and hesitations, and conscious of the total dependence of his
little country on Germany, this certainly was an act of courage.

Boris went even farther than that. In Berchtesgaden he
promised von Ribbentrop he would deport some Jews—whom he
defined as "a small number of Bolshevik-Communist elements"—to
Poland.[18] He never did that. No Bulgarian Jews were deported as
"Bolshevik elements," and no such plans were ever made.

The king's critics claim that the main reason for his reversal
was the crucial German defeat in Stalingrad, which was the turning
point in the war. We found this argument in the accounts of many
writers. However, they should brush up on their history. The defeat
of Fieldmarshall von Paulus in Stalingrad occurred on February 2,
1943. (The other turning point of the war, Rommel's defeat at El
Alamein, took place between October 23 and November 2, 1942.)
Its results became known the following day. This was twenty days
before the signing of the Belev-Dannecker agreement and more than
a month before the planned deportation of the Bulgarian Jews. If the
Stalingrad debacle had indeed influenced Boris's decision, he
shouldn't have allowed Belev to sign the agreement in the first place.
But to claim that a month after the agreement was signed, and after

the deportation from Thrace and Macedonia had begun, Boris suddenly remembered the battle of Stalingrad and changed his policy is more than ludicrous.

True, he might have been influenced by the Allied warnings to Bulgaria and by the course of the war; but nothing dramatic happened on the battlefields between February 22 and March 9, 1943, that could explain Boris's reversal. The only dramatic event in this period was the rebellion of some of the staunchest supporters of the king and of the government against the planned deportation.

The fact remains, however, that on March 9, 1943, Boris did indeed sharply reverse his Jewish policy. From that moment until the day he died, he stuck firmly to his new course and defeated the plans for a new deportation in May. He could have acted differently. On March 9 he could have merely delayed the deportation and carried it out later. On April 1 he could have agreed to von Ribbentrop's demands. On April 13 he could have refrained from sending all the able Jewish men to labor units, in order "to avoid the deportation."[19] On May 20 he could have approved Belev's "plan A."

But he did not.

Boris's actions in March and in May of 1943 were triggered by Peshev, Stefan, and other brave Bulgarians. Without them, the Bulgarian Jews were doomed. However, the final responsibility was the king's, and his decisions saved the Jews of Bulgaria.

Not one Bulgarian Jew was sent to the death camps in Poland.

The Bulgarian Jews became the only Jewish community in the Nazi sphere of influence whose number increased, during World War II.

# NOTES

## CHAPTER ONE: Alarm

[1] Maurice Lazar (Buko Lazarov's brother), interview by author, July 9, 1997; see also Buko Lazarov, "Who and How Saved the Bulgarian Jews," a series of articles in *Narodno Delo*, Tel-Aviv (in Bulgarian), 180–86; and Buko Lazarov, testimony, Yad Vashem, Jerusalem, August 1977, 03/3970.

[2] Ibid.

[3] Buko Lazarov, testimony before People's Court VII, March 1945.

[4] Guy Haskell, *From Sofia to Jaffa* (Detroit: Wayne State University Press, 1994), 87–96, 108.

[5] *Encyclopaedia Judaica*, Keter, Jerusalem, 1971 vol. 4, 1479–82.

[6] Ibid., 1481.

[7] Ibid.

[8] *Encyclopaedia of the Jewish Diaspora* (in Hebrew), vol. 10, Bulgaria, Jerusalem, 1967, 31–34.

[9] Ibid., 32.

[10] Ibid., 59.

[11] Ibid.

[12] *El Amigo del Puevlo* (in Ladino), bi-weekly, Russe, fifth issue, year 7, no date.

[13] Peter Meyer, *The Jews in the Soviet Satellites* (Syracuse University Press, 1953), 1967; also *Encyclopaedia of the Jewish Diaspora*, op. cit., 86.

[14] Haim Keshales, *Korot Yehudey Bulgaria Betkufat Hashoah* (*History of Bulgaria's Jews During the Holocaust* [in Hebrew]), *Korot Yehudey Bulgaria*, Davar, Tel-Aviv, 1969 vol. 3, 20.

[15] Benyamin (Bubi) Arditi, *Vidni Evrei V Bulgaria* (*Eminent Jews in Bulgaria* [in Bulgarian]), 3 vols., Tel-Aviv, 1969–1971, vol. 2, 111; and in Keshales, op. cit. 22.

## CHAPTER TWO: The Fox

[1] Stephane Groueff, *Crown of Thorns* (Maryland: Madison Books, 1987), 141.

[2] Ibid., 242.

[3] Ibid., 63.

4 Stilian Noykov and Valentin Radev, *Tzar Boris III v Tainite dokumenti na Tretia Reich* (*King Boris III in the Secret Documents of the Third Reich*) (Sofia: Publishing House of the St. Klement Ohridski University, 1995), 7.

5 Groueff, op. cit., 320.

6 Richard Dunlop, *Donovan, America's Master Spy* (Chicago: Rand McNally, 1982), 249–51; see also I. Dimitrov, *Bulgarian Historical Review*, vol. 4, 1978.

7 Dunlop, op. cit.

8 Ibid.

9 Groueff, op. cit., 320.

10 Parvan Draganov, diary, quoted in *Crown of Thorns*, op. cit., 193–194; also Peter Konstantinov, *History of Bulgaria* (in Bulgarian), (Sofia: Phoenix, 1993), 254.

11 Liubomir Lulchev, diary, *Taynite na Dvortzovia Jivot* (*The Secrets of the Palace Life*) (Sofia: Veselie, 1992), 243.

12 *New York Times*, September 17, 1939.

13 Frederic Chary, *The Bulgarian Jews and the Final Solution* (Pittsburgh: University of Pittsburgh Press, 1972), 17.

## CHAPTER THREE: The Law for the Defense of the Nation

1 Natan Grinberg, *Hitleristkiat Natisk za Unishtojavane na Evreite ot Bulgaria* (*The Hitlerist Pressure for the Annihilation of Bulgaria's Jews* [in Bulgarian]) (Tel-Aviv: Amal, 1961), 34.

2 Derjaven Vestnik, the Official State *Gazette*, January 23, 1941, 1–5.

3 Joseph Geron, letter, October 21, 1940, CDIA, f. 173, op. 6, a.e.1087, 29–39.

4 Haim Oliver, report of Police Director, Colonel Pantev, *Nie Spasenite* (*We, the rescued* [in Bulgarian]) (Sofia: Izdatelstvo za literatura na Chujdi ezitzi, 1967), 50–51.

5 Buko Levi, testimony (memoirs), Yad Vashem, Jerusalem, November 21, 1967.

6 Ibid.

7 Joseph Geron, testimony (memoirs), Yad Vashem, Jerusalem, June 18, 1958.

8 Buko Levi, memoirs, op. cit.

9 Ibid.

10 Joseph Geron, memoirs, op. cit.

11 CPA (Central Communist Party Archives), f.18, op. 2.a.e.92, 1–2.

12 CDIA (Central Historical State Archives), f.173, op. 6.a.e.1087, 27–28.

13 CDIA, f.173. op. 6.a.e.1087, 82–83, 84, 85, 88, 89, 90, 91–92, 93, 94–95, 96–97.

14 CDIA, f.173, op. 6.a.e.1087, 113.

15 CDIA, f.173, op. 6.a.e.1087, 263–64.

16 CDIA, f.173, op. 6.a.e.1087, 55–58.

17 CDIA, f.173, op. 6 a.e.1087, 108–18.

18 CDIA, f.173, op. 6.a.e. 1087, 25.

19 AMVR (Archives of the Ministry of Interior), K 117623, 12–16.

20 Haim Oliver, op. cit., 62–64.

21 Ibid., 57–58.

22 CDIA, f.173, op. 6.a.e. 1087, 114–15.

23 Dimiter Peshev, diary, CDIA, f.1335, op. 1, a.e.156, 141–67.

24 Bulgarian writers, letter, October 22, 1940, CDIA, f.173, op.6.a.e.1087, 25.

25 Lulchev, letter to the king, November 9, 1940, *Tainite na Dvortzovia Jivot*, 239–43.

26 Lulchev, diary, November 9, 1940, op. cit. 242–43.

[27] Lulchev, diary, January 26, 1941, op. cit., 270–71.

[00] Noykov and Radev, *Tzar Boris III v Tainite Dokumenti na Tretia Reich*, 7.

## CHAPTER FOUR: The Commissar

[1] Politisches Archiv des Auswartigen Amt, F.17, Bl. 035-039.

[2] Reports from Sofia to the S.D., transferred to the Ministry of Foreign Affairs, September 25, 1940, and October 24, 1940, Politisches Archiv des Auswartigen Amto, Inland II geheim, Bd. 347, Bl. 52–57 and Bl. 140–41.

[3] Bogdan Filov, Dnevnik (diary [in Bulgarian]), Otechestvenia Front, Sofia, 1990, November 18, 1940, 211.

[4] Bogdan Filov, diary. Filov quoted the king's words in German. "Sie haben da unten einen kleinen treuen Freund tun Sie ihn nicht abschiessen," November 18, 1940, 211.

[5] Bogdan Filov, diary, November 18, 1940, 211.

[6] Bogdan Filov, diary, January 7, 1941, 221–223.

[7] Ibid.

[8] Bogdan Filov, diary, March 1, 1941, 271.

[9] Karl Claudius, report to Ribbentrop, April 28, 1941, Politischen Archiv des Auswartigen Amts, Unterstaatssekretar, Aktenband 11, Akten betreffend Bulgarien, Bl. 311381-311383, quoted in *Tzar Boris III v Tainite Dokumenti*.

[10] Bulletin of the Central Consistory, year XXI, no. 36–37, June 13, 1941, 3, 4.

[11] Ibid.

[12] Ibid., no. 32, May 2, 1941.

[13] Keshales, *Korot Yehudey Bulgaria*, vol. 3, op. cit. 59.

[14] Beckerle, diary, Bulgarian edition (Sofia: Christo Botev, 1992), 5–8.

[15] Colonel Carl-August von Schoenebeck, diary, quoted in *Crown of Thorns*, op. cit. 378.

[16] Beckerle, telegrams, Political Archives, Sofia, c.178874, tel. 793, July 24, 1941 and c.178886, tel. 828, July 31, 1941. They are also quoted by Benyamin Arditi, *Yehudey Bulgaria Bishnot Hamishtar Hanazi* (*The Jews of Bulgaria during the years of Nazi regime* [in Hebrew]) (Holon: Tel-Giborim, 1962), 227–28), and mentioned in *The Diary of Beckerle*, 12.

[17] Ibid.

[18] Bogdan Filov, diary, July 30, 1941, 380–81.

[19] Cabinet's resolution of August 12, 1941, CDIA, f.284, op.1, a.e.7707, 28–29.

[20] *Zora* (Bulgarian daily), August 21, 1941.

[21] Bulletin of the Central Consistory, year XXI, number 10, December 5, 1941, 4.

[22] Benyamin Arditi, *Yehudey Bulgaria*, 59.

[23] Order of June 25, 1941, CDIA, c.p.#247, 6.

[24] Order 6401 of December 29, 1941, quoted in Natan Grinberg, *Hitleristkiat Natisk za Unishtojavane na Evreite ot Bulgaria*, op. cit., 35.

[25] Benyamin Arditi, *Yehudey Bulgaria*, 396.

[26] Yaroslav Kalitzin, Interrogatory by People's Court VII, March 9, 1945.

[27] Benyamin Arditi, *Yehudey Bulgaria*, 70–73.

[28] Ibid., 396.

[29] Report presented at the Deliberations of the People's Court VII, Sofia, 1945, 2020.

[30] Natan Grinberg, *Dokumenti* (Documents [in Bulgarian]), Central Consistory of the Jews in Bulgaria, Sofia, 1945, 7, report presented at the Deliberation of the People's Court VII, Sofia, 1945, 2028.

[31] Frederic Chary, op. cit., 52.

[32] Ibid., 51.

[33] Durjaven Vestnik, text of the law (State *Gazette*), July 9, 1942.

[34] Durjaven Vestnik (State *Gazette*), no. 192, August 29, 1942; and Natan Grinberg *Hitleristkiat Natisk*, op. cit. 36–37.

[35] Liliana Panitza, interrogatory by the People's Militia, September–October 1944.

[36] Maria Pavlova, interrogatory by the People's Militia (3 protocols) no date, F. 190, op. 3 a.e.21. Also *Dokumenti*, 184–185 and AMVR vol. 187, 16 (90a).

[37] S. Nikolov, former KEV employee, interrogatory by People's Court VII, vol. I, PNS, file 179, 33.

[38] Benyamin Arditi, *Yehudey Bulgaria*, 72–78, and Frederic Chary, 56–57.

[39] Haim Keshales, *Korot Yehudey Bulgaria Betekufat Hashoa*, vol. 3, 76–79.

[40] Frederic Chary, op. cit. 57–58.

[41] Schellenberg, letter to Luther, November 9, 1942, quoted in Benyamin Arditi, *Yehudey Bulgaria*, 90–93, also in Frederic Chary, op. cit. 73–74.

[42] Bulletin of the Central Consistory, July 7, 1942; also in Natan Grinberg, *Hitleristkiat Natisk*, 40–42.

[43] Haim Keshales, *Korot Yehudey*, vol. 3, 88.

[44] Beckerle, diary, August 22, 1942, 27. The meeting between the king and Rabbi Hanan'el hasn't been reported by other reliable sources.

[45] Ibid.

[46] Politisches Archiv des Auswartiges Amts, Inland II Geheim, Bd. 183, Akten Betreffend Judenfrage in Bulgarien, Bl. 486251-486257, November 9, 1942, also quoted in *Tzar Boris III v Tainite Dokumenti*, 177–79, and in Frederic Chary, 73–75.

[47] Peshev, diary, CDIA, f.1335, op.1 a.e. 158, 141–67.

[48] Nuremberg documents, #1517.

[49] Telegram 1769, October 16, 1942, Yad Vashem K 207522/3.

[50] Bogdan Filov, diary, October 26, 1942, 536.

[51] Beckerle, telegram, #1839, November 2, 1942, Yad Vashem K 207525.

[52] Beckerle, report to Berlin, #A 4318/42, November 16, 1942, Yad Vashem K 207547.

[53] Adolf Eichmann, letter to Luther, IV B 4 a 3564/42 geheim/1484/, December 10, 1942, Yad Vashem K 207555/6.

[54] Yad Vashem K 207557.

[55] Beckerle, reports of conversation to the foreign ministry, Berlin, A 88/43, January 22 1943, Yad Vashem K 207564/6, and A 154/43, February 8, 1943, Yad Vashem K 207571/3.

[56] Warrant 3156 on the citizenship, approved by the cabinet, paragraph 4, published in the State *Gazette*, no. 124, June 10, 1942.

[57] Dannecker, report to Eichmann, February 2, 1943, Yad Vashem K 207571/3.

[58] Ibid.

[59] Natan Grinberg, *Hitleristkiat Natisk*, 88–89.

## CHAPTER FIVE: An Order for Deportation

[1] Liliana Panitza, interrogatory by the People's Militia, September 27, 28, October 5, November 2, full transcripts; also Belev, report to Gabrovski, February 4, 1943.

[2] Liliana Panitza, interrogatory by the People's Militia, Ibid.

[3] Liliana Panitza, interrogatory by People's Court VII, March 12, 1945.

[4] Liliana Panitza, interrogatory by the People's Militia.

[5] Liliana Panitza, interrogatory by the People's Militia and by the People's Court.

[6] Belev, report to Gabrovski, February 4, 1943; Natan Grinberg, *Dokumenti*, 8–11.

[7] Belev, report to Gabrovski, February 4, 1943, 11-12.

[8] Ribbentrop, telegram to Beckerle, #293, March 26, 1942, Politisches Archiv . . . Handakten Ritter, Bulgarien, Bd. 2, Bl. 282708-282710, also quoted in *Tzar Boris III v Tainite Dokumenti*, 154–56.

[9] Luther, report, April 6, 1942, and Ribbentrop, telegram to Beckerle, April 8, 1942, op. cit.

[10] Bogdan Filov, diary, February 17, 1943, 557–58.

[11] Yaroslav Kalitzin, written testimony before the People's Militia, quoting a conversation with Belev, AMVR, Papers of The People's Court, vol. 188, n.d.

[12] Bogdan Filov, diary, February 17, 1943.

[13] Bogdan Filov, diary, Ibid., 558–59.

[14] Dannecker, report to Eichmann, countersigned by Beckerle, February 16, 1943, Yad Vashem K 207579/80.

[15] Liliana Panitza, interrogatory by People's Court VII.

[16] Liliana Panitza, interrogatory by People's Court VII, vol. II, file 180, 119.

[17] Kalitzin, interrogatory by People's Court VII, File PNS 179, 313.

[18] Belev, telegram to the KEV delegates, *Dokumenti*, op. cit. 11–12.

[19] Yaroslav Kalitzin, report to Alexander Belev, February 16, 1943, *Dokumenti*, 12–14.

[20] Hausner Gideon, *Justice in Jerusalem* (New York: Harper and Row, 1966), 124.

[21] Das Reich, Berlin, October 18, 1942.

[22] Liliana Panitza, interrogatory by People's Court VII, Ibid., 119.

[23] Boris III, message to Metropolitan Stefan, quoted in Stefan's Memoirs, handwritten, Institute of Balkanistic studies, inv. 8804.

[24] Yaroslav Kalitzin, testimony before the People's Militia, AMVR.

[25] Dannecker, report to Eichmann, February 23, 1943, Yad Vashem K 207583/5, accompanied by Beckerle's letter from the same day, A235/43 T.

[26] Beckerle, diary, March 3, 1943, 85.

[27] Liliana Panitza, interrogatory by People's Court VII.

[28] Alexander Belev, reports, following reports by Peter Gabrovski, Cabinet Resolutions 2 5, March 1943, *Dokumenti*, 23–44.

[29] Decision of March 1943, *Dokumenti*, 42–44.

[30] Gabrovski, report for Warrant 113, approved on March 2, 1943, quoted in *Dokumenti*, 25.

[31] Ibid., report for Warrant 29, approved on March 5, 1943, quoted in *Dokumenti*, 39–41.

[32] Ibid., report for Warrant 116, approved on March 2, 1943, quoted in *Dokumenti*, 30–32.

[33] Warrant 3156 on the citizenship, approved by the cabinet, paragraph 4, published in the State *Gazette*, no. 124, June 10, 1942.

[34] Ibid., *Dokumenti*, 43.

## CHAPTER SIX: The Lovers

[1] Ilya Dobrevski, interrogatory by the People's Militia (before the trial), n.d., vol. 187, 181–83.

[2] Ibid., September 27, 1944.

3 Ibid.
4 Liliana Panitza, interrogatory by People's Court VII, March 23, 1945.
5 Liliana Panitza, interrogatory by the People's Militia, October 2, 1944, October 5, 1944; Ilya Dobrevski, interrogatory by People's Court VII.
6 Dobrevski, interrogatory, Ibid.
7 Ilya Dobrevski, reports to his department head, March 1, 1943, and to Commissar Belev, March 22, 1943; see *Dokumenti*, 74–80.
8 Liliana Panitza, interrogatory by the People's Militia, October 2, 1944.
9 Maria Pavlova, interrogatory by the People's Militia.
10 Yaroslav Kalitzin, written testimony before the People's Militia, op. cit.
11 Buko Levi, testimony at Yad Vashem, 03/3458 (also referred to as memoirs), November 1967, 21–22; also a hint in his deposition as Panitza's defense witness before the People's Tribunal VII, March 24, 1945. "By her behavior toward us, and by her convictions, she actually couldn't have been a clerk in the Commissariat for Jewish affairs . . . [Yet] Particular reasons, strictly personal, kept her working in this institution."
12 Maria Pavlova, interrogatory by the People's Militia, n.d., f.190, op.3, a.e.21, second protocol, 14.
13 Liliana Panitza, interrogatory by the People's Militia, October 2, 1944.
14 Ibid., September 27, 1944.
15 Ibid., October 2, 1944.
16 Dobrevski, interrogatory, Ibid.
17 Liliana Panitza, interrogatory by the People's Militia, September 27, 1944.
18 Liliana Panitza, interrogatory by People's Court VII, March 12, 1945, V. 180, 112.
19 Maria Pavlova, interrogatory, op. cit.
20 Liliana Panitza, deposition before the People's Militia.
21 Liliana Panitza, draft letter (to Belev) handwritten, pencil, n.d., found in the People's Militia archives.
22 Ibid.
23 Liliana Panitza, interrogatory by the People's Court, March 23, 1945.
24 Bulgarian Jew, interview, Jaffa, March 15, 1996; interview with another source, November 24, 1997.
25 Jack Benaroya, interrogatory by the People's Court VII, March 24, 1945, vol. 1, 1577–80.
26 Yaroslav Kalitzin, written testimony before the People's Militia.
27 Yaroslav Kalitzin, written testimony before the People's Militia; also interview with Maria Pavlova by Albena Taneva.
28 Buko Levi, testimony at Yad Vashem, Ibid.
29 Buko Levi, testimony at Yad Vashem, Ibid.
30 Buko Levi, testimony before the People's Court, March 24, 1945.
31 Buko Levi, testimony before the People's Court, Ibid.
32 Liliana Panitza, plea of the defense at trial at People's Court VII, Sofia.
33 Buko Levi, testimony before the People's Court.
34 Buko Levi, testimony before the People's Court, March 24, 1945.
35 Ibid.
36 Frederic Chary, op. cit. 91.
37 Buko Levi, testimony at Yad Vashem, Ibid.
38 Buko Levi, testimony before the People's Court.
39 Ibid.

## CHAPTER SEVEN: A Thracian Nightmare

1. Benzion Solomon Kadmon, testimony, *Dokumenti*, 80–81.
2. For a collection of the main documents, see *Dokumenti*, 44–113.
3. Testimony, *Dokumenti*, 96-II, 96-III.
4. Ibid., 98–99.
5. Joseph Konfino, testimony before People's Court VII; also *Dokumenti*, 102–3.
6. Nora Levi, testimony, *Dokumenti*, 100–102.
7. Ibid.
8. Quoted in Arditi, *Vidni Evrei*, op. cit. vol. 2, 134.
9. Written testimony, *Dokumenti*, 88–89, 99.
10. Harry Nissimov, *Sas Zubi I nokti* (With Teeth and Nails) (Columb 92 Sofia, 1995), 75–76.
11. Ibid., 76.
12. Telegram 2663, March 8, 1943, vol. 187, photocopy of the original. The texts of the telegrams, printed, appear also in *Dokumenti*, 96-III, 96-V.
13. Telegram 2843, March 8, 1943, Ibid.
14. Telegram 2844, March 8, 1943, Ibid.
15. Telegram 2624, March 8, 1943, Ibid.
16. Telegram 3193, March 8, 1943, Ibid.
17. Telegram 3255, March 6, 1943, Ibid.
18. Telegram 3370, March 6, 1943, Ibid; and in *Dokumenti*, 96-V.
19. Telegram 6, 8.3.43, Ibid; and in *Dokumenti*, 96-VI.
20. Dobrevski, testimony, *Dokumenti*, 96-VI, confirmed by Kalitzin's written testimony before the People's Militia.
21. Joseph Konfino, testimony before People's Court VII; also *Dokumenti*, 109–10.

## CHAPTER EIGHT: Boxcars at the Station

1. Boris Tasev, report to Dr. Ivan Popov, March 1943, *Dokumenti*, 180–84.
2. Buko Lazarov, testimony; and series of articles in *Narodno Delo*, op. cit., confirmed by Maurice Lazarov, interview, op. cit.
3. Buko Lazarov, Ibid.
4. Boris Tasev, letter to Kyustendil's Mayor, March 5, 1943, *Dokumenti*, 180–81.
5. Protocol established by Boris Tasev and Pinhas Comfort, March 6, 1943, *Dokumenti*, 181.
6. Haim Rahamim Behar, testimony, Yad Vashem, Jerusalem.
7. Depositions of several KEV employees—Yaroslav Kalitzin, Maria Pavlova, and Yordan Lazanov—and of several Jewish witnesses—Moshe Nissim, Tamara Beracha, Aharon Beracha, Boris Oliver, and Nissim Haim, NA BAN Ebraistika, doc. 55.
8. Haim Rahamim Behar, testimony, Yad Vashem, Jerusalem; Buko Lazarov, "Who and How Saved the Bulgarian Jews," a series of articles in *Narodno Delo*; Buko Lazarov, testimony, Yad Vashem.
9. Buko Lazarov, testimony, Yad Vashem, August 1977.
10. Haim Rahamim Behar, testimony, Ibid.
11. Haim Rahamim Behar, Ibid.
12. Yako Baruch, testimony, Yad Vashem, Jerusalem.

13  Samuel Baruch, letter to his brother, Yako Baruch, presented to People's Court VII, vol. 12, file 54, 2066.

14  Buko Beracha, interview with Nir Baruch, *The Survival*, ed. David Cohen, Shalom, Sofia, 1995, 300–301.

15  Buko Beracha, interview, op. cit.

16  Buko Lazarov, op. cit.

17  Buko Beracha, op. cit.

18  Haim Rahamim Behar, testimony, op. cit.

19  Peter Mikhalev, interrogatory by People's Court II, vol. V, file 47, 873. Also interview of Parka Mikhaleva (Peter Mikhalev's widow) with the author and Albena Taneva, September 4, 1997.

20  Yako Baruch, testimony, People's Court VII, 2066.

21  Peter Mikhalev, testimony, NA BAN, f.111, op. 1, a.e.47, 1–5.

22  Ibid.

23  Buko Lazarov, testimony, op. cit.

24  Mikhalev, op. cit.

25  Ibid.

26  Lazarov, op. cit.

27  Mikhalev, op. cit.

28  Gregor Suichmezov (son of Assen Suichmezov), interview, 2.7.1996, 29.8.1996 (assisted by Dr. Sonia Levi).

29  Assen Suichmezov, recollections, December 19, 1976, ODA (Regional State Archives), Kyustendil, f. 278. "k," op.1, a.e.1, 1–9.

30  Gregor Suichmezov, interview, op. cit.; also Buko Beracha, interview, op. cit.

31  Gregor Suichmezov, Ibid.

32  Albert Alfandari, interview by Dr. Sonia Levi, Kyustendil, July 1, 1996.

33  Assen Suichmezov, recollections, Ibid.

34  Dr. Momchilov (Ivan Momchilov's son), interview by Albena Taneva, April 2, 1997.

## CHAPTER NINE: An Order from the Highest Place

1  Dr. Liuben Diukmedjiev, testimony before People's Court II, 19.1. 1945.

2  Svetoslav Peshev (Peshev's nephew), interview, July 3, 1996, Kyustendil; and with his two other nephews, Kichka and Kaludka Kiradjiev, Sofia, September 29, 1996.

3  Svetoslav Peshev, interview, August 29, 1996.

4  Peshev, depositions before People's Court II, vol. V, file PNS 69, and file PNS 47, 828–41.

5  Yako Baruch, testimony before the People's Court, vol. XII, file 54, 2066.

6  Peshev, memoirs, CDIA, f.1335, op.1, a.e.158, 141–67.

7  Ibid.

8  Peter Mikhalev, testimony, BAN, f.3, op.1, a.e. 47, 1–5, original.

9  Ibid.

10  Buko Beracha, interview by Nir Baruch, "The Survival," op. cit.

11  Ibid.

12  Assen Suichmezov, testimony, ODA, Kyustendil, f.278 "k" op.1 a.e.1, 1–9, original.

13  Yako Baruch, testimony before People's Court VII, vol.V, 912-19; deposition at Yad Vashem, 03/1705; BAN, Hebraistika, doc. 62.

[14] Yako Baruch, testimony before People's Court II, in presence of Dimiter Peshev. Peshev also mentions the name of Yako Baruch in his testimony at the People's Court, as a witness for his defense. (There are three different testimonies of Yako Baruch—before the People's Court, at Yad Vashem, and at the Bulgarian Academy of Sciences. They are not identical and differ at several points.) Strangely enough, though, neither Peshev nor the other participants in the Kyustendil delegation mention Peshev's early meeting with Yako Baruch. Buko Lazarov, a close friend of Peshev, doesn't mention such a meeting either. Following his later conversations with Peshev, Lazarov claims that Peshev didn't know anything about the deportation before the arrival of the Kyustendil delegation. (Lazarov's testimony at Yad Vashem, op. cit.)

[15] Ibid.

[16] Suichmezov, op. cit.

[17] Instead of "Mister," the Bulgarians living in small towns and villages used the more informal "Bai" (pronounced Buy).

[18] Suichmezov, op. cit.

[19] Dr. Momchilov (Ivan Momchilov's son), interview by Albena Taneva, op. cit., based on his notes.

[20] Dimiter Peshev, memoirs (handwritten), SDIA, f.1335, op.1, a.e.158, 170–84, original, 1969-1970.

[21] In his memoirs, Peshev writes that the meeting with Ikonomov had taken place at the very beginning of March 1943. The first Jews arrived in Dupnitza on March 5, a Friday. As the Parliament was closed on this Saturday and Sunday, the earliest date when Ikonomov could have met Peshev was Monday, March 8.

[22] Dimiter Peshev, Memoirs, op. cit.

[23] Ibid.

[24] Peshev says that he later visited Kyustendil and learned of the forthcoming deportation (before receiving the Kyustendil delegation). He is mistaken. There is no record of his visiting Kyustendil in the days preceding the planned deportation. His emotional reaction, which he describes in his memoirs, "following his visit to Kyustendil," probably took place following his meeting with the Kyustendil delegation.

[25] Dimiter Peshev, op. cit.

[26] Mikhalev, op. cit.; Suichmezov, op. cit.

[27] Peter G. Kenderov, notes on the role of his father, Georgi Petrov Kenderov, in the rescue of the Bulgarian Jews, BAN, f.111, op.1, a.e.52, 1, original manuscript.

[28] Peshev, op. cit.

[29] Mikhalev, op. cit.

[30] In his handwritten memoirs, Peshev claims that he had visited Kyustendil before March 10 and had kept in touch since then with the regional governor who informed him of the forthcoming deportation. There is no evidence this ever happened. Buko Lazarov, a good friend of Peshev's, who continued to visit him after the war in Sofia, discussed the issue with him in detail and categorically denies in his testimony (Yad Vashem 3585-284-1 03/3970, August 1977) that Peshev knew of the planned deportation before the arrival of the Kyustendil delegation.

[31] Mikhalev, op. cit.

[32] Ibid.

[33] Benyamin Arditi, *Yehudey Bulgaria bishnot hamishtar hanazi, 1940–1944 (The Jews of Bulgaria Under the Nazi Regime 1940–1944)* (Tel-Aviv: Israel Press, 1962), 287. Arditi says the meeting took place at nine o'clock. This is not correct. He also says that

Peshev participated at that meeting. This is a mistake as well. Frederic Chary, in his book *The Bulgarian Jews and the Final Solution 1940–1944* (University of Pittsburgh Press, 1972), quoting the same page of Arditi's book, writes that the meeting took place at Peshev's office. This is a mistake, Arditi says that the meeting took place at a Sofia café.

34 Arditi, Ibid.

35 Mikhalev, op. cit.

36 Suichmezov, op. cit.

37 Ibid.

38 Peshev, op. cit.

39 Suichmezov, letter to the Presidium of the Bulgarian Parliament, 1969, Suichmezov's family private archives.

40 Mikhalev, op. cit.

41 Ibid.

42 Peshev, op. cit.

43 Buko Lazarov, "Who and how saved the Bulgarian Jews," op. cit.

44 Suichmezov, petition for a pension, addressed to the presidium of the Bulgarian Parliament, 1969 (no exact date), private archives of the Suichmezov family.

45 Mikhalev, op. cit.

46 Mikhalev, testimony delivered before People's Court II, 873.

47 Ibid.

48 Buko Lazarov, op. cit.

49 Suichmezov, op. cit.

50 Ibid.

51 Ibid.

52 Gregor Suichmezov, Assen's son, interview, op. cit.

53 Suichmezov, op. cit.

54 Dr. Momchilov (Ivan Momchilov's son), op. cit.

55 Minutes of the Saint Synod meeting, April 2, 1943.

56 Letter 138, March 7, 1943, by the Plovdiv delegate of the KEV, accompanying a list of 616 people subject to deportation, *Dokumenti*, 177.

57 Frederic Chary, op. cit. 90.

58 Kyril, telegram to King Boris, March 10, 1943, Archives of the Saint Synod.

59 Frederic Chary, op. cit. 90.

60 Rina Shaashua Hasson, interview, Ramat Hasharon, Israel, August 1994. Beka Lazarova, an official at the Shalom Jewish organization in Sofia, told us on January 9, 1998, that her mother had been rounded up in Plovdiv, that day, and remembered "a man in a priest's cloak" who came to speak to the Jews and encourage them.

61 Metropolitan Kyril, testimony at the meeting of the Saint Synod, April 2, 1943.

62 Ibid.

63 Peter Kenderov (Gheorgi Kenderov's son), testimony, NA BAN, f.111, op.1, a.e. 52, 1. This testimony suffers from several inconsistencies, but this part is credible.

64 Report signed by Hoffmann, countersigned by Beckerle, April 5, 1943, Yad Vashem Jerusalem, K 207604-207609.

65 Maria Pavlova, testimony before People's Court VII; also interview with Albena Taneva, for this book, November 20, 1997.

66 Dimiter Peshev, testimony before People's Court II, manuscript, n.d., vol. 69, 109.

## CHAPTER TEN: Trains

1 Liliana Panitza, interrogatory by the People's Court, March 23, 1945.
2 *Dokumenti*, 184–85.
3 Ibid.
4 Liliana Panitza, interrogatory by the People's Militia, October 2, 1944.
5 Yaroslav Kalitzin, written testimony, op. cit. Kalitzin mistakenly places this incident and Dannecker's flight to Germany in the period before the deportation.
6 Yaroslav Kalitzin, written testimony before the People's Militia, op. cit.
7 Pavlova, testimony before the People's Militia, AMVR; and *Dokumenti*, 184–85.
8 Ibid.
9 Maria Pavlova, testimony before the People's Militia, vol. 187, 16 (90a).
10 Kalitzin, written testimony before the People's Militia, op. cit.
11 Borislav Tasev, report to Dr. Ivan Popov, *Dokumenti*, 182–84.
12 Ibid.
13 Berta and Miko Noach, testimony, *Dokumenti*, 152–53.
14 Albert Sarfati, testimony, *Dokumenti*, 160–62.
15 Liubomir Panev, testimony, *Dokumenti*, 159.
16 Sarfati, op. cit.
17 Leon Nissim Shalom, testimony, *Dokumenti*, 150.
18 Joseph Levi, testimony, *Dokumenti*, 147–50.
19 Report of the Swiss embassy in Bulgaria, Sofia, March 11, 1943, copy at NA BAN, f. 111, op. 1, a.e. 53, 1–6.
20 Filov, diary, March 11, 1943, 560–61.
21 Ibid.
22 Ibid.
23 Redard, report of the Swiss Embassy, op. cit.
24 Ibid.
25 Ibid.
26 Filov, diary, March 15, 1943, 561.
27 Metropolitan Stefan, memoirs, op. cit.
28 Ibid.
29 Ibid.
30 Simcho Isakov, "Trains," 1943, *Andarta*, a collection of poems, Traklin, 1973, Ramat Gan, 35–38.
31 Nadejda Vasileva, "On the catastrophe of the Thracian Jews: Recollection," Yad Vashem Studies on the European Catastrophe and Resistance, 3 (1959), 295–302; also, the original text of her testimony.
32 Dr. Ivan Mendizov, interrogatory by the People's Militia, October 22, 1944, vol. 187, 80–81.
33 Albert Sarfati, testimony, *Dokumenti*, 164–65.
34 Some sources count the people who died during the deportation, others don't, which explains the slight discrepancies between the numbers of deported Jews.

## CHAPTER ELEVEN: Forty-Three Signatures

1 Dimiter Peshev, memoirs, op. cit. 170–265.
2 Ibid.
3 Ibid.

4   Frederic Chary, op. cit. 90.
5   Dimiter Peshev, testimony before People's Court II, op. cit., handwritten, 10a.
6   Dimiter Peshev, memoirs, op. cit.
7   Dimiter Peshev, testimony, op. cit. 11.
8   Dimiter Peshev, the last word before People's Court II, vol. 69, 68.
9   Dimiter Peshev, memoirs, op. cit.
10  Ibid.
11  Jacob Baruch, interrogation before People's Court VII, vol. 12, file 54, 2066.
12  Peshev, testimony before People's Court II, vol. 5, file 47, 828.
13  Peshev, memoirs, op. cit.
14  Photocopy of the note appears in the *Encyclopedia of the Jewish Diaspora*, vol. X, *Bulgaria*, 859, and in the documents concerning Dimiter Peshev in the People's Court II files.
15  Dimiter Peshev, memoirs, op. cit.; and Peshev, testimony before People's Court II, op. cit.
16  Bogdan Filov, diary, 561.
17  Dimiter Peshev, memoirs, op. cit.
18  Dimiter Peshev, testimony before the People's Court II, 828.
19  Dimiter Peshev, testimony before the People's Court, op. cit.
20  Filov, diary, entry of March 25, 564.
21  Ibid., entry of March 19, 1943, 561.
22  Ibid.
23  Ibid., entry of March 20.
24  Ibid., entry of March 23, 563.
25  Dimiter Peshev, memoirs, op. cit.
26  Filov, diary, entry of March 26, 563–64.
27  Dimiter Peshev, memoirs, op. cit.
28  Ibid.
29  Filov, diary, entry of March 26, 564.
30  Ibid., entry of March 26, 563; also reported by Peshev, memoirs, op. cit.
31  Minutes of the Parliamentary proceedings, March 26, 1943.
32  Ibid.
33  Ibid., March 28, 1943; *The Survival*, op. cit., footnote, 228; Filov, diary, entry of March 28, 1943, 564.
34  Peshev, speech, Plenary session, Minutes of the Parliamentary proceedings, December 26, 1943.
35  Dimiter Peshev, testimony before the People's Court, op. cit.
36  Minutes of the Parliamentary proceedings, December 26, 1943.

## CHAPTER TWELVE: The Bluff

1   Filov, diary, op. cit., entry of March 29, 1943, 565.
2   Adolf-Heinz Beckerle, diary, Bulgarian edition, Sofia, 1992, entry for March 10, 1943, 90.
3   Ibid., entry for March 23, 100.
4   Quoted in Filov's diary, entry for April 4, 1943, 567.
5   Ribbentrop, telegram to Beckerle, April 4, 1943, Yad Vashem, Jerusalem, URO 94–95.

[6] Filov, diary, op. cit. 567.

[7] Filov, diary, April 13, 1943, op. cit. 568–69.

[8] Haim Keshales, *Korot Yehudey Bulgaria*, 1969, vol. 3, 163.

[9] Hoffman, report, countersigned by Beckerle, April 5, 1943, Yad Vashem, Jerusalem, K 207604-207609.

[10] Ibid.

## CHAPTER THIRTEEN: The Metropolitans

[1] Stephane Groueff, *Crown of Thorns*, op. cit. 86.

[2] Ibid.

[3] Professor Nikolai Shivarov, interview by Albena Taneva, Sofia University, November 11, 1997.

[4] Metropolitan Stefan, diary, March 22, 1942, quoted in "Exarch Stefan I," by Dimiter Lozov, 252.

[5] Stephane Groueff, op. cit. 172–73, 178.

[6] Metropolitan Stefan, diary, April 9, 1942.

[7] Metropolitan Stefan, diary, March 8, 1942.

[8] Walter Schellenberg, note to Luther, June 13, 1941, quoted by Frederic Chary, 189, n.d.

[9] Radio Sofia, March 3, 1942.

[10] Minutes of the Saint Synod meeting, April 2, 1943.

[11] Frederic Chary, op. cit. 189.

[12] Leon Madjar, interview by Albena Taneva, Sofia, February 23, 1997.

[13] Minutes of the Saint Synod meeting, April 2, 1943.

[14] Ibid.

[15] Keshales, op. cit. 157–58.

[16] Minutes of the Saint Synod meeting, April 3, 1941, CDIA, f. 791, op. 1, a.e. 67.

[17] Minutes of the Saint Synod meeting, December 10, 1942, f. 791, op. 2, l.e.10.

[18] Minutes of the Saint Synod meeting, April 2, 1943.

[19] Keshales, op. cit. 157–58.

[20] Letter quoted in full at the Saint Synod meeting, June 22, 1943, f. 791, op. 1, a.e. 70, 84–88.

[21] Filov, diary, April 14, 1943, 569.

[22] Ibid.

[23] Ibid., April 15, 1943, 570–71.

[24] Report on the meeting with the king, read at the Saint Synod meeting, June 22, 1943, f. 791, op. 1, a.e. 70, 88–89.

[25] Saint Synod meeting, June 22, 1943.

[26] Filov, diary, April 13, 1943, 568–69.

[27] Saint Synod meeting, June 22, 1943.

[28] Ibid.

## CHAPTER FOURTEEN: Belev's Devious Plan

[1] Belev, Circular 11, April 14, 1943, quoted in Benyamin Arditi, *Yehudey Bulgaria*, 203.

[2] Benyamin Arditi, *Yehudey Bulgaria*, 203.

[3] Haim Keshales, *Korot Yehudey Bulgaria*, 160.

4   Benyamin Arditi, *Yehudey Bulgaria*, 203.
5   Buko Levi, testimony before the People's Court, March 24, 1945.
6   Stefan, memoirs, October 17, op. cit., King Boris's message to Metropolitan Stefan.
7   Ribbentrop, telegram 422 to the German Embassy in Sofia, April 4, 1943, op. cit.; and Bogdan Filov, diary, April 5, 1943, 567.
8   Bogdan Filov, diary, April 15, 1943, 571.
9   Ibid., April 13, 1943.
10  Beckerle, diary, April 20, 1943, 106.
11  Gunther, letter to counselor Von Thadden at the German Foreign office, May 17, 1943, following telephone conversation of May 14, 1943 between counselor Von Thadden and Hauptsturmfuhrer Bosshammer, K-207618/20, Yad Vashem, Jerusalem.
12  Gunther, op. cit.
13  Beckerle, diary, May 10, 1943, 107.
14  Sofia's Newspaper *Zora*, May 15, 1943. Also telegram from the German embassy in Sofia to the Ministry of Foreign Affairs in Berlin, May 15, 1943, K-208523/4, Yad Vashem, Jerusalem.
15  Belev, deportation plan (n.d.), Haim Grinberg, *Dokumenti*, 185–87.

## CHAPTER FIFTEEN: Despair

1   Benyamin Arditi, *Yehudey Bulgaria*, op. cit, 207.
2   Ibid., 207–8.
3   Ibid. The description that follows is also based on the same passages in Arditi's book.
4   Haim Keshales, *History of the Bulgarian Jews*, vol. 3, 168.
5   Benyamin Arditi, op. cit., 209.
6   Keshales, op. cit.
7   Queen Giovanna, interview by King Simeon, September 11, 1997; also Stephane Groueff, op. cit., 319–20.
8   Queen Giovanna, op. cit.
9   Evdokia Filova, diary, Christo Botev, Sofia, 1992, February 6, 1942, 121.
10  Ibid., 158–59.
11  Liliana Panitza, Yaroslav Kalitzin, testimonies, op. cit.
12  Interview with a supplier to the royal palace (who escaped to Albania with King Boris's help), Miami, December 14, 1994.
13  Velchev/Boboshevski, text of letter published by B. Arditi in "Izgrev," June 7, 1946.
14  Zvetan Boboshevski, testimony before the People's Court, AMVR, Case 108/1946, 45–49.
15  AMVR, C-101522, vol. 4, 198; Central Communist Party archives, F.1., O.4. a.u. 238, 1.
16  Joseph Geron, testimony, Yad Vashem; also Keshales, op. cit. 169.
17  Benyamin Arditi, op. cit., 212.
18  Benyamin Arditi, *Rolyata na Tzar Boris III pri Izselvaneto na evreite ot Bulgaria (The role of king Boris III in the deportation of Bulgaria's Jews)*, Tel-Aviv., n.p. 1952, 49.
19  For the personality of Rabbi Daniel Tzion, see Haim Keshales, op. cit. 170–73, and Frederic Chary, , 147–50. Also Daniel Tzion, *Pet Godini pod Fashistki gnet (Spomeni) [Five years under Fascist oppression (memoirs)]*, Sofia 1945.
20  Daniel Tzion, op. cit., 52–55.
21  Menahem Moshonov, memoirs, testimony at Yad Vashem, Jerusalem, n.d.

[22] Rabbi Asher Hananel, testimony before People's Court VII, 805–17.
[23] Daniel Tzion, *Pet Godini*, 54–60.
[24] Rabbi Asher Hananel, testimony before People's Court VII, 806.
[25] Metropolitan Stefan, memoirs, handwritten, October 17, 1950, Institute of Balkanistic studies, unit 8804.
[26] Metropolitan Stefan, memoirs.
[27] Rabbi Asher Hananel, testimony, 807.
[28] Metropolitan Stefan, memoirs.
[29] Metropolitan Stefan, memoirs.
[30] Lora Bracha Farhi, article in *Al Hamishmar* in Bulgarian, Issue 210, June 1961.
[31] Rabbi Asher Hananel, testimony, 807.
[32] Rabbi Asher Hananel, testimony, 807.
[33] Rabbi Asher Hananel, testimony, 807.
[34] Metropolitan Stefan, memoirs.
[35] Metropolitan Stefan, memoirs.
[36] Metropolitan Stefan, memoirs.
[37] Metropolitan Stefan, memoirs.
[38] Metropolitan Stefan, memoirs.
[39] Metropolitan Stefan, memoirs.
[40] Nikola Mushanov and Petko Staynov, letter to the king, May 24, 1943, Central Party Archives, F. 250, File "On the Jewish Question."
[41] Mushanov and Staynov, letter to the king.
[42] Solomon Leviev, *Nashata Obshta Vina (Our Common Guilt)*, Evreiski Vesti, Sofia, April 24, 1990.
[43] Benyamin Arditi, *Yehudey Bulgaria*, 216.
[44] Solomon Leviev, op. cit.
[45] Benyamin Arditi, *Yehudey Bulgaria*, 216; also interview with writer Victor Baruch, who participated at the protest, April 30, 1997.
[46] Betty Danon, interview, April 10, 1997, Jaffa.
[47] Peko Takov (the late Vulka Goranova's husband) and her son, interview, Sofia, April 26, 1997.
[48] Solomon Leviev, op. cit.
[49] Benyamin Arditi, *Yehudey Bulgaria*, 217.
[50] Daniel Tzion, testimony before People's Court VII, 804–5.
[51] Asher Hananel, testimony before People's Court VII, 808–9.
[52] Ratnik flyer, May 26, 1943, Hoffman's report to Berlin.
[53] Asher Hananel, testimony, 810.
[54] Asher Hananel, testimony, 809.
[55] KEV report, 26, quoted by Benyamin Arditi, *Yehudey Bulgaria*, 218.
[56] Monsignor Roncalli, letter to King Boris III, June 30, 1943; *Actes et Documents du Saint-Siege, relatifs a la Seconde Guerre Mondiale*, 9, Libreria Editrice Vaticana, 1975, 372.
[57] Lawyers Union, letter to Interior Minister Peter Gabrovski, March 20, 1943; Keshales, op. cit. 175–76.
[58] Letter of the Lawyers, Ibid.
[59] Keshales, op. cit. 178.

## CHAPTER SIXTEEN: The King Has Vanished

1  Belev, deportation plan (undated), Grinberg Haim, *Dokumenti*, 185–87.
2  Beckerle, report to the German foreign ministry, June 7, 1943, Yad Vashem, Jerusalem, K-207646-207648.
3  Hoffman, report to the fourth department (Gestapo), Section IV B 4 (Jewish Questions) at the S.D., reviewed and countersigned by Beckerle, June 7, 1943, Yad Vashem, Jerusalem, K-207839-207645.
4  Hoffman, report, op. cit.
5  Hoffman, report, op. cit.
6  Sava Djevrev, *Az Biach do Negovo Velichestvo* (*I Was Beside His Majesty*), (Sofia: Gal-Iko, 1993).
7  Sava Djevrev, *Az Biach*, 56-58.
8  Sava Djevrev, *Az Biach*, 57.
9  Resolution 70 of the Cabinet, May 21, 1943, protocol 74.
10 Minutes of the Saint Synod meeting, 29.6.1943, f.791, op.1, a.e.70, 122.
11 Yaroslav Kalitzin, written testimony before the People's Militia, op. cit.
12 Minutes of the Saint Synod meeting, 24.6.1943, f.791. op.1. a.e.70, 106.
13 Minutes of the Saint Synod meeting, 28.5.1943, f.791, op.1.,a.e.69, 201-2.
14 Ibid.
15 Bogdan Filov, diary, April 13, 1943.
16 Minutes of the Saint Synod meeting, 24.6.1943, 106-7.
17 Yaroslav Kalitzin, written testimony, op. cit.
18 Yaroslav Kalitzin, written testimony, op. cit.
19 Minutes of the Saint Synod meeting, 29.6.1943, 125-26.
20 Ivan Dimitrov Strogov, *What Did I Say to King Boris about the War and about Our Jewry* (in Bulgarian), Sofia, 1944, 29.
21 Ibid., 31.
22 Keshales, op. cit., 168.
23 Ellin Pellin, testimony before People's Court VII, 1504–5. Confirmed by Boyan Ivanov (Ellin Pellin's son), interview by Albena Taneva, Sofia, October 2, 1997.
24 Pellin, testimony before People's Court II, 1505–6.
25 Boyan Ivanov (Ellin Pellin's son), op. cit.
26 Ellin Pellin, op. cit.
27 In two interviews by Albena Taneva, on November 21, 1997, and November 27, 1997.
28 Maria Pavlova, op. cit.
29 Charles-Arthur Redard, Swiss chargé d'affaires, report, June 17, 1943, supplied by Mr. Mikhail Kolarov, Sofia.
30 Eli Ashkenazi, chairman of the Jewish Scientific Institute in Sofia, letter to Dr. Shapuissa, May 7, 1948; answer of Dr. Shapuissa, June 8, 1948, archives of Mr. Mikhail Kolarov, Sofia.
31 Hoffman, report to Berlin #927, June 24, 1943, URO 168, Israel Police.

## CHAPTER SEVENTEEN: Belev's Revenge

1  Ratnik flyer, May 26, 1943.
2  Daniel Tzion, testimony before the People's Court VII, March 16, 1945; also Daniel Tzion, *Pet Godini pod Fashistki gnet*, memoirs, op. cit., 60–61.
3  Rabbi Daniel Tzion, testimony before the People's Court VII.

[4] Buko Levi, testimony at Yad Vashem, and deposition before the People's Court VII, op. cit.

[5] Keshales, 205.

[6] Jacques Benaroya, testimony before the People's Court VII, also quoted in the final sentences.

[7] Yaroslav Kalizin, written testimony before the People's Militia, op. cit.

[8] Rabbi Daniel Tzion, testimony, Ibid.

[9] Rabbi Daniel Tzion, *Pet Godini*, op. cit. 61–75.

[10] *Dokumenti*, 184.

[11] Albert Varsano, testimony, published in *Phar* newspaper (in Bulgarian, in Israel), 1955, quoted in Keshales, 205–9.

## CHAPTER EIGHTEEN: The Last Effort

[1] Beckerle, telegram to the foreign ministry in Berlin, May 25, 1943; Keshales, op. cit. 186.

[2] Keshales, op. cit. 187; and Von Thadden report of June 1, 1943, Yad Vashem doc. K 207636.

[3] Belev, conversation with Dannecker, reported to Berlin by Police attaché Hoffman, June 7, 1943, Keshales, op. cit. 188–90.

[4] Hoffman, report, June 7, 1943, Yad Vashem, K-207646/48.

[5] Beckerle, report, June 7, 1943, Yad Vashem, K 207639/45.

[6] Hoffman, report, June 24, 1943, Yad Vashem, URO 168, Bureau 06, Israeli Police.

[7] Wagner, telegram 1243, August 15, 1943, URO II, Bureau 06, Israeli Police.

[8] Beckerle, report to Berlin, August 18, 1943, URO 190.

[9] Ibid.

[10] Beckerle, telegram 1223, August 19, 1943, URO II.

[11] Beckerle, report to Berlin, August 18, 1943, URO 190.

## CHAPTER NINETEEN: The Mysterious Death of Boris III

[1] Stephane Groueff, *Crown of Thorns*, 355.

[2] Ibid. (based on interview of Groueff with Balan)

[3] Ibid., 358.

[4] Filov, diary, August 15, 1943, 601.

[5] Ibid.

[6] Quoted in Stephane Groueff, *Crown of Thorns*, 360.

[7] Hugh Trevor Roper, *Hitler's Table Talk*, 630.

[8] Schoenebeck, diary, quoted in *Crown of Thorns*, 378.

[9] Groueff, *Crown of Thorns*, 363.

[10] Groueff, *Crown of Thorns*, 370.

[11] Groueff's quotes from Colonel Schoenebeck's diary for August 1943. Mr. Groueff corresponded with Colonel Schoenebeck and obtained a copy of his diary. Confirmed by Stephane Groueff to the author, February 8, 1998. *Crown of Thorns*, 376–79.

[12] Beckerle, report to von Ribbentrop, telegram #1292, August 29, 1943.

[13] Ibid.

[14] Dr. Frederic Chary, interview, November 1965, quoted in *The Bulgarian Jews and the Final Solution*, 160.

15 Beckerle, report to von Ribbentrop, telegram #1304, August 30, 1943.
16 Testimony before the People's Court, January 1945, reported in *The New York Times*, January 13, 1945.
17 Queen Giovanna memoirs (in Bulgarian), Sveti Kliment Ohridsky, Sofia, 1991, 124.
18 Member of the Royal family, interview, January 1995.
19 Groueff, *Crown of Thorns*, 370.
20 Joseph Goebbels, diaries, Hamish Hamilton, London, 1948, entry for September 11, 1943.
21 Groueff, *Crown of Thorns*, 351–52.
22 Yaroslav Kalitzin, written testimony, op. cit.
23 Minutes of Christov's speech, October 2, 1943, CDIA, op.l.a.e.1299, 8–9.

## CHAPTER TWENTY: A Body in a Ditch

1 Frederic Chary, 164–65.
2 Frederic Chary, 155, 196–97.
3 Filov, diary, July 7, 1944, 718.
4 Vitali Haimov, testimony, Yad Vashem Jerusalem, quoted in Keshales, 219–21.
5 Keshales, 221.
6 Liliana Panitza, interrogatory by the People's Militia, October 2, 1944.
7 Ibid., September 27, September 28, October 5, 1944.
8 Ilya Dobrevski, interrogatory, op. cit.
9 Ibid.
10 Ibid.
11 Ibid.
12 Liliana Panitza, interrogatory before the People's Militia, complemented by her interrogatory before the People's Court, March 23, 1945.
13 Ibid.
14 Liliana Panitza, interrogatory before the People's Court, March 23, 1945.
15 Liliana Panitza, draft letter (to Belev,) handwritten, pencil, n.d., found in the People 's Militia files, MVR archives.
16 Liliana Panitza, interrogatory before the People's Militia, March 23, 1945.
17 The account is furnished by numerous sources and interviews. See Haim Keshales, op. cit. 250.
18 Keshales confirms that Belev was executed by partisans after his capture in Kyustendil but doesn't mention the name of "Belo." Ibid., 250; Arditi also mentions Belev's killing, with no details. Benyamin Arditi, *Yehudey Bulgaria*, 322.

## CHAPTER TWENTY-ONE: The Hour of Reckoning

1 Haim Keshales, op. cit. 242–43. He claims that "tens of thousands" were killed.
2 Minutes of People's Court VII.
3 Maria Pavlova, Liliana Panitza's sister, interview by the author and Dr. Sonia Levi, September 26, 1996.
4 Ibid., August 25, 1996, by Dr. Sonia Levi and September 25, 1996.
5 Maurice Lazar, interview, op. cit.

[6] Dr. Garben, testimony, indictment of Adolf Heinz Beckerle by the Supreme Regional Court at Frankfurt on Main, June 20, 1960.

[7] Beckerle, indictment, June 20, 1960, Supreme Regional Court at Frankfurt on Main.

[8] Exarch Stefan's Will, supplied by his godson Mr. Ivan Mlnev, to Albena Taneva.

[9] Betty Danon, interview, April 10, 1997.

[10] Vulka Goranova and Betty Danon, statement, July 20, 1990.

[11] Solomon Leviev, *Nashata Obshta Vina*, op. cit.

[12] Peko Takov, interview, April 25, 1997, Sofia.

[13] President Todor Jivkov, interview, April 29, 1997, Sofia.

[14] Todor Jivkov, Memoirs, Sofia, 1997, 100, Siv-Abagar.

[15] Ibid., 101.

[16] Ibid.

[17] Ibid., 102.

[18] Resolution #172 of the Supreme Court, August 26, 1996.

[19] Guy Haskell, *From Sofia to Jaffa*, op. cit., 7.

# EPILOGUE

[1] Beckerle, conversation with Gabrovski, reports to the foreign ministry, Berlin, A 88/43, January 22, 1943, Yad Vashem K 207564/6 and A 154/43, February 8, 1943, Yad Vashem K 207571/3.

[2] Beckerle, report to Berlin, June 7, 1943, Yad Vashem K 207639/45.

[3] Hoffman, report to Berlin, April 5, 1943, Yad Vashem, K 207604-207509.

[4] Beckerle, indictment, June 20, 1960, op. cit.

[5] Testimony quoted at the Indictment of Beckerle, op. cit.

[6] King Boris, report to Filov, Filov's diary, April 4, 1943, 567.

[7] Interviews with Bulgarians, taken at random, between the years 1995-1998.

[8] Peshev, letter of March 17, signed by 43 MPs, op. cit.

[9] Buko Lazarov, "Who and how saved the Bulgarian Jews," op. cit.; also Buko Lazarov, article in the Israeli newspaper *Israelski Phar* (in Bulgarian), March 9, 1977, "March 9, 1943—day of Rescue of Bulgaria's Jewry"; also articles and letters from the Archives of Dr. Moise Avrahami.

[10] Filov, diary, February 17, 1943, 558.

[11] Frederic Chary, op. cit. 43.

[12] Peshev, memoirs, op. cit. 141-67.

[13] Metropolitan Stefan, memoirs, op. cit.

[14] Liliana Panitza, interrogatory before the People's Militia, October 2, 1944.

[15] Chary, op. cit. 45.

[16] Filov, diary, February 17, 1943, 557-58.

[17] Yaroslav Kalitzin, written testimony delivered before the People's Militia, op. cit.

[18] Ribbentrop, telegram to Beckerle, April 4, 1943, Yad Vashem, Jerusalem, URO 94-95.

[19] Filov, diary, April 13, 1943, 568-69, reporting the king's words to him and Gabrovski.

# INDEX

NOTE: Bold page numbers indicate photographs

**A**

Abadjiev, Michael, 1–2, 106
Administrative Council of the War
    victims, 33
Agrarian party, 16, 249
Aktzia, 88–89, 91, 266
Albrect and Nadejda, 24–25
Alexander, King Ivan, 5
Alexander Nevski Church, 167, 195
Alexander Nevski Square, 191
Alexander, Tsar II, 20
Alexandrov, Dr., 232
Alfasa, Avraham, 84
"Aliya Beth," 36
Allies
    American bombers, 226–227
    European landings, 225
Anavi, Pressiado, 105
anti-Semitic legislation, political
    practicality of, 23–24, 223–224
Arditi, Benyamin, 121, 188, 190, 198,
    211
Argentina, immigration to, 188
Ashkenazi Jews, 6
assassinations, 14, 21, 67–68, 174,
    182–183, 221, 235–239
Assenov, Dragomir, 198
Astruk, Betty, 199–200
Auschwitz, 52

**B**

Bachkov monastery, 253
Bagrianov, P.M. Ivan, 242, 243, 249
Bakerdjiev, Christo, 63, 136
Balan, Stanislav, 83, 229
Balkan Entente, 13, 19
Balkan Wars, 7, 11, 12
Baruch, Jacob (Yako), 105–106, 115,
    117–118, 121, 147
Baruch, Samuel, 105, 117
Battenberg, Prince Alexander, 7, 9
Bauer, Hans, 229
Bavaria, Jewish emigration from, 5
Bayazid, Sultan II, 6
Beckerle, Adolf-Heinz, 46, 48, 56,
    59–60, 74, 158, 161, 180, 205, 219,
    222–226, 228, 229, 233–236, 252,
    259–261
Beckerle, Frau, 188
*Beit Yosef* (Caro), 6
Belev, Alexander, 3, 77–78, 179–184,
    **236–237**, 239. *See also* Panitza, Liliana
    anti-Semitism, 27–28, 51–54, 201,
    263
    deportation order activities, 63–75,
    82, 88–89, **95**, 97, 103, 105,
    129, 131–134, 144, 145, 161,
    183, 185, 190, 205–206, 208,
    215–218, 219–228, 265–266

dismissal and disappearence, 243–248, 250
and King Boris, 213
relationship with Panitza, 77–85
Belev-Dannecker agreement, 2–3, 62, 63–75, 145, 245, 247, 264–265, 267
Belo, 248
Belzec, 52
Ben-Elijah, Rabbi Jacob, 5
Benaroya, Dr. Jacques, 82, 217
Benvenisti, Stella, 199
Beracha, Buko, 106, 107
Berchtesgaden, 157, 220, 267
Beshkov, Ivan, 241
Betar organization, 198
Bitola, deportation of Jews, 135
black market, 78, 201, 239
blood libel, 7, 260
Bojilov, P.M. Dobri, 30, 239, 241–242
"Bolshevization" threat, 20, 22. See also Communist party; Soviet Union
Boris, King I, relations with Jews, 4
Boris, King III
    biography, 9, 10, 11, 13–20, **17, 18**
    death, 232–239, 241
    and Dunovism, 38–39
    and Ellin Pellin, **211**–213
    internal affairs, 67–68, 151, 175–176
    Jewish policy, 23–25, 56, 73, 128–130, 132, 139–140, 159–162, 183, 189–190, 196, 201, 204, 206, 209, 211–213, 226, 257, 261, 263–268
    marriage to Princess Giovanna, **17, 18**, 166–167
    political agenda, 17–18, 21–26, 68, 73
    relations with Church, 172–174
    relations with Filov, **23**, 68, 128, 139, 157, 160, 163, 180, 212
    relations with Hitler, 15–16, 21, 27, 40, 41, **43**, 157–159, 207, 212, 220, 229–232, 237–238
    on Saints Kyril and Methodius day, 206–207
    superstitions, 229
    and ZZN, 38–40

Bozhilov, P.M., 249
Bozukov, Boris Gheorghiev, 91
Brannik organization, 8, 99, 102–103, 125, 168, 191, 249, 260
bribes, 107, 188, 241
Britain, offers for refugees, 68
Buchenwald, 238
Bulgaria. See also Boris, King III; Sofia
    citizenship benefits, 76, 264
    Constitution, 7, 9, 12, 262
    German occupation of, 42–43, **45**
    relations with Germany, 20–23, **24**, 25–26, 37–38, 41, 42–43, 53, 57, **183**, 220, 230–231, 236, 241–242
    tolerance toward Jews, 8, 56–57, 60, 102, 107, 223–226, 259–261
Bulgarian armed forces, 226–227, 230–231, **254**
Bulgarian Doctors Union, 33
Bulgarian Jews
    aid to foreign Jews, 95–97, 99–100
    conversion to Christianity, 5, 29, 34, 126, 168, 169, 173, 176, 188, 208–210
    defined under racial law, 28, 53
    deportation agenda, 2, 58–61, 66–75, 101–112, 131–133, 182–183, 185–204, 205–206, 208, 213, 215–218, 219–228, 239, 264
    "Family card" requirements, 179
    as freedom fighters, 50
    history, 3–7
    immigration to Israel, 257
    labor units, 44–48, **47**, 58–59, 61, 62, 66, 76, 94, 140, 158, 175, 180–181, 188, 221–222, 243
    military participation, 5–6, 7–8, 29–30, 32, 46–48, 121
    partisan activities, 174, 182–183, 247–248, 249
    patriotism of, 198, 201
    pensions for political friends, 251–252
    population numbers, 8, 29, 179
    propaganda against, 174–175, 215–216, 221, 223–224

property confiscation and taxes, 28,
49–**50**, 52–53, 55, 66, 103–104,
134, 171, 187, 190, 239
recovery of rights, 242–243
relocation, **31**, 53–**54**
as Sephardic Jews, 6, 159
Star of David requirements, **31**,
55–56, 92, 93, 168
violence against, 77, 95, 126, 168,
198, 200, 212, 216–218
ZZN restrictions on, 28–29, 44–46,
48, 49–51
Bulgarian kingdom, 4–5. *See also* Boris,
King III
Bulgarian Lawyers Union, 32, 203
Bulgarian National Bank, 99
Bulgarian Painters Union, 33
Bulgarian State Railways, 75
Bulgarian Writers Union, 146, 212
Bulgars, 4
Byzance, 5

**C**

Caro, Rabbi Joseph, 6
censorship, 167–168, 227n, 239
Cham Koriya palace, 10
Chapuissa, Dr. Edouard, 213–214
Charron, Rene, 238
Chavdarov, 132
Chilingirov, Stilyan, 146
Christiani, Pablo, 5
Christianity
Jewish conversion to, 5, 29, 34, 126,
168, 169, 173, 176, 188, 208–210
Jewish influence on, 4–5
"Christo Botev," 50, 257
Christov, Docho, 239
Church. *See* Stefan, Metropolitan; Vatican
Ciano, Count Galeazzo, 41–42
circumcision, 144
Clementine, 9
Comforty, Pinhas, 103 104, 105, 106,
107
Commissariat for Jewish Questions, 2, 53,
74, 75, 121, 124, 146, 196–197,
243, 264

Communist party, 16, 20, 224, 254–255,
256–257, 262. *See also* Soviet Union
opposition to ZZN, 32
partisan activities, 50–51, 68, 182,
189, 199, 221, 247–248, 249
Coronel Manuscript, 5
Crinis, Dr. Maximilian de, 233
curfew laws, 3, 49, 116, 125, 186, 187
Czechoslovakia, 36

**D**

Dalakchiev, Kyril, 250
Dannecker, Theodore, 3, 59, 62, 63,
164, 180, 182, 220–221, 228, 242,
252, 264
and Belev, 62, 63, 67–74, 131–132,
135, 145, 205–206, 219, 223
Danon, Betty, 199, 255–256
Daskalov, Dr., 232, 234
death-sentence decrees, 14–15, 16, 249
Dede Agach, deportation of Jews, 88,
91, 98
Demir Hissar, deportation of Jews, 91–92
Denmark, deportation of Jews, 58
Djevrev, Sava, 206–207
Dobrevski, Ilya, 78–80, 89, 100, 244
Dobrovitch, Strashimir, 231
Dobrudja, 13, 20–21, 27, 43, 76, 232,
262, 264–265
Donovan, Col. William J., 22
*Dorian II,* 37
d'Orleans, Louis Philippe, 9
Draganov, Nikola, 182
Draganov, Parvan, 18
Dragoitcheva, Zola, 199
Drama, deportation of Jews, 88, 91, 97,
98
Dukmedjiev, Dr. Liuben, 114
Dulles, Allen, 238
Dunov, Peter, 38–39
Dunovism, 38, 191–192
Dupnitza
deportation activities, 2, 99, 104, 105–
106, 116, 124, 168–169, 217
transit camp, 69, 89, 91, 94, 100,
118–120, 139

**E**

Eagle's Nest, 41, 157, 220
Efremov, Mayor, 103, 106
Eichmann, Adolf, 59, 74, 219
El Alamein, 267
Elazar, David, 255
Eleonore, Queen, 10
Emmanuele, King Vittorio, 18
Eppinger, Dr. Hans, 233, 234–235, 237
Evdokia, Princess, 188, 234
Evksinograd palace, 10
Evlogi of Sliven, opposition to ZZN, 127, 172
Exarch Joseph, 166

**F**

Fallieres, Pres., 11
Farhi, Leon, 185
Farhi, Lora, 194
Fascist National Students Union, 35
Ferdinand, King
    alliance with Germany, 13, 22, 166, 231
    biography, 9–11, 12, **17**
Fernandes warehouse, 2, 103, 116
Filaret of Lovetch, 169–170
Filov, P.M. Bogdan
    and Belev, 68–69, 73, 76
    death sentence, 249, 257
    deportation activities, 114, 120, 129–130, 222, 226
    meeting with Redard, 137–139
    and Metropolitan Stefan, 195–196, 208–210
    and Parliament letter, 146, 148–155
    politics, **24**, 25–26, 30–31, 33–34, 38, 41, 239, 242, 262, 263
    relations with Church, 173–174
    relations with Jews, 30, 169, 187
    relations with King Boris, **23**, 68, 128, 139, 157, 160, 163, 180, 212, 230, 236
    relations with Nazis, 41–44, 48, 53, 58–59, 175–176, 230
Filova, Evdokia, 188–189
Finzi, 198
France, Jewish emigration from, 5

**G**

Gabe, Dora, 7, 216
Gabe, Peter, 7
Gabrovski, I.M. Peter, 23, 26, 51, 104, 180, **236–237**, 244, 263
    and Belev, 51–52, 69, 73–74, 131–133, 179, 213
    death sentence, 249, 257
    deportation activities, 115, 120–124, 128–130, 158, 161–162, 183–184, 205–206, 209–210, 222, 265–266
    and Filov, 68–69, 148, 160
    politics, 27, 30–31, 35, 37–38, 44, 49, 59–62, 203, 221, 239, 241
    relations with Jews, 53, 57, 85, 187
Ganev, Spas, 148
George, King V, 11
Georgiev, Col. Kimon, 16
Gerdjikov, Gov., 124
Germany. *See also* Hitler, Adolf
    Bulgarian deportation order, 69–72
    defeat, 243
    relations with Bulgaria, 20–23, **24**, 25–26, 37–38, 41, 42–43, 53, 57, **183**, 220, 230–231, 236, 241–242
Geron, Joseph, 190, 216
    efforts against ZZN, 29–30
Gioshev, 131
Giovanna, Queen, **17**, **18**, 166–**167**, 188, 237, 253, 257
Giumurdjina. *See also* Thrace
    deportation of Jews, 78–79, 87–89, 91, 97, 98
Goering, Hermann, 67, 159
Goranova, Vulka, **199**–200, 255–256
Gorna-Djumaya, transit camp, 69, 89, 91, 100, 106, 139
Gorsko Slivovo, **31**
Greece. *See also* Macedonia; Thrace
    forced labor camps, 181
    German occupation of, 43, **45**, 157, 230
Groueff, Stephane, 166
Grouev, Pavel, 19, 24, 30, 194, 230, 250
Gypsies, aid to Jews, 143

# H

Haimov, Vitali, 191, 198, 211
Hananel, Rabbi Asher, 56, 192–193, 195, 200–202, 219
Haskovo, deportation activities, 127
Hausner, Gideon, 69–70
Heydrich, Reinhard, 52
Himmler, Heinrich, 180–182
Hisarluka Hill, 101
Hitler, Adolph, 19, 42, 46. *See also* Germany
    relations with King Boris, 15–16, 21, 27, 40, 41, **43**, 157–159, 207, 212, 220, 229–232, 237–238
Hoffman, Adolf, 59, 63, 161–163, 180, 205, 214
Hoffman, Karl, 220–222, 224, 252, 260
Hungary
    deportation of Jews, 58, 227, 242
    Jewish emigration from, 5, 36

# I

Ianev, Sotir, 174
Iasi camp, 242
Ikonomov, Dimiter, 118–120, 124, 147
IMRO, 16
intellectuals, 261–262
International Red Cross, 213
Isakov, Simcho, 140
Isakova, Nastia, 199
Israel. *See also* Palestine
    immigration of Bulgarian Jews to, 257–258
Italy
    Allied landings, 225
    deportation of Jews, 228, 242
    immigration to, 188
    invasion of Abyssinia, 19
    surrender, 241

# J

Jaffa, 257
Jewish Central Consistory, 28, 56, 83, 243
Jewish Legions, 7
Jewish National Fund, 257
Jewish problem, "final solution" to, 52–53, 58, 158

Jewish tomb, 6
Jews. *See also* Bulgarian Jews; Sofia
    property confiscation, 87–88, 98–99, 136, 144
    violence against, 88, 91–94, 99–100, 135–136
Jivkov, Todor, 199, 255–256
Joseph of Varna, opposition to ZZN, 171

# K

"Kailuka" camp, 218
Kalfov, Christo, 148, 154
Kalitzin, Yaroslav, 63, 69, 79, 82–83, 89, 97, 100, 131, 210, 217
*Kara Georgi* (steamship), 144
Karadjov, 96
Karavelova, Mrs. Ekaterina, support for Jews, 168, 187, 194–195
Katowicz, 90, 144
Kavala, deportation of Jews, 88, 91, 97, 98
Kazasov, Dimo, 33, 217
Keitel, Wilhelm, 230
Kenderov, Georgi Petrov, 120, 127
KEV. *See Komisarstvo za Evreiskite Vuprosi*
Khandjiev, Dr., 190, 211, 233
Kiosseivanov, Georgi, 23, 25, 114, 238
Kiosseivanov, Peter, 151, 152, 215
Kiradjiev, Kichka and Kaludka, 251
Klement of Stara Zagora, opposition to ZZN, 172
Kojukharov, Alexander, 147
Kojukharov, Todor, 154
*Komisarstvo za Evreiskite Vuprosi* (KEV), 53–55, 241, 250, 253
    deportation agreement, 67, 69, 75, 78–79, 88–89, 97–100, 104, 107, 125, 133, 136, 143, 185, 201–202, 216–217
Konfino, Dr. Baruch, 36
Konfino, Dr. Joseph, 91, 93–94, 100
Konstantinov, Chief, 209
Kristallnact attacks, 8, 51
Ksanti, deportation of Jews, 88, 91, 96, 97, 98
Kunev, Trifon, 146
Kurtev, Vladimir, 104, 107, **111**, 121, 250
Kyril and Methodius, Cyrillic alphabet creation, 5

Kyril and Methodius day, gatherings and
    protests, 191, 195, 197–198, 206,
    254–255
Kyril of Plovdiv
    as Metropolitan, 252–253
    opposition to ZZN, 34, 126–127,
        169–170
Kyril, Prince, 10, 11, 233, 234, 237, 239,
    249, 257
Kyustendil
    death of Belev, 247–248
    delegation to Sofia, 108–112,
        113–130, 132, 251–252
    deportation activities, 1, 2, 101–112,
        133, 186, 217


**L**

Ladino dialect, 6, 102
Landau, 242
Lapovo, 90
Law of Civilian Mobilization, 105
Law for the Defense of the Nation
    cancellation, 243
    Church opposition to, 165–177
    inception, 27–40, 52, 53, 115, 264
    King Boris III feelings about, 25,
        175, 263–264
    public response to, 31–35, 262
Lazarov, Anka, 1, **2**, 107
Lazarov, Buko, 1, **2**, 3, 105–109, 251–252
League of Nations, 18–19, 102
Legionnaires, 8, 57, 67, 69, 249, 260
Leonov, Buko, 124
Levi, Dr. Nissim (Buko), 30, 83–85, 102,
    179, 185, 187, 216
Levi, Joseph, 136
Levi, Nora, 93–94
Leviev, Solomon (Gosho), 197–198, 200,
    254–255
Levkov, Ivan, 107
Lisetz Mountains, 101
Lod, 257
Lom
    "blood libel" incidents, 7
    transit camp, 139, 143, 183–184,
        186, 187–188
Losenetz district, citizen protests in, 32

Lovetch
    Church opposition to ZZN, 34
    deportation activities, 120
Lukov, Gen. Christo, 67–68, 131, 174, 182
Lulchev, Col. Liubomir, 25, 38–40, 192,
    250
Luther, Martin, 58


**M**

Maccabee organization, 198
Macedonia
    abandonment, 13
    Bulgarian claim to, 21, 262
    Bulgarian occupation of, 43, 73, 232,
        265
    deportation of Jews, 3, 61–62, 66–75,
        82, 84–85, **90**, **95**, 131,
        135–137, 143–144, 161, 180,
        253–254, 257–258, 264
    revolutionary movement, 16, 165
Madjar, Nora, 257
Mafalda, Princess, 238
Magistrati, Count, 188
Maidanek, 52
"Malinarka" (Leviev), 216
Mann, Thomas, 168
Maria-Louisa, Princess, 10, **18**, 57, **167**,
    253
Marinov, Spas, 151
marriage, 114
*Mashil* (steamship), 144
Melamed, Jacques, 198
Mendizov, Dr. Ivan, 144
Metaxas, P.M., 235
Metropolitans. *See also* Stefan,
    Metropolitan
    opposition to ZZN, 34–35
Mevorach, Nissim, 211
Meyer, Dr. Arthur, 24
Mihov, Nikola, 239, 249
Mikhalev, Peter, 107–112, **108**,
    121–123, 133, 251–252
Miltenov, Gov. Liuben, 103–105, 107,
    109, 124
Ministry of Education, 244
Ministry of Religions, 208–209
Mizrahi, David, 7

Momchilov, Ivan, 107, 111, 118, 122, 125, 252
Murad, Sultan III, 6
Muraviev, P.M. Konstantin, 243
Mushanov, Menahem, 192
Mushanov, P.M. Nikola, 36, 148, **197**
Mussolini, B., 241

**N**

Nazi S.A., 25, 46
Nehardea, Matti, 199
Neofit of Vidin, opposition to ZZN, 169–170, 173–174, 177, 209
Neuilly treaty, 13, 19, 20
Nevski, Alexander, 20
"New Order" politics, 30
Nicholas, Pope I, 4
Nikolai, Tsar II, 10
Nikolov, Svilen, 207
Nissimov, Harry, 95–96
Nissimov, Mancho, 30
Noach, Berta and Miko, 135
Nuremberg laws. *See* Law for the Defense of the Nation

**O**

Oliver, Haim, 255
Operation Barbarossa, 43, 50. *See also* Soviet Union
Osogovo Mountains, 101
"Otez Paissi" Christian-Fascist youth movement, 35
Ottoman Empire, relations with Jews, 5–6
"Our Common Guilt" (Leviev), 255
Ovcharov, Atanas, 92, 93, 100

**P**

Paissi of Vratza, opposition to ZZN, 34, 171
Palestine. *See also* Israel
immigration to, 36–37, 49, 68, 116, 137, 163, 242
Panev, Liubomir, 136
Panitza, Liliana (Lily). *See also* Belev, Alexander
after Belev's dismissal, 243–247, 250

duties to Belev, 63, **64**, 69, 73, 74, 89, 201, 213, 264
relationship with Belev, 77–85, 131–132, 243–247
warning to Jews, 76, 82–83, 179–180, 185, 217
Pantev, Col. Atanas, 182
Papal Nunzio, 188, 202
Papo, Menahem, 182, 221, 249
Papon, Maurice, 253
Pardo, Jack, 187
Parliament. *See* Sobranie
Pavlova, Maria, 79–80, 131, 132, 213, 250
Paytashev, Mr., 99
Pazardjik
"blood libel" incidents, 7
deportation activities, 116, 120, 127–128, 217
Peev, Peiu, 250
Pellin, Ellin
and King Boris, **211**–213, 267
opposition to ZZN, 33
People's Court, 249–250, 253
People's Militia, 246–247
Peretz, Marko Aaron, 94
Peshev, Dimiter, 16, 108, 189
after liberation, 250–251
anti-deportation activities, 113–124, **114**, 129, 145–148, 151–155, 187, 266–268
letter to Parliament, 145–155, 158, 174
pension fund for, 251–252
on ZZN, 37–38
Petev, Mayor, 97
Pirot
deportation of Jews, 136, 144
transit camp, 89, 139
Piti, Buko, 211
Pleven, transit camp, 186, 218
Ploesti, 227
Plovdiv
citizen protests, 32, 146
deportation activities, 2, 116, 120, 125–128, 217

Popov, F.M. Ivan
    anti-Semitism, 48, 53, 153, 250
    deportation activities, 93–94, 97,
        100, 103, 133, 136
    relations with King Boris, 22, **23**
Pravoslav Catholic Church. *See* Stefan,
    Metropolitan
Prokopiev, Mr., 133
propaganda, 174–175, 215–216, 221,
    223–224
Protich, Justice, 243
Prudkin, Anton, 36
Punev, Christo, on opposition to ZZN, 33
Puntev, Slavi, 143

**Q**
Queen Theodora, 5

**R**
radio sets, 49, **50**
Radomir
    army revolt, 13
    transit camp, 3, 69, 89, 100, 104–106
Rahamim, Haim, 104–105, 106, 107, 241
railroads, 89–91, 126
Ramla, 257
rape, 136
Ratnik organization, 132, 246, 249, 260
    Kristallnacht attacks, 8, 51
    political involvement, 26, 27, 54, 57,
        77, 102–103, 125, 215
    propaganda, 215–216
Razgrad, transit camp, 186
Redard, Charles-Arthur, intercession
    efforts, 137–139, 163
Reichsicherheitshauptamt (RSHA), 52,
    55–56, 134, 162, 238
revenge, Jew's refusal to commit, 5
Ribbentrop, Joachim von, 41–42, 46, 58,
    67, 158–161, 175, 180, 220, 230,
    231, 234, 261, 267
Richthofen, Baron von, 46
road construction, 44–48, **47**, 58–59, 61,
    62, 66, 76, 94, 140, 158, 160, 162,
    175, 180–181, 188, 221–222, 243
    Todt organization, 138n

Romania
    bombings, 227
    deportation of Jews, 139, 227, 242
    relations with Bulgaria, 20, 27, 264
Romaniots. *See also* Bulgarian Jews
    settlements in Bulgaria, 4
Rommel, 267
Roncalli, Monsignor Angelo, 202–203
Rubenova, Mati, 249
Russe
    "blood libel" incidents, 7
    deportation activities, 217
    partisan activities, 221, 249
    transit camp, 186, 188
Russia. *See also* Soviet Union
    relations with Bulgaria, 7, 20, 77–78

**S**
Saint Synod. *See also* Stefan,
    Metropolitan
    opposition to ZZN, 34, 168–177
Sajitz, Dr. Rudolf, 233, 234
*Salvador* tragedy, 36–37
Samokov, deportation of Jews, 105, 127
Sara-Shaban, deportation of Jews, 88
Sarafov, Mr., 208–209
Sarah, wife of Alexander, 5
Sarfati, Albert, 135
*Saturnus* (steamship), 144
Schellenberg, Walter, 56–57
Schoenebeck, Col. Carl-August von, 67,
    233–235
Sephardim, 6, 159. *See also* Bulgarian
    Jews
Serbia, 157
    war with Bulgaria, 7
Serdika Bank, 246
Seres, deportation of Jews, 88
Sevov, Iordan, 151, 234, 238
Shakov, Dr. Sammy, 94
Shekerdjiski, Emil, 249
Shipliev, Mayor, 97
Shokov, Stoian. *See* Stefan, Metropolitan
*Shpanioli*, 6, 159
Shtip, deportation of Jews, 136
*Shulhan Arukh* (Caro), 6

Shumen
    deportation activities, 127
    transit camp, 186
Simeon, Crown Prince (King), **18**, 56, 57,
    239, 242, 253
Simitli, deportation of Jews, 91, 93
Simov, Alexander, 147
Skopje
    deportation of Jews, 135, 144
    transit camp, 89, **90**, 136
Slavs, 4, 77–78, 165
Sliven
    Church opposition to ZZN, 34, 127
    deportation activities, 116, 128
Sobibor, 52
Sobolev, Arkadi, 22
Sobranie, 7, 12, **15**, 16, 107, 241,
    249–250
    letter of forty-three signatures,
        145–155, 174, 262, 267
    response to deportation, 120–122,
        145–155
Sofia. *See also* Bulgaria; Bulgarian Jews
    Allied bombardments, 241
    deportation of Jews, 82–85, 104, 105,
        116, 132, 184, 185–186, 188,
        202, 208, 216–217, 219, 224
    German Army presence, **183**
    Kristallnact attacks, 8
    modernization of, 12
Sofroni of Turnovo, opposition to ZZN, 172
Sokolov, Nahum, 24
Somovit, transit camp, 79, 183–184, 200,
    217
Soviet Union. *See also* Communist party;
    Russia
    German offensive against, 43, 50,
        225, 230, 267
    invasion of Bulgaria, 243, 246
    relations with Bulgaria, 22, 41, 51,
        230–232, 237
Spain, expulsion of Jews, 6
Spaniols, emigration to Ottoman Empire,
    6
Stainov, Prof. Petko, 36, 154
Stalin, Joseph, 19
Stambolisky, Alexander, 14
Stanishev, Prof. Alexander, 121

Stankov, Dimiter, 146
Star of David requirements, **31**, 55–56,
    92, 93, 168
Staynov, Prof. Petko, 147, 197
Stefan, Metropolitan
    anti-Fascist views, 167–168
    biography, 165–166
    as Exarch, 252–253
    and King Boris, **35**, 207, 264
    opposition to deportation, 139–140,
        165–177, 180, 187, 190,
        193–197, 200, 208–210, 262,
        266–268
    opposition to ZZN, 34, 57, 168
    and Queen Giovanna, **167**
    support for rabbis, 192–193,
        200–201, 216
Stoianchevski, Spas, 250
Stoika, Liliana, 79–80, 244
Stolypin, Prime Minister, 14
Stomanyakov, Christo, 241, 243–244, 250
Strogov, Dr. Ivan, 211
Struma Valley, 101
suicide, 187, 237, 246, 252
Suitchmezov, Assen, 107, 109–112,
    116–117, 122, 124–125, 251–252
Suitchmezov, Gregor, 110
Sveta Nedelya bombing, 14, 166
Swiss embassy, 68, 137–138, 163, 202,
    238

**T**
Tadjer, Col. Avraham, 102, 121, 124,
    169, 187, 243
Tadjer, Leon, 249
Tasev, Borislav, 100, 103–104, 107, 109,
    133, 134, 250
Theodorus of Salonika, 5
Thrace
    Bulgarian claim to, 21, 262
    Bulgarian occupation of, 43, 73, 232,
        265
    deportation of Jews, 3, 61–62, 65–75,
        82, 84–85, 87–100, 119, 131,
        135–137, 143–144, 161,
        169–170, 180, 253–254,
        257–258, 264
tobacco warehouses, **90**, 103

Todt organization, 138n
"Trains" (Isakov), 140–142
Treaty of Neuilly, 13, 19, 20
Treblinka, 52, **90**, 144
Tripartite Pact. *See also* Germany
    Bulgaria participation in, 22, 38,
        41–42
Turkey, 157. *See also* Macedonia; Thrace
    occupation of Bulgaria, 5–7, 9, 12
Turnovo
    Church opposition to ZZN, 34
    Turkish occupation of, 5–6
Tzankov, Alexander, 147
*Tzar Dushan* (steamship), 144
Tzaribrod, 13
Tzarska Bistritza palace, 207
Tziber, transit camps, 184, 205
Tzion, Rabbi Daniel, 79, 191–193,
    199–200, 216–217, 256

U
Utgren, 260

V
Varna, Church opposition to ZZN, 34
Vasileva, Nadejda, 143
Vatev, Dr. Iosif, 104, 241
Vatican, opposition to deportation, 202–203
Vazov, Ivan, 241
Velchev, Col. Damian, 16, 114, 189, 202
Velkov, Zakhari, 1–3, 131
Ventura, Annie, 249
Vidin
    opposition to ZZN, 169
    transit camps, 186, 188
Vladigerov, Pancho, 216
*Voivoda* (steamship), 144
von Paulus, 267
Von Thadden, Counselor, 180
Vrajdebna Airfield, 229
Vrana palace, 10, 174, 241
Vratza
    "blood libel" incidents, 7
    transit camp, 186

W
Wagner, Horst, 225
Wannsee Conference, 52

Warrant 116, 76
Warrant 127, 75. *See also* deportation
    agreement
Wasserman, Albert, 168
Wolf's Lair, 230
women
    Bulgaria women's movement, 187
    Communist party membership, 182,
        199–200
    friendships with Jews, **31**
    German admittance of, 245
    support for Jews, 188–189
    violence against, 92, **95**
World War I, 8, 13, 20, 22, 166, 231
World War II, 8, 18–19. *See also*
    Germany; Soviet Union
writers and poets, opposition to ZZN, 33
Wurttemberg, Duke, 24–25

Y
Yakova, Rosa, 92
Yakova, Violeta, 174, 182, 249
Yambol, partisan activities, 249
Yanakiev, Kulcho, 182–183, 221
Yanev, Sotir, 182
Yastrebetz chalet, 207
Yeremiev, Georgi, 107
Yoan Assen, King II, 5
Yuch Bunar Communist party, 199
Yuch Bunar neighborhood, 186, 199–200
Yuch Bunar synagogue, 192, 197, 254–255
Yugoslavia
    German occupation, 43, **45**
    relations with Bulgaria, 19, 21

Z
Zaharna Fabrika district, citizen protests
    in, 32
*Zakon za Zashita na Natziata* (ZZN). *See*
    Law for the Defense of the Nation
Zionism, 8, 106, 198, 261
Zveno republicans, 16
Zweig, Stefan, 168
ZZN. *See Zakon za Zashita na Natziata*

To Treblinka

Vienna

GERMANY

*Danube*

*River*

AUSTRIA

Budapest

H U N G A R Y

Zagreb

*Danube*    *River*

Belgrade

C R O A T I A

Y U G O S L A V I A

S E R B I A

M O N T E N E G R O

Skopje

A L B A N I A

M A C

A d r i a t i c   S e a

N

I T A L Y

0 Miles                50

0 Kilometers          100

Jeffrey L. Ward